Design Better and Build Your Brand in Canva

A beginner's guide to producing professional branding, marketing, and social content for businesses

Laura Goodsell

BIRMINGHAM—MUMBAI

Design Better and Build Your Brand in Canva

Group Product Manager: Rohit Rajkumar

Publishing Product Manager: Vaideeshwari Muralikrishnan

Senior Content Development Editor: Feza Shaikh

Technical Editor: Joseph Aloocaran

Copy Editor: Safis Editing

Project Coordinator: Sonam Pandey

Proofreader: Safis Editing

Indexer: Rekha Nair

Production Designer: Prashant Ghare

Marketing Coordinator: Nivedita Pandey

First published: January 2023

Production reference: 1161222

Published by Packt Publishing Ltd.

Livery Place

35 Livery Street

Birmingham

B3 2PB, UK.

ISBN 978-1-80056-933-1

www.packt.com

To every small business owner out there who's following their passion, their dream, and working hard to make it happen, this is for you. If I can help you in any small way, that's a goal accomplished for me. Read and enjoy this book, put it to good use and let it help you in your business with all of your graphics and marketing materials.

-Laura Goodsell

Contributors

About the author

Laura Goodsell is an award-winning Canva design coach and Canva **Creator Ambassador** (**Canvassador**) based in the UK. She helps small business owners to use and utilize Canva for their business and create branded graphics on a budget, as well as teaching them how to create passive income through digital products and template and element creation. Encouraging women to enter the digital world is one of Laura's passions.

She has built her business around helping make design accessible and simple for all small business owners.

Laura's aim is to help businesses become more visible on social media, focusing on design-based services, such as creating courses and challenges, training business groups, writing books, and creating templates and elements for Canva.

I would like to thank the people who have been so very supportive and encouraging during the writing of this book, especially my partner, James, for always supporting and encouraging me to achieve my dreams. To my parents, for their support and encouragement, and to my children, Oliver and Alfie, just for being the wonderful people they truly are – please never change, you inspire me daily.

About the reviewer

Naomi Johnson is a self-employed digital designer and video creator. Her mission is to provide solo business owners with a comprehensive range of affordable design-based products, services, and training that enable them to simplify their lives and boost their income in a variety of ways. Entirely self-taught, she has particular expertise in designing journals, planners, and notebooks in both traditional and digital formats.

Foreword

I became aware of Laura Goodsell through her online work under her Business Design Academy brand and knew that she was one of a limited number of Canva experts here in the UK. Being a Canva Creator Ambassador reflects her knowledge and the trust that this global design software company has in Laura. In this book, *Design Better and Build Your Brand in Canva*, Laura takes you through the journey of creating your own visual branding – from the absolute starting point with an idea through to a full suite of digital assets, images, and expert tips to make the most of the software.

With easy-to-follow, step-by-step guides, you'll be able to create your own range of professional images and graphics so that you and your business can stand out! As a business mentor, I recommend Canva to my clients, especially if they don't have the budget or the like to know how to do things for themselves. This book will help to give you the skills, knowledge, and confidence to use this platform effectively.

From creating the essential elements for your business (logo design, social media designs, and designing with print in mind), expert tips on how to use the creative tools from within Canva, and Laura's expert advice, you really will create the brand and images that will help you stand out in your field. You'll feel more confident and be able to design your brand better!

As well as building your skills and knowledge of Canva, you'll learn how easy and quick it is to create and develop your designs and brand, enabling you to build your business and increase your visibility – essential in the business world of today.

Become your own digital and brand developer, build your images, and build your business with Laura Goodsell, Canvasador.

Janine Friston

Founder and CEO, Female Business Network

Since I started *More Than Just Mum Coaching and Mentoring* in 2020, I have had a love for Canva. I use it almost daily for my life and my business. It's one of the apps I use regularly for my membership program to create goal boards and many other designs too, such as social media graphics, posters for my in-person events, workbooks, lead magnets, goal tracker journals, my annual planners that I create and sell on Amazon, and presentations too. I literally use it for everything!

As a life coach and business mentor who mainly uses social media to grow my audience, and engage and communicate, it is important that I have a quick and easy-to-use application such as Canva.

Having grown up well into my mid-30s telling myself I wasn't creative, Canva has unleashed a new version of creativity for me. I am passionate about creating vibrant, on-brand graphics that are in alignment with me, and that's exactly what I get with Canva.

I first came across Laura in 2020 when she was recommended to me by a friend. Since then, we have supported each other in business, and she has always been so helpful. Laura has also delivered guest sessions for my membership program, to help the ladies that are members with the basics of Canva.

Over these past few years, I have watched Laura build her brand and business via social media, supporting hundreds, if not thousands, of small business owners to create a sideline semi-passive income, or to set up a new digital business through template and element creation. More recently, she has set up a membership program and created courses for all levels and challenges, one-to-one coaching, and graphics for the Canva library.

She is the go-to expert when it comes to anything Canva; she offers so much value and support to her community, and has an incredible amount of knowledge when it comes to this app.

In this book, Laura provides a step-by-step guide on *how to Canva*! As a daily user, I consider myself pretty good, but I have still picked up loads of super simple hacks and tips that are going to save me time and energy in the future. So, even if you think you know Canva, I'd highly recommend this book.

The book is broken down into simple chapters with summaries, making it really easy to follow. There are also screenshots relating to each step – Laura has definitely kept it simple! As a busy mum of two, I LOVE to keep things simple.

Even if you think you're pretty good on Canva (like I did), I would highly recommend you make the investment today!

This book will save you time, and time is money!

Laura is the go-to expert for everything Canva, and I hope you love this book as much as I did.

Heather Palfreyman

Founder, More Than Just Mum Coaching and Mentoring

Helping women unlock their potential for growth and expansion in life and their career or business

`www.morethanjustmum.com`

Table of Contents

3

4

Part 2: Creating Your Brand and Design Tips

5

6

Expert Hacks to Create Your Own Professional-Looking Designs 127

7

Five Graphic Design Principles You Need to Know 149

Part 3: Let's Get Creating

8

Creating Your Perfect Logo 163

9

Making Social Media Graphics with Canva 179

10

Leveraging Video and Animation within Your Business Marketing 205

11

Downloading and Sharing Your Designs 229

12

Tips and Tricks for Printing 253

Preface

This book will help you to use Canva, set up your branding, and create consistent, well-designed graphics for your business. But what is Canva? And why should you use it? Well... Canva is a graphic design platform that has grown significantly in popularity in only a few short years. Its aim is to make design accessible to everyone, regardless of your design ability. On Canva, you can create any number of designs for work and home on the platform, on both desktop and the mobile app, using pre-made templates or creating them from scratch. It also allows you to edit both video and images, create animations, schedule content to social media, and create presentations for work. There is a growing number of apps being incorporated into Canva, giving you so much more flexibility and scope for growing your business. Canva, above all, is a very visual platform, simple to get to grips with, and great fun to use.

Who this book is for

This book is ideal for aspiring designers, social media managers, virtual assistants, service-based businesses, and solopreneurs with basic experience in Canva who are looking to advance in a new skill, while creating their brand and perfecting their social media and marketing materials on a budget. A basic understanding of Canva, such as knowing how to set up a free Canva account, create a basic design using a template, add images and text boxes, and change the color of fonts, is assumed but not essential.

What this book covers

Chapter 1, Setting Up Canva on Desktop and Mobile, looks at what Canva is, setting up the platform, as well as the difference between Free and Pro accounts and creating folders to help you get organized from day one.

Chapter 2, Discovering and Editing Templates, helps you discover how to find and use Canva templates, as well as how to start one from scratch.

Chapter 3, Tools and Features for Using Elements and Images, helps with understanding the use of elements and backgrounds and discovering the full range of editing tools available for imagery within a design.

Chapter 4, Designing Eye-Catching Graphics through Useful Features, teaches you how to use the features that define Canva and allow you to create amazing eye-catching designs.

Chapter 5, Exploring the Awesome Creative Tools for Branding, looks at branding, how it is built, and what we need to create our own brand, as well as getting your branding set up in the Canva brand kit.

Chapter 6, Expert Hacks to Create Your Own Professional-Looking Designs, provides five tutorials for you to have a go at, which will help you to use and understand backgrounds, grids, frames, color, images, text, and graphs.

Chapter 7, Five Graphic Design Principles You Need to Know, outlines design principles that will help you to create amazing-looking designs.

Chapter 8, Creating Your Perfect Logo, shows you how to create a logo and sub-logos and understand the use of elements within a logo.

Chapter 9, Making Social Media Graphics with Canva, shows you how to create five different-style graphics needed for social media and business use.

Chapter 10, Leveraging Video and Animation within Your Business Marketing, teaches you how to use video and animation within Canva for your business needs.

Chapter 11, Downloading and Sharing Your Designs, shows you how to download and share your designs so you can get your business out there.

Chapter 12, Tips and Tricks for Printing, shows you how to print your designs through Canva or a third-party printer, as well as creating multi-page documents for book design.

To get the most out of this book

For this book to have the greatest impact, it would be best if you had a basic understanding of Canva and what the platform is used for.

You may already have a free Canva account set up and can create a basic design using a template.

You may know how to add an image, add text boxes, and change the color of fonts, but beyond that, you are looking to learn more.

Software/hardware covered in the book	Operating system requirements
The Canva platform	Any operating system will work An internet connection is required A computer, laptop, or tablet will work best
Canva Pro	A Canva Pro subscription will be required to use any of the Pro features

For certain aspects of this book, you will need to have a Canva Pro account, for example, to use the Background Remover tool or the vast majority of the Smartmockups tool, as mentioned in *Chapter 3, Tools and Features for Using Elements and Images*. To use any other Pro elements and images, a Pro account is required. I have tried to include as much content as possible that is available on a Free account.

After you have completed this book, I would love for you to continue on your Canva journey, creating graphics and growing your business. I have a free Facebook group for Canva users, full of support and advice, that you are welcome to join: `www.facebook.com/groups/createoncanva`.

Download the color images

We also provide a PDF file that has color images of the screenshots and diagrams used in this book. You can download it here: `https://packt.link/sVTuR`.

Conventions used

There are a number of text conventions used throughout this book.

Bold: Indicates a new term, an important word, or words that you see onscreen. For instance, words in menus or dialog boxes appear in **bold**. Here is an example: "Click the **Share** button, then for sharing options, click **more**."

> **Tips or important notes**
> Appear like this.

Get in touch

Feedback from our readers is always welcome.

General feedback: If you have questions about any aspect of this book, email us at `customercare@packtpub.com` and mention the book title in the subject of your message.

Errata: Although we have taken every care to ensure the accuracy of our content, mistakes do happen. If you have found a mistake in this book, we would be grateful if you would report this to us. Please visit `www.packtpub.com/support/errata` and fill in the form.

Piracy: If you come across any illegal copies of our works in any form on the internet, we would be grateful if you would provide us with the location address or website name. Please contact us at `copyright@packt.com` with a link to the material.

If you are interested in becoming an author: If there is a topic that you have expertise in and you are interested in either writing or contributing to a book, please visit `authors.packtpub.com`.

Share Your Thoughts

Once you've read, we'd love to hear your thoughts! Scan the QR code below to go straight to the Amazon review page for this book and share your feedback.

`https://packt.link/r/1800569335`

Your review is important to us and the tech community and will help us make sure we're delivering excellent quality content.

Download a free PDF copy of this book

Thanks for purchasing this book!

Do you like to read on the go but are unable to carry your print books everywhere? Is your eBook purchase not compatible with the device of your choice?

Don't worry, now with every Packt book you get a DRM-free PDF version of that book at no cost.

Read anywhere, any place, on any device. Search, copy, and paste code from your favorite technical books directly into your application.

The perks don't stop there, you can get exclusive access to discounts, newsletters, and great free content in your inbox daily

Follow these simple steps to get the benefits:

1. Scan the QR code or visit the link below

`https://packt.link/free-ebook/978-1-80056-933-1`

2. Submit your proof of purchase
3. That's it! We'll send your free PDF and other benefits to your email directly

Before we really get started with graphic creation in Canva, there are a few things we need to set up in preparation. They will help us save time, find our way around the platform easier, and make our business more consistent through our graphics. So, in this section, we're going to focus on getting you set up on Canva on both desktop and mobile, as mobile on-the-go graphics work really well for busy business owners. We're also going to look at how you can edit and use Canva's ready-made templates, as well as creating your own from scratch, and how to use the various different tools and features to end up with great-looking, consistent templates.

This part includes the following chapters:

1

Setting Up Canva on Desktop and Mobile

Canva is a fantastic platform that is available to everyone and is, in particular, ideal for small business owners. In this chapter, you will be introduced to Canva as well as how to set up your account, and we will go through the main differences between Free and Pro, so you can decide which is best for you. You will also have the chance to look at both mobile and desktop platforms, as there are some slight differences, and we will look at the Content Planner, which is Canva's social media scheduling tool.

In this chapter we are going to cover the following main topics:

- What is Canva?
- Free versus Pro – what's the difference?
- Setting up your Canva account
- Using the mobile version of Canva
- Scheduling content with the Content Planner
- Setting up folders for organization

By the end of this chapter, you will have set up your Canva account, created folders to organize your designs, understood the difference between the two different accounts as well as the desktop and mobile versions, and will be ready to get creating and schedule your content.

Technical requirements

To complete this chapter, you only need to have a working desktop computer or laptop and mobile phone (if you would like to look at the mobile version, but not compulsory) as well as access to an internet connection. There are no requirements when it comes to design experience; Canva has been created to be accessible by everyone, and anyone of any age or ability can use and create with Canva. This is why it has become such a popular platform – anyone can create beautiful designs.

What is Canva?

Canva is a design platform where you can create your own designs using a drag-and-drop system. It includes hundreds of thousands of images, elements, fonts, shapes, and templates; the majority are available free for you to use, but you can upgrade to a paid subscription to gain access to everything.

The things you can create include social media designs, book covers, calendars, planners, t-shirt designs, and posters. Every type of design has its own sizing within Canva so you can just pick the size, choose a suitable template, and get designing. Templates and elements are created by freelance designers as well as in-house designers at Canva. It is a multi-purpose platform, meaning it is available both as a website, desktop app, and mobile app, all connected to help make designing easier for the everyday person.

Now you know what you need to set up an account and you have an understanding of what Canva is, let's look at the different types of accounts that are available to you.

Free versus Pro – what's the difference?

Canva has two main accounts, Free and Pro. Free is a free-to-open account and you have access to a lot of features to get designing straight away. With the option of purchasing Pro elements and templates if you would like to, Pro is a paid account that gives you access to everything including some amazing features that are really useful to those wanting to use Canva daily. The Pro account is, at the time of writing this book, $12.99 per month or $119.99 per year (`www.canva.com`).

Canva Free benefits

The following are the benefits of Canva Free:

- 250,000+ templates
- Hundreds of thousands of free photos and graphics
- 5 GB of cloud storage space
- Unlimited folders
- 100+ design styles: social media posts, posters, invites, banners, and more

Canva Pro benefits

The following are the benefits of Canva Pro:

- In Pro, you get everything that you get for Free, plus the following:
    - Resize your designs with the Magic Resize tool
    - 610,000+ templates, with new designs added daily

- 100+ million images, videos, audio, and graphics
- Full access to the complete brand kit
- Background Remover tools for both images and video
- Full access to the Content planner
- Unlimited folders
- 100 GB cloud storage space

Let's look at how you can now set up your Canva account.

Setting up your Canva account

To set up a Canva account (you may already have one), follow these steps:

1. Go to `www.canva.com` on your computer or tablet; once there, you will see the screen as shown in *Figure 1.1*:

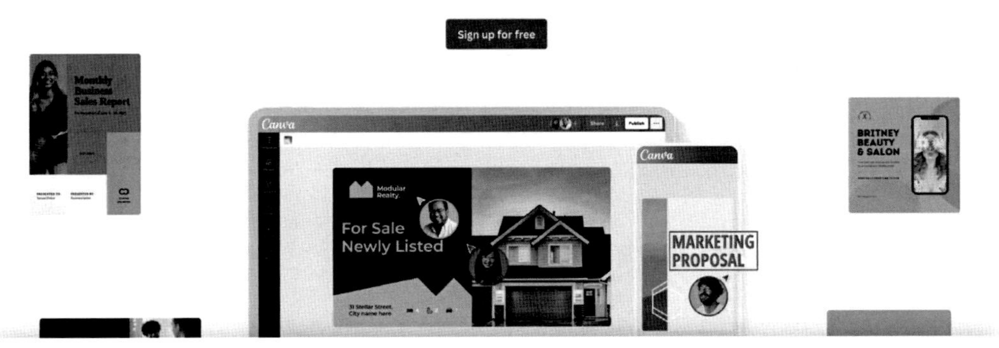

Figure 1.1 – Home page screen in Canva

You then have a choice of signing up for a Free Canva account or starting a free 30-day trial of Pro. I would recommend going for the Free account with a view of trying the free trial later once you are familiar with the platform.

2. Next, select the **Sign up** button in the top-right corner and the popup will appear as shown in *Figure 1.2*:

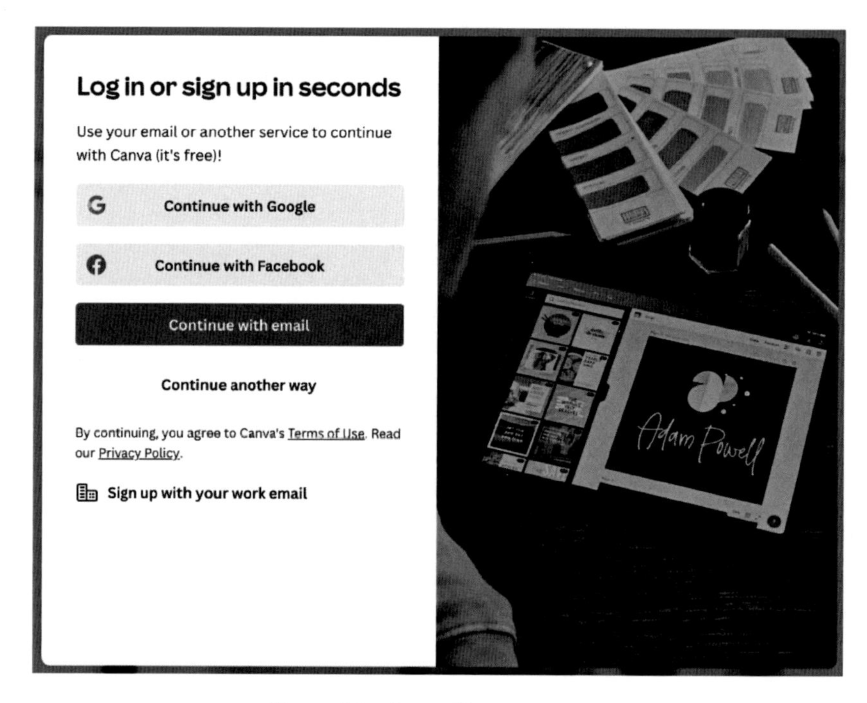

Figure 1.2 – Canva Sign-up popup

You will then be able to select how you would like to sign up. I would recommend using an existing email address by clicking the purple box that says Continue with email. This will then take you to a password screen where you can create a secure password for the account. Don't forget to make a note of which email address you have used and the password created.

3. You will then be taken to the Canva home screen ready to get your new account set up; it will look like this:

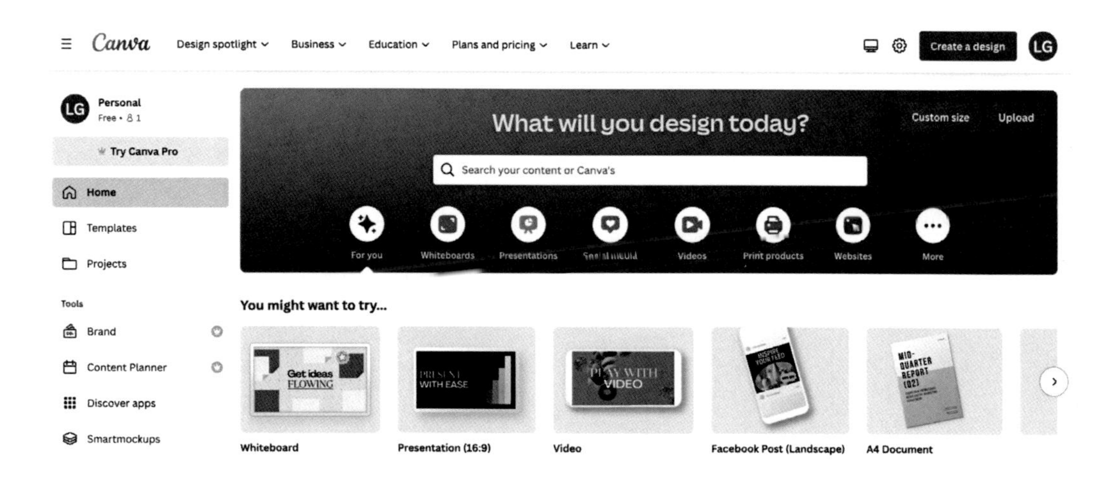

Figure 1.3 – The Canva home screen after logging in

Once you have your new account set up and you are logged in, I would always advise you to have a good look around, check out the menu on the left, scroll through the sections under the search bar in the middle, and familiarize yourself with the layout of the home screen; you will see this a lot on your design journey. Don't worry about going too deep into the features as we will be covering these later in the book, but for now, check out your new design platform.

Next, we'll have a look at setting up and using the mobile version of Canva as this works really well with the website.

Using the mobile version of Canva

At this point, I would like to talk a bit about the Canva mobile app, as the majority of people are now using mobiles over desktop computers for everyday life and work, so it is important to get this app set up as well. You can use the same login details that you used for the desktop/web version of Canva and when you do, all of your designs, uploads, images, and branding are carried across, so anything you create on your desktop will be available to you through the mobile app on your phone. There are a few small differences and not all features are carried over to the mobile app. The main difference is the obvious one really: the screen size. On our computers and desktop screens, we can see so much more and can design more complex projects this way. Using your mobile, you are restricted to a smaller screen, so it's perfect for downloading designs and scheduling or uploading to social media on the go.

To get the Canva mobile app, you will need access to either the App Store on Apple or Google Play Store on Android phones. It will often appear as an advert at the top of the page. Select Canva and log in using your Canva login details.

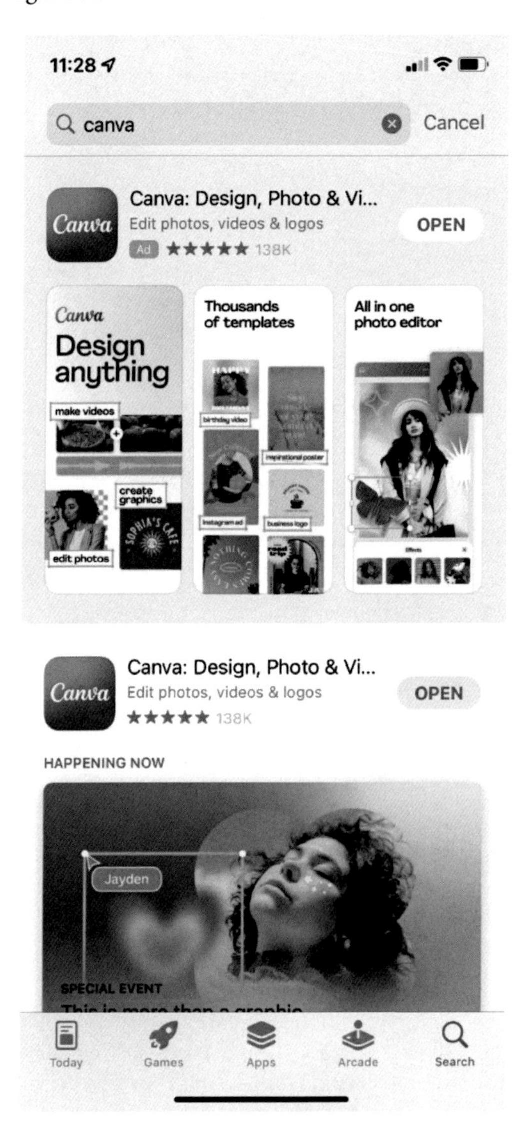

Figure 1.4 – Canva App Store view

It will then open up on your phone and you will see a screen similar to this one:

Figure 1.5 – Canva for mobile home screen

There are a few small differences between the desktop version and mobile version of Canva, including the following:

- The main menu is across the bottom rather than the left side, and the **Create a design** button is the small purple circle in the bottom-right corner:

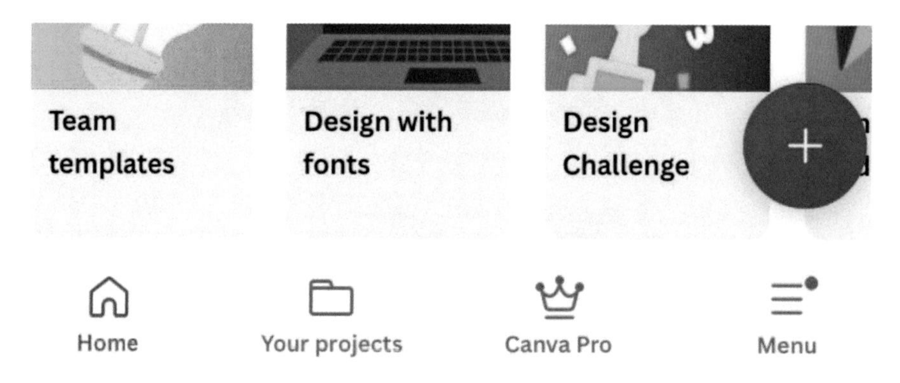

Figure 1.6 – Mobile version main menu

- When designing, all the template features are along the bottom rather than the top:

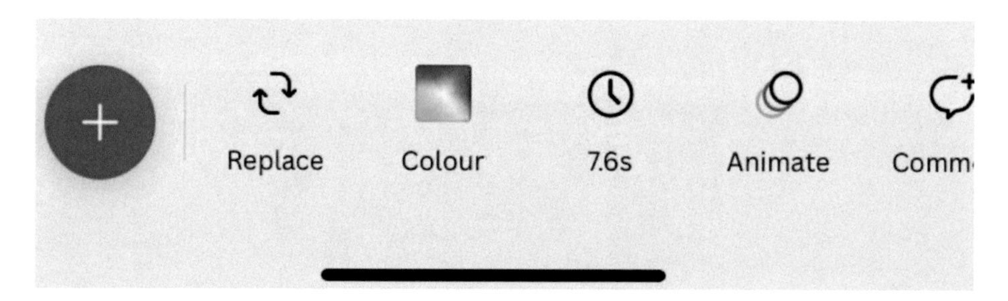

Figure 1.7 – Mobile version design features

- To access features when you are working on a design, you select the small purple circle in the bottom left and the elements are accessible from there, and to view all your pages together, there is a white circle with a number in a square in it, on the right of the screen:

Figure 1.8 – Mobile version create button and view all pages button

Overall, they are very similar, and any differences have been put in place to accommodate the difference in screen sizes.

The mobile version is great for being on the go and being able to find your designs quickly, which is why we will now look at setting up folders and getting organized.

Setting up folders for organization

So now we've set up our Canva account and know how the mobile version works, it's time to get organized. In Canva, you can create folders to organize your designs into various parts of your business or home life, view your recent designs, and quickly see your uploaded content all on the **Your projects** tab. This can be found on the left-hand menu under the **Home** tab.

The order of sections on this page goes as follows:

- **Recent**
- **Folders**
- **Designs**
- **Images**
- **Videos**

This can be seen in the following screenshot:

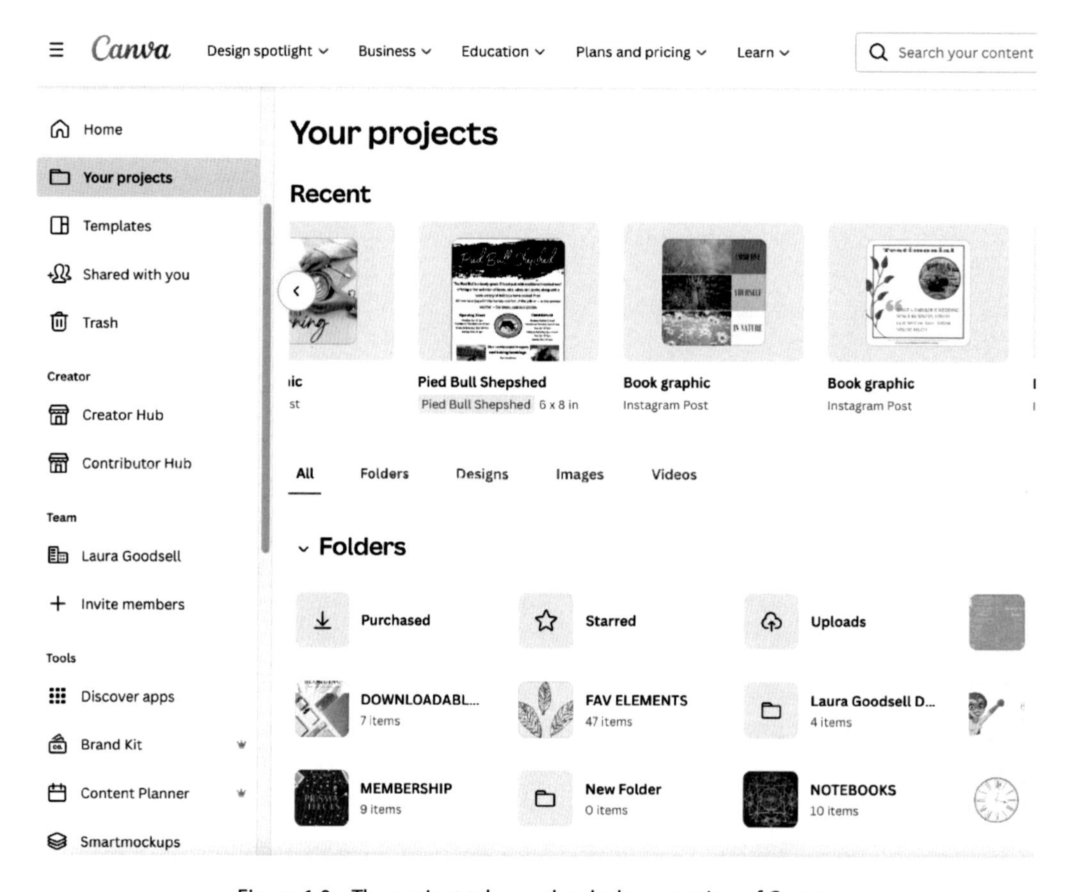

Figure 1.9 – The project tabs on the desktop version of Canva

Scroll down the page and you will see anything you've uploaded or created here. This is the best place to access everything, a central hub for your account.

Creating folders

You get three folders already in the account, as follows:

- **Purchased** – Anything you have purchased outside of the Pro subscription
- **Starred** – Any elements or images that you have favorited and would like to use later are saved here
- **Uploads** – Everything you upload to your account, including images and video

With the Pro version and the Free version, you get unlimited folders along with the existing three mentioned previously and you can name them whatever you would like. To create a new folder, follow these instructions:

1. Click on the cross in the top-right corner. This will open up an **Add new** menu:

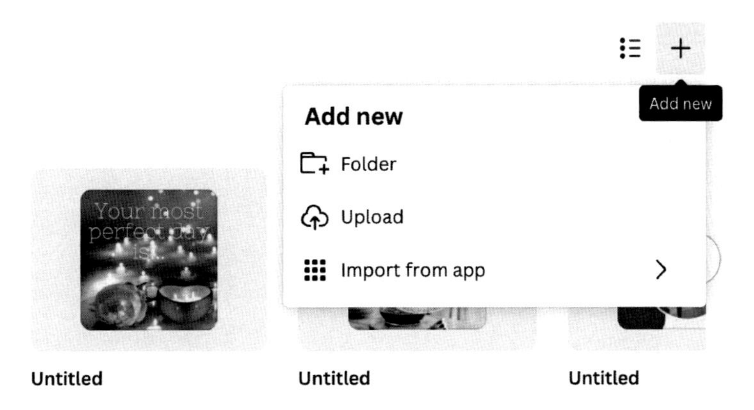

Figure 1.10 – Creating a new folder on desktop

2. Click on the **Folder** icon.
3. Add a name for your folder:

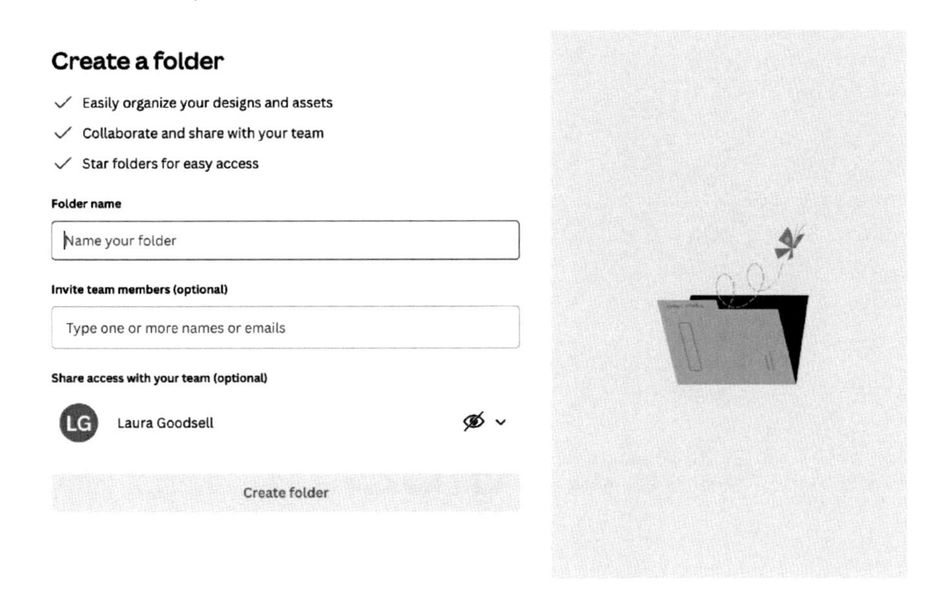

Figure 1.11 – Naming your folders

Ignore the second option, unless you are creating a team, but for this exercise, we are just looking at setting up a basic folder.

4. Then, select the **Create folder** button at the bottom.
5. It will now add your folder to the **Folders** section on the page. You can customize a folder by clicking on the three dots next to it or by selecting the folder itself:

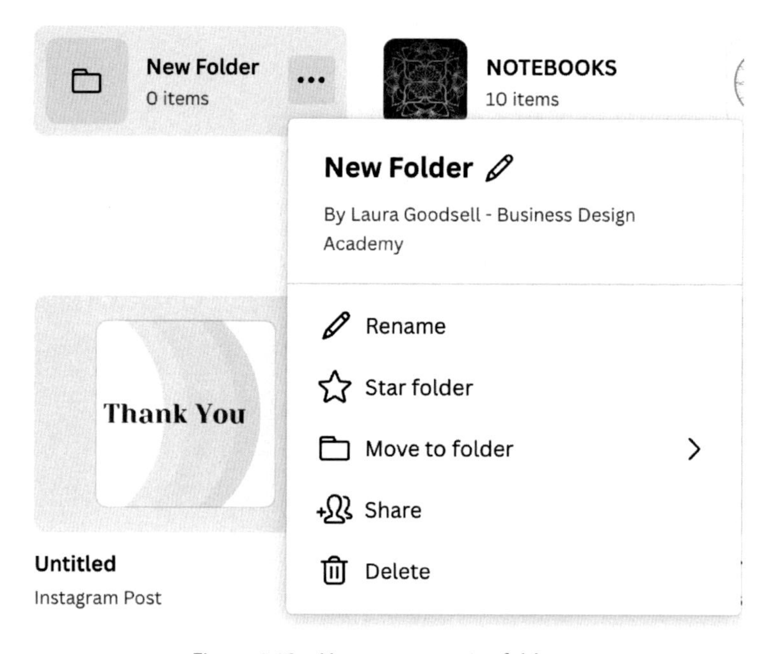

Figure 1.12 – How to customize folders

You can also have your new folder as a top-level folder by selecting the star icon next to its name, which will turn the star yellow. It will now appear in the menu bar on the left. This is perfect for all users, and you can create as many folders as you would like. You can also create folders within folders up to five deep for extra organization.

New Folder ★

Figure 1.13 – Adding a star to create a top-level folder

Finally within the **Folders** options, you can share a folder with a team member, but they do need to have been set up as a member within your Canva account; you can't share a folder with someone outside of your team.

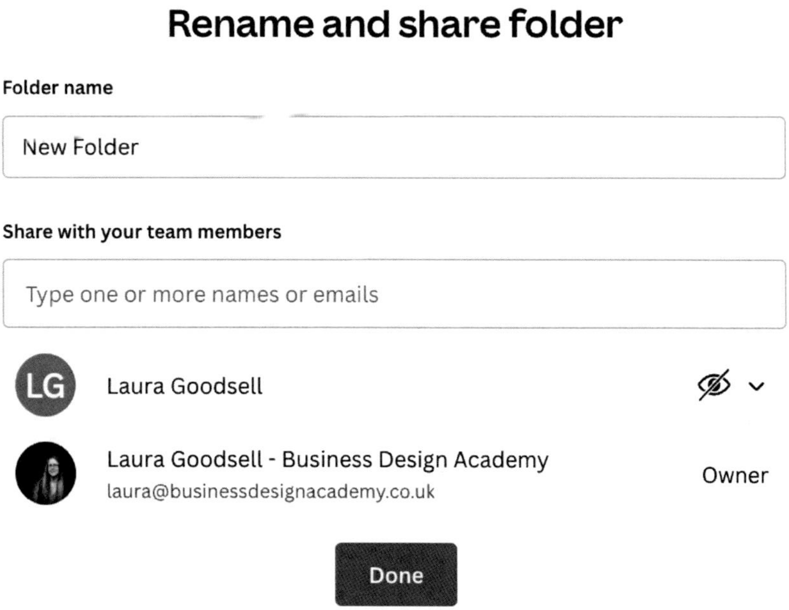

Rename and share folder

Folder name

New Folder

Share with your team members

Type one or more names or emails

LG Laura Goodsell

Laura Goodsell - Business Design Academy
laura@businessdesignacademy.co.uk
Owner

Done

Figure 1.14 – Sharing a folder with a team member

So far, we have covered what Canva is and how it can be used, how to set up our account on desktop and mobile, and we have also looked at the differences between the two main Canva accounts. We've gotten ourselves organized with folders for our designs, so next, we're going to look at the Content Planner.

Scheduling content with the Content Planner

The Canva Content Planner is a brilliant feature for anyone who uses and schedules social media. It helps you to create and schedule multiple social platforms all from within Canva. You don't need to sign up to third-party apps and websites to get your content into your accounts.

It can be located in the main menu on the right. This is a Pro feature only, so if you are on Free, you will not have access; however, you can sign up for a 30-day free trial and have a look to see whether you would be interested in using it in the future.

The Content Planner is laid out like a calendar, with the option to toggle between months at the top, and you can see at a glance where you have scheduled your posts and when. It also has important holidays and world events on, so if you ever wanted to create for an occasion, you can click on the name and it will give you a selection of templates already created for that date:

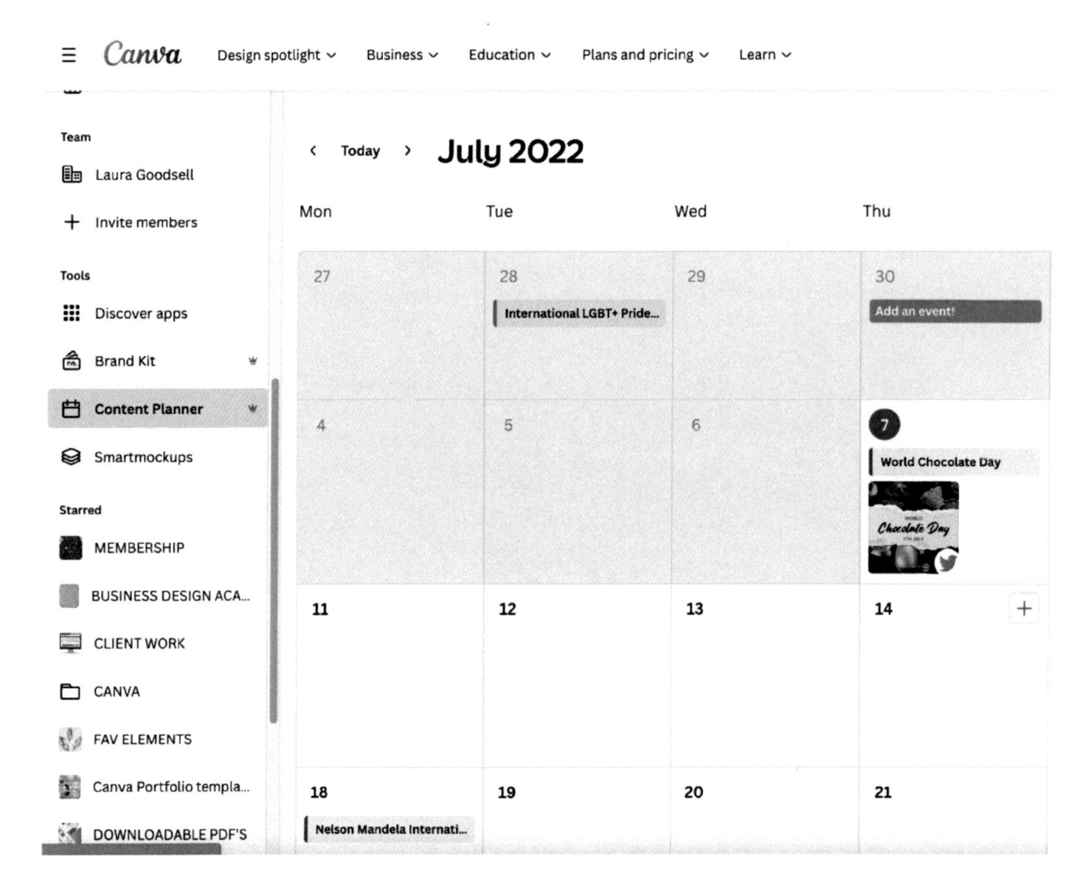

Figure 1.15 – Canva Content Planner

Here, I have clicked on the **International Yoga Day** link, and I can then click on one of these options to start creating my post in relation to International Yoga Day:

International Yoga Day

International Yoga Day is a holiday to celebrate the practice of yoga and mindfulness.

Figure 1.16 – View of Templates available for different holidays in the Content Planner

Creating and scheduling a post

Here, I will go step by step through how to schedule content for your socials, as there are a couple of ways you can do this through Canva. The simplest and best way is to pick a date from the calendar that you would like to post to and then create your design.

Here, I have clicked on the date I would like to use, and it has brought up my own designs at the top to choose from, a selection of pre-made templates at the bottom, plus the option (in the middle to the right) to create a design from scratch. For this example, I will select a pre-made template:

Figure 1.17 – Templates in Canva

Once I have selected my template, it will open up in the normal template editing view. I can now change the text, swap out any images, or adjust the colors to suit my brand (we will cover branding in *Chapter 5, Exploring the Awesome Creative Tools for Branding*).

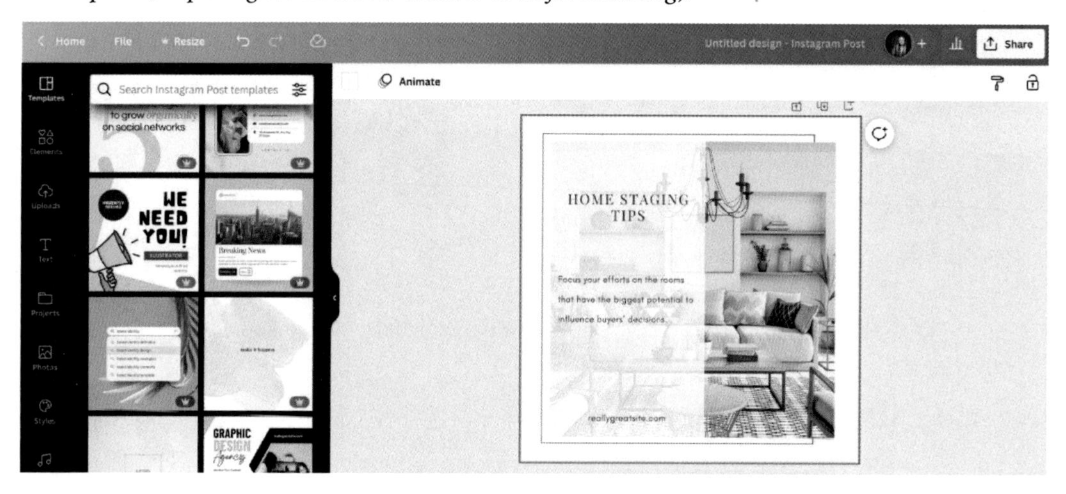

Figure 1.18 – Canva design screen

Once you have finished editing your template (we will cover editing in *Chapter 2, Discovering and Editing Templates*), you are ready to schedule. Click on the **Share** button in the top-right corner:

Figure 1.19 – View of the Share button

You will see a drop-down menu; you will often need to select the **More** option at the bottom to find the **Schedule** button:

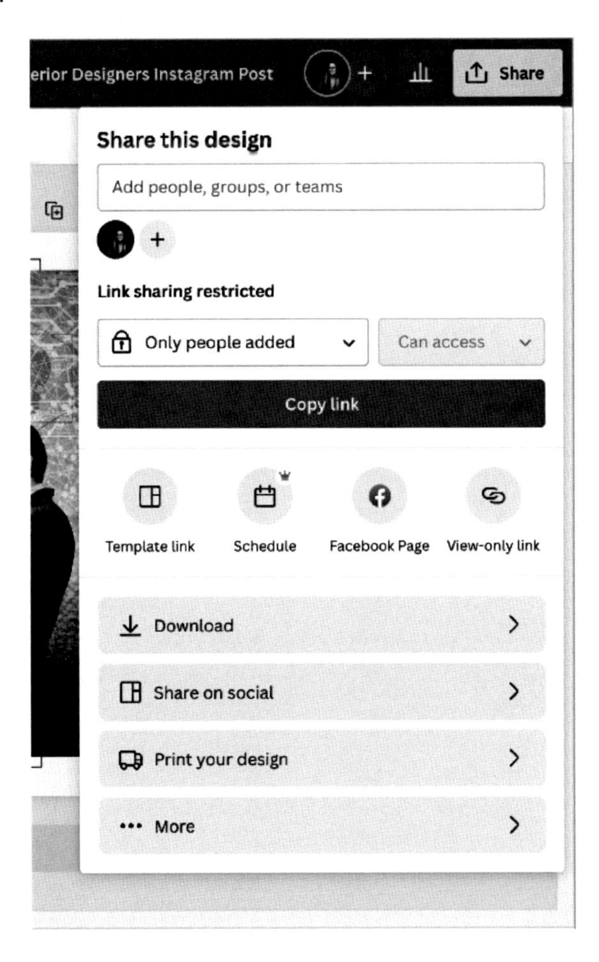

Figure 1.20 – Share dropdown

Once you have selected the **More** button, you will then see all of the available options, including every social media platform that you can directly post to, as well as the **Schedule** tab, as shown here:

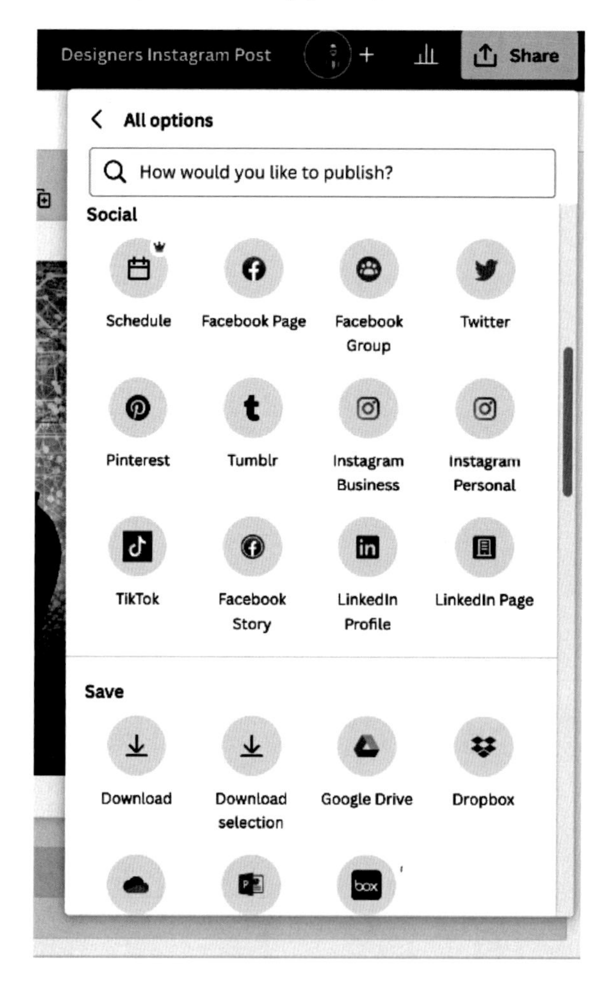

Figure 1.21 – Schedule option in the Share dropdown

Here, you will find every option available to you within Canva. Scroll down until you find the **Schedule** option and select it. It will be in the **Social** section. Next, it will bring up boxes for you to write out your content, select your channel, and change the date and time you want the post to go out:

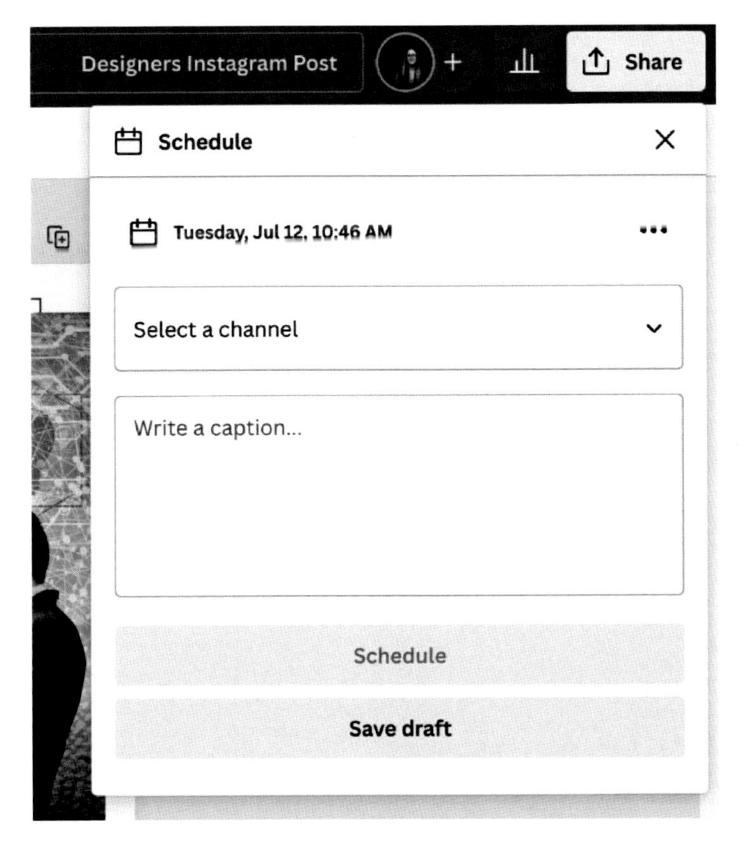

Figure 1.22 – Dropdown to create your social media post

Click on the date and a calendar will appear. Select your date, and at the bottom, you will find the option to select the time:

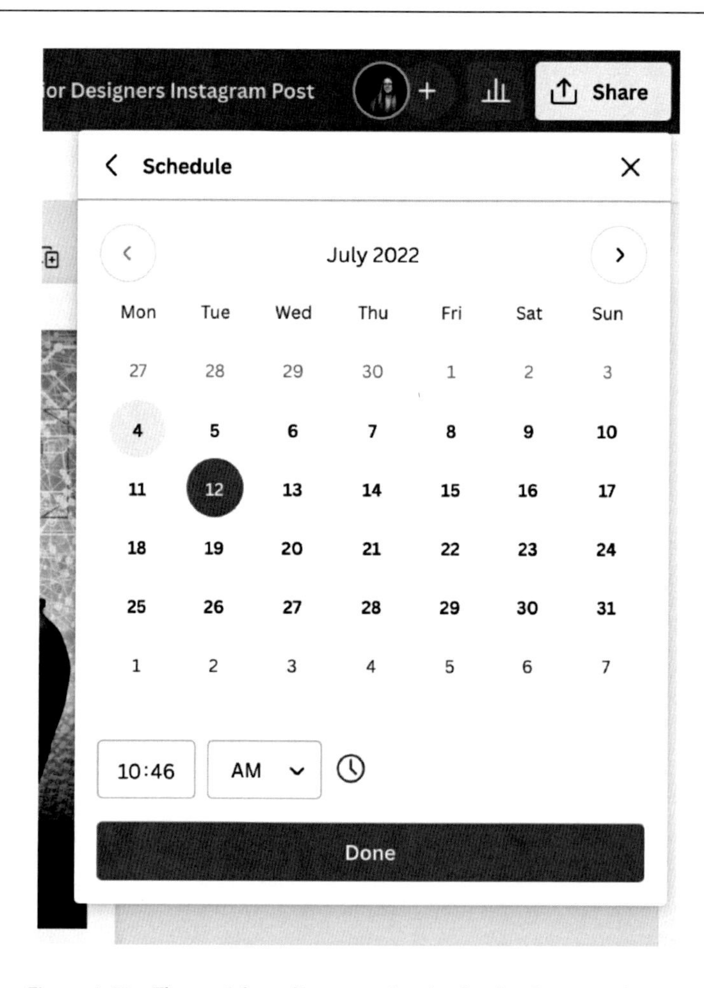

Figure 1.23 – The social media post calendar for the Content Planner

Next, select your channel. You will need to connect your social channels to Canva at this point. They are mostly easy to do apart from Facebook; you will have to log in to your Facebook account and grant Canva permission. You can also connect to Instagram, which is the most popular platform to post directly to, however, you can only connect to either a Business or Personal account, and not a Creator account.

But mostly, they just require your login details from within Canva, or if you are on a device already logged in, it can connect automatically. This can be done by selecting the **Select a channel** option at the bottom of the drop-down option. Once connected, it will appear at the top and you can just select the channel you need:

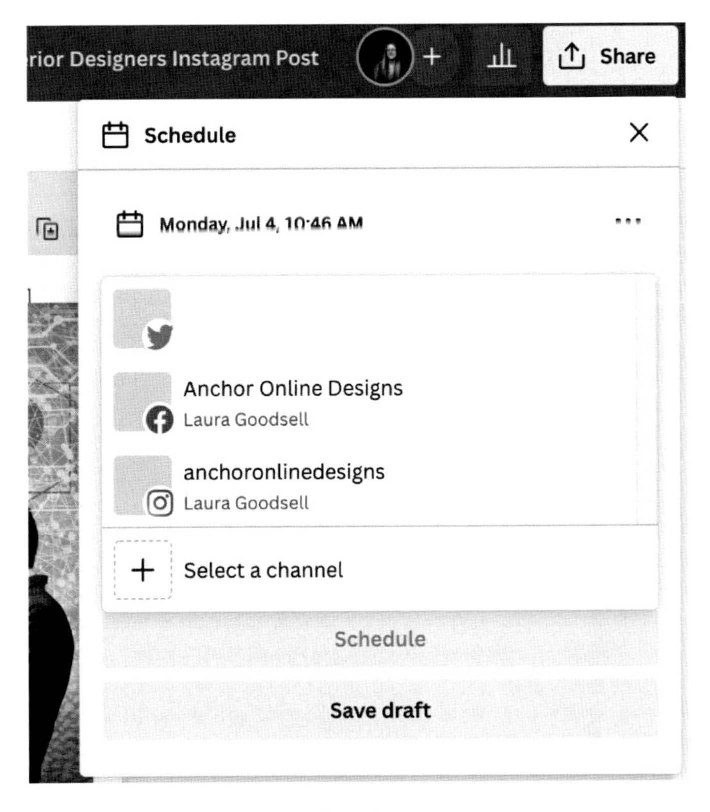

Figure 1.24 – Selecting the social media account to post your content to

Lastly, you are required to write your caption as you would directly on your social channel. Canva has even made it possible for you to stay within your character count. As you change the social platforms, the word count in the bottom-right corner will change; Twitter, for example, is 280 characters and Facebook is 5,000 characters:

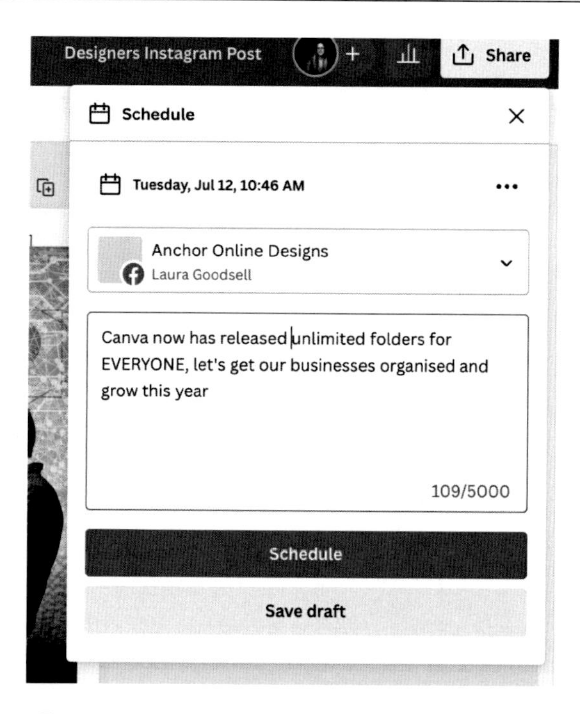

Figure 1.25 – Writing your social media post caption

Now is the time to click **Schedule** or save your post as a draft to come back to at a later date. These options can be found directly on the Content Planner calendar.

If you would like to schedule the same post to another platform, you will need to click the **Make a copy** button of the design, as you can only use it once per platform:

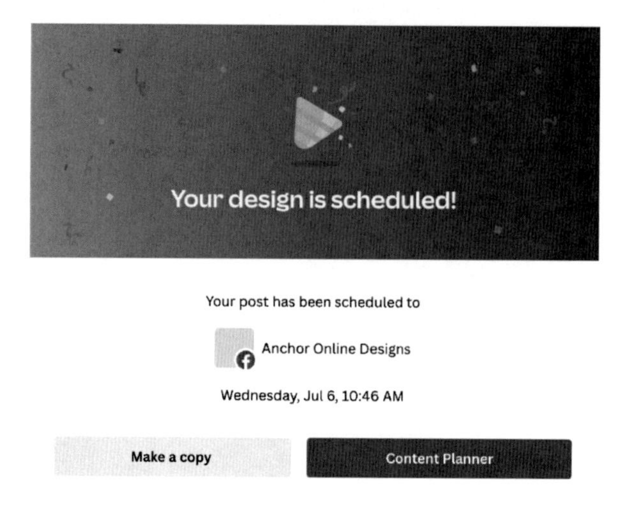

Figure 1.26 – Your design is scheduled screen

Let's go over to the Content Planner and see our post. I now have a view of my scheduled posts, and if you hover over one, it will tell you the time and platform it has been scheduled to. You can schedule multiple posts on different platforms on the same day. It will show you smaller icons of each platform, so you can easily see at a glance where everything is set to post:

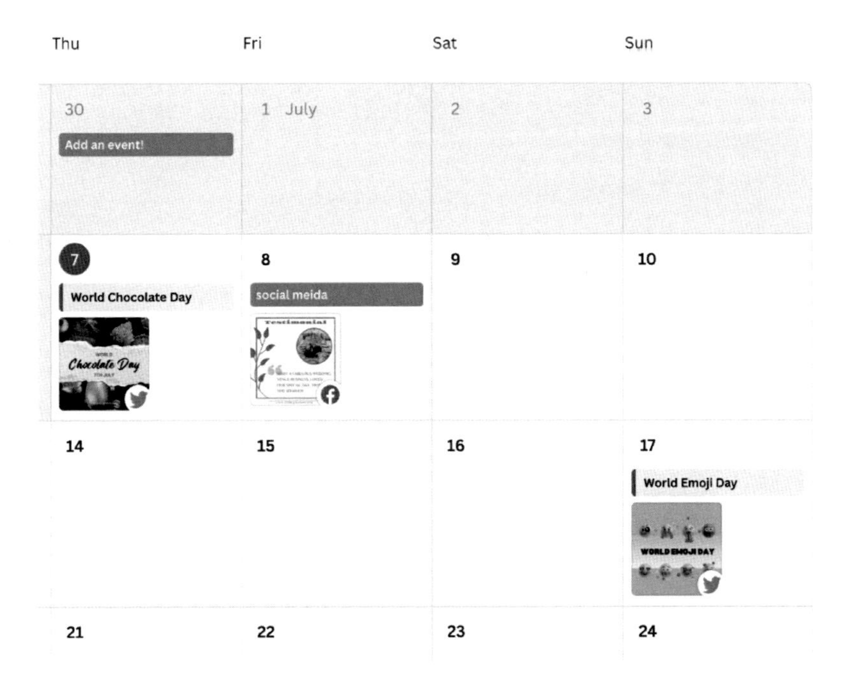

Figure 1.27 – View of the Content Planner with scheduled posts

All scheduled posts can be edited if needed. Just click on the post on the Content Planner and it will bring up the scheduled post for you to edit. Click **Save and schedule** and you're done.

Other ways to schedule and post

There are a couple of other ways to schedule and post posts to social platforms through Canva that achieve the same goal and are quite similar in process, but I thought it would be beneficial to briefly explain them. Both of these ways can be done on mobile or desktop versions of Canva:

- The first way is to create your design first, without selecting a date through the Content Planner. You can open up a blank template and create your design, then choose the **Schedule** option in the menu.

- Second, you don't have to schedule at all; you can post directly to your chosen platform. Just click on the **Share** option and select your platform from the drop-down menu. A similar screen will appear as if you are scheduling but with a **Publish now** button instead. This saves you having to download your designs, save them to your phone or computer, and then upload them to your socials. However, you can still schedule from this drop-down if you want, by clicking the small calendar icon in the bottom-left corner:

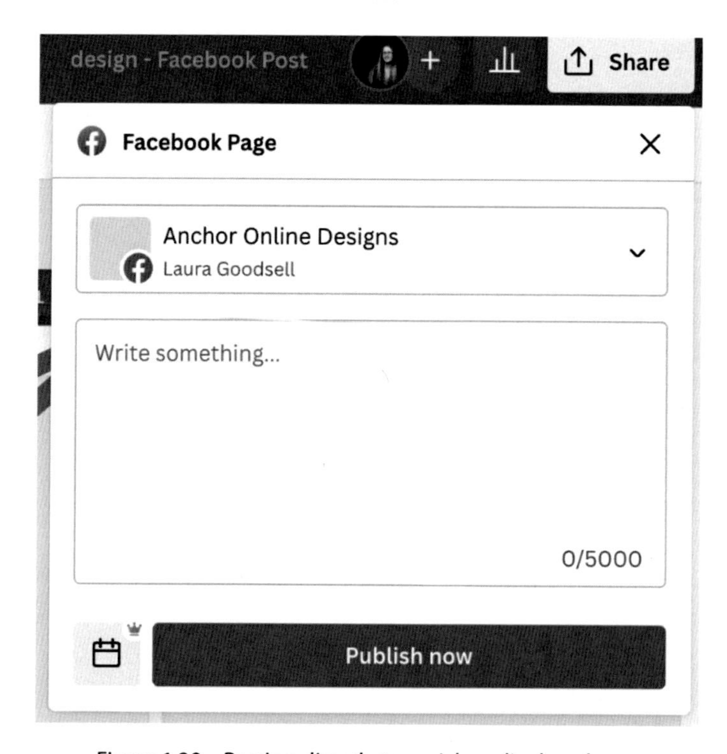

Figure 1.28 – Posting directly to social media dropdown

Creating and scheduling your posts to social media in bulk saves a lot of time when it comes to what to post each day. The Content Planner is here to help you and is a great feature to implement into your business. As it's included in Pro, there are no additional costs either.

We've now come to the end, so let's look at what we have learned in this chapter.

Summary

It's a wrap for the first chapter! By now, you will have a good understanding of what Canva is and the differences between the Free and Pro accounts. You have learned how to create and set up your Canva account, and how to set up and use the mobile app. Then, you learned how to create folders ready to get going with your designs and we looked at how to use the Content Planner to schedule your posts to social media. Although this is a Pro-only feature, I thought it would be beneficial to mention it in this book, as a lot of Canva users start on the Free account (which is awesome and getting better) but often find the benefits of Pro are required within their business, so you may make the switch over at some point in the future.

So that's it for this chapter. In the next chapter, we will be discovering templates that are available in Canva, how to edit them, and the wonderful use of elements and imagery, building on our knowledge from this chapter.

2

Discovering and Editing Templates

Templates are the main draw of Canva – that and its ease of use. Canva has hundreds of thousands of templates for every aspect of business and home life, from social media posts to poster, logo, and t-shirt designs. Along with the templates, you also have elements and images that you can add to your template to help make it unique. These are available to both Free and Pro users and many of them are also editable, making Canva a very versatile platform.

In this chapter, we are going to cover the following main topics:

- Finding and editing your templates
- Starting and finding your designs
- Using lines and shapes
- Text effects and fonts

By the end of this chapter, you will have gained a good amount of knowledge on using and editing templates. You will know where to search for templates that are aligned with your business, how to create a design from scratch, and where to find and edit simple lines and shapes.

Finding and editing your templates

Canva templates have been designed with you in mind. They are easy to edit and constructed in a way that, in some instances, requires no editing at all, or you can create a design from scratch. But how do you find a template that's suitable for your business needs? That is what we are going to find out in this section.

So, let's head over to the Canva dashboard. From here, you have a couple of options to search for your template. Use either the **Create a design** button in the top-right corner or the search bar in the middle.

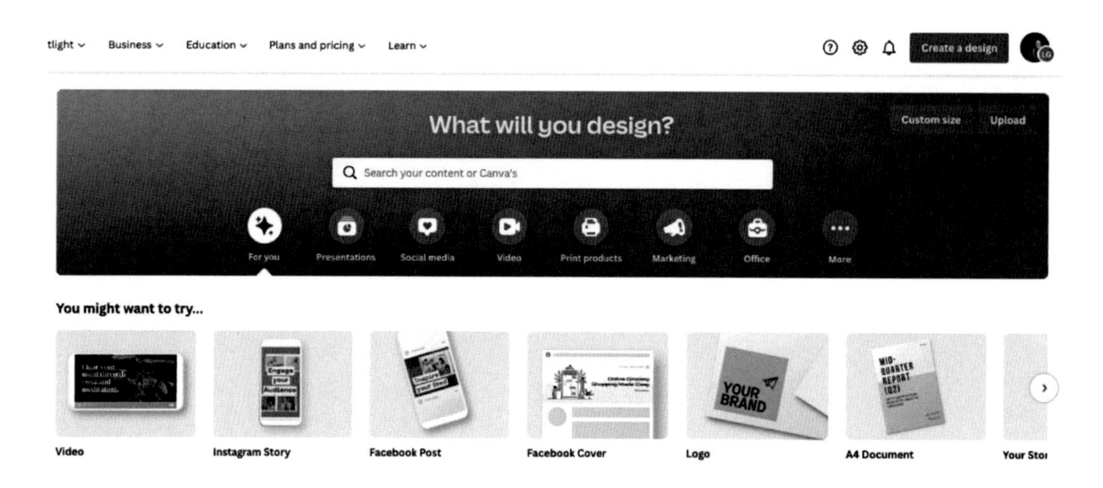

Figure 2.1 – Home page screen, showing the search bar and design buttons

If you know what you want to search for, for example, a Facebook story post, you can use the search bar, but if you're not sure, select the **Create a design** button, and it will give you a dropdown to choose from, which is what we are doing here:

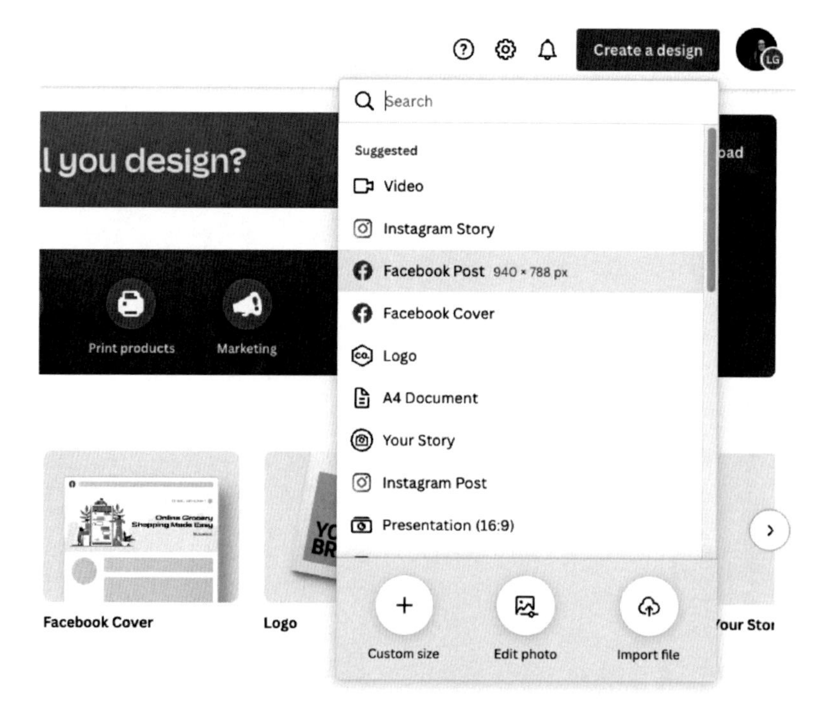

Figure 2.2 – Create a design dropdown

Here, we have several options. You can either search for a template, select an option in the dropdown, create a custom-sized template, or import a file directly into Canva. This option allows you to upload a PDF document, which will turn into a completely editable design.

For this example, we're going to select a Facebook post from the dropdown. Facebook and Instagram posts are the most used templates in Canva.

Once selected, a new screen will open, giving you the option to create from scratch or select a template.

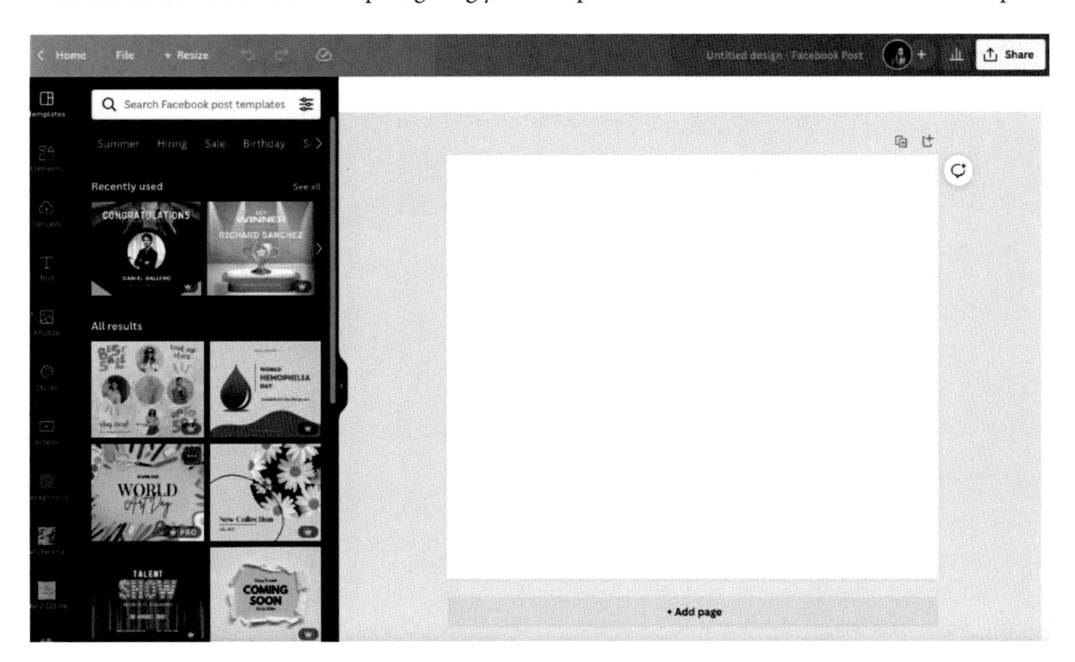

Figure 2.3 – Blank template

Click on the **Template** option in the top left corner and it will bring up the templates available, starting with any recently used ones, then all results sorted by most popular.

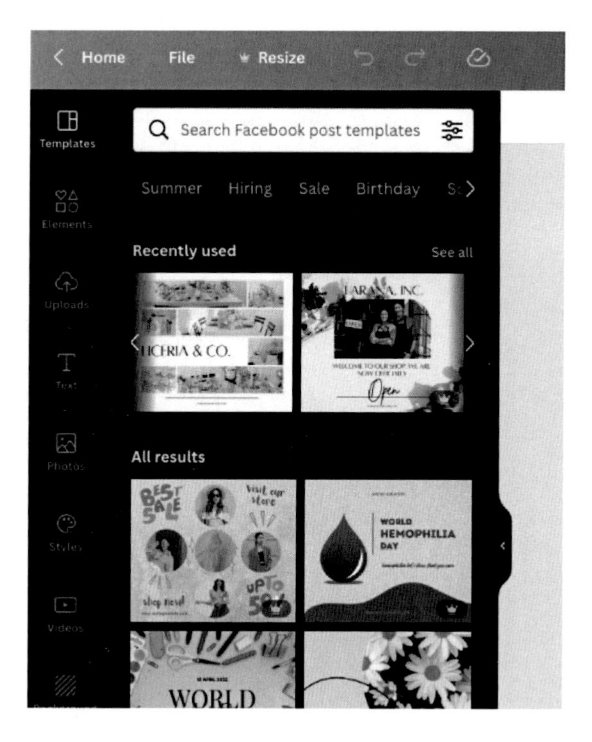

Figure 2.4 – Closeup of the template options

Scroll through these to get an idea of what's available and see whether there are any that catch your eye. You can also choose a style of template using the options along the top; for example, we have **Summer**, **Hiring**, **Sale**, and **Birthday**.

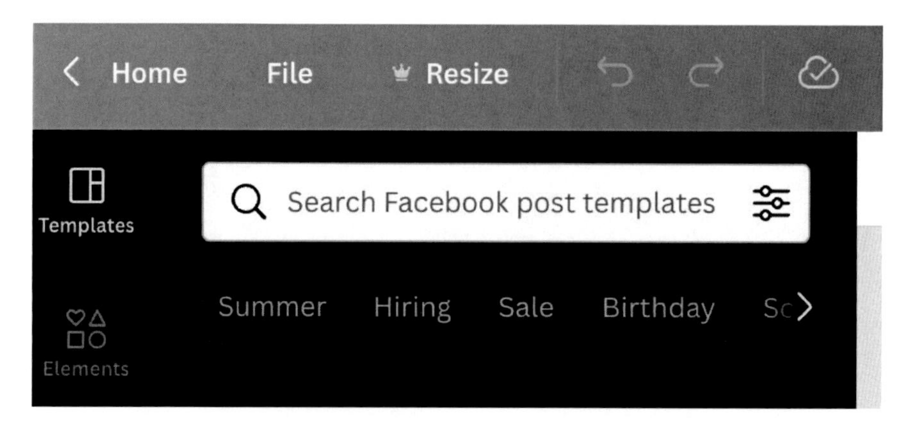

Figure 2.5 – Closeup of different style template buttons

Going back to the main page, I have selected a template from the options on the left that has caught my eye. For this example, my business is a social media manager, so I am looking for a template that is professional, clean, and clear to help promote my message. Canva will display the template automatically on the blank template screen. Now, I would like to edit it to suit my business.

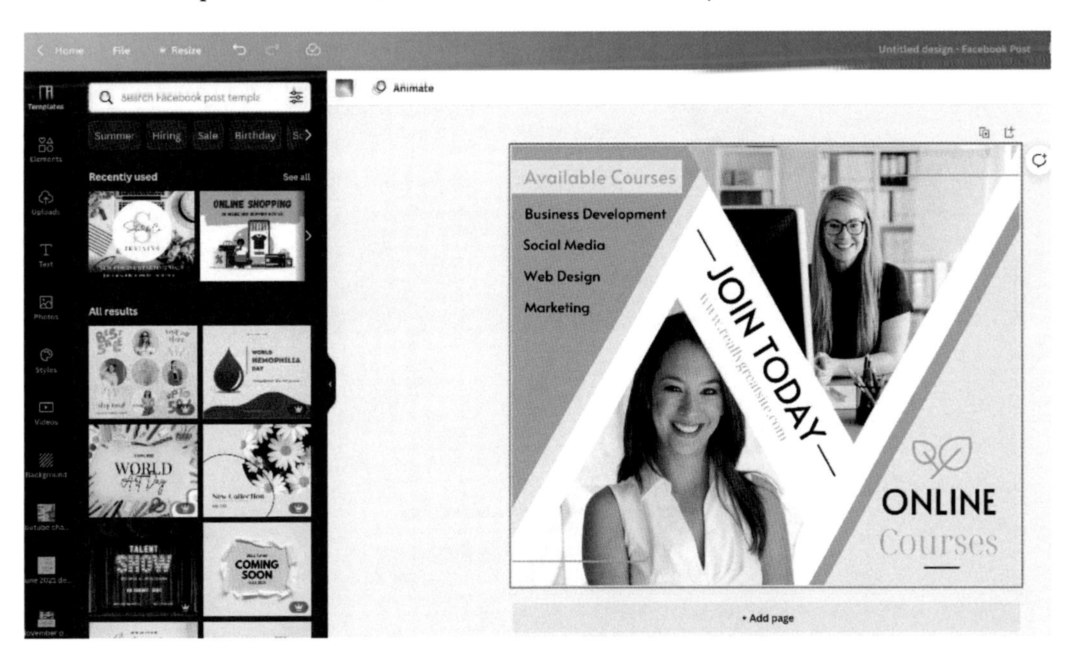

Figure 2.6 – Selected template ready for editing

I could use this template as is; it's a lovely designed template and could only need minimal editing to suit my business. Hover your mouse over the template and you will see lots of purple squares appear. These represent every element, shape, image, and text block that is within your design. To change any of these, you need to highlight and then select the box in question.

> **Tip**
>
> Canva has an automatic save option so you don't need to worry about saving your designs, but if you would like to, click on the **File** tab at the top and scroll down to **Save**.

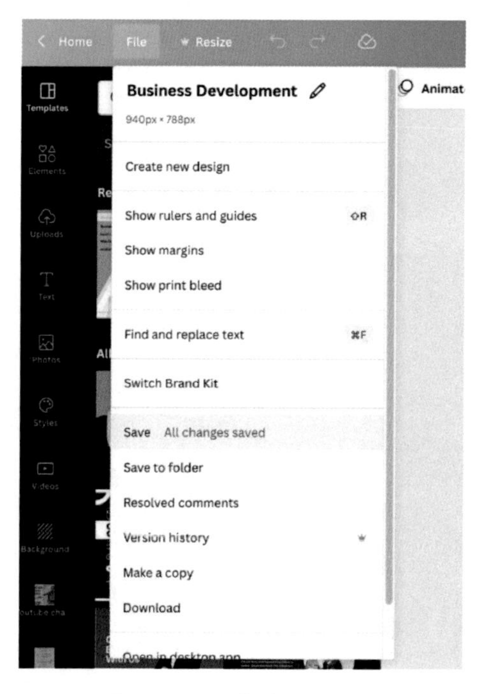

Figure 2.7 – File dropdown

Changing the colors

Follow along with these steps to edit a template in Canva:

1. First of all, let's start with the color choices; for example, I want my business brand colors to be cream, teal, and light gray, so I would want to change the ones on the template. I can do this by selecting a block of color and then clicking on the color block icon in the top-left corner.

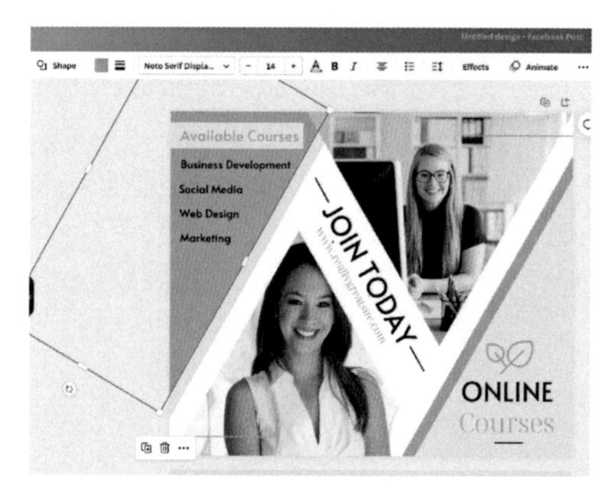

Figure 2.8 – Selecting a block of color to change

2. This will bring up the color palettes, which includes your branding colors (we will cover this in *Chapter 5, Exploring the Awesome Creative Tools for Branding*), colors taken from the photos, default colors, and the option to create your own color.
3. I've selected the cross icon under the **Document Colors** section, as this will let me choose my own color. I can now move the white circles around to find the ideal color for my shape.

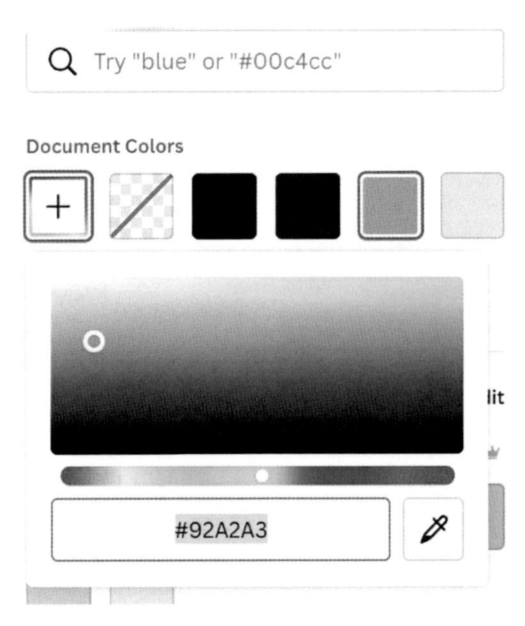

Figure 2.9 – Color option to select own color

4. As you move the circles around, you will notice the color changing on your design, so you can see how it will look before selecting it.

5. Once you have decided on the color, just take your cursor off of the color box and it will keep the option on your design.

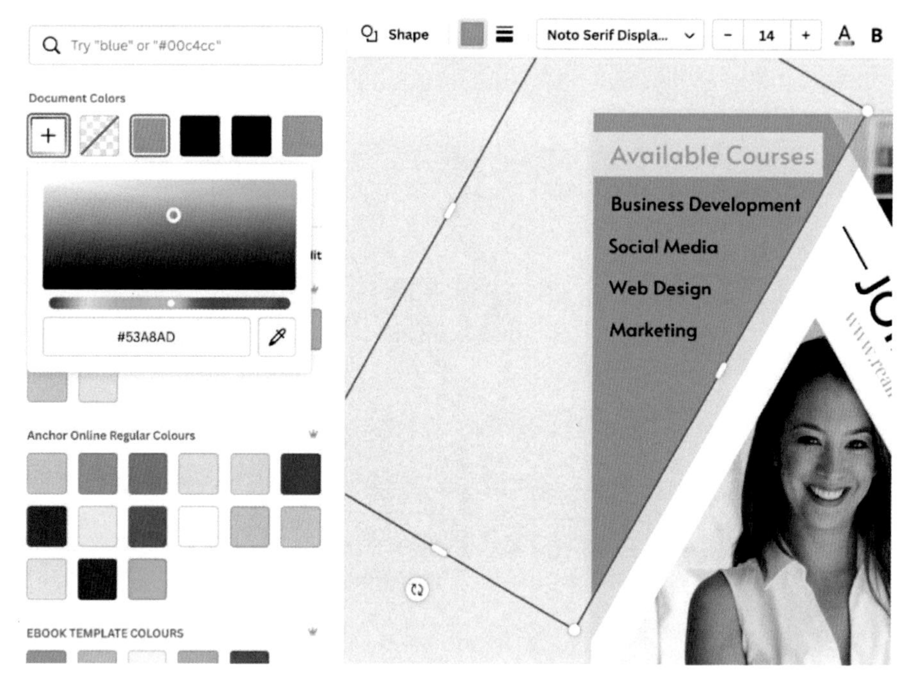

Figure 2.10 – Changing the color of blocks in Canva

You can now repeat the same steps for any other part of your design. This will also work for changing the color of fonts and icons.

> **Tip**
> If you have a lot of the same color on the template, a box will appear at the bottom of the color palette, to allow you to change all from one color to the next. This works on all pages within your design, saving you from changing the color individually.

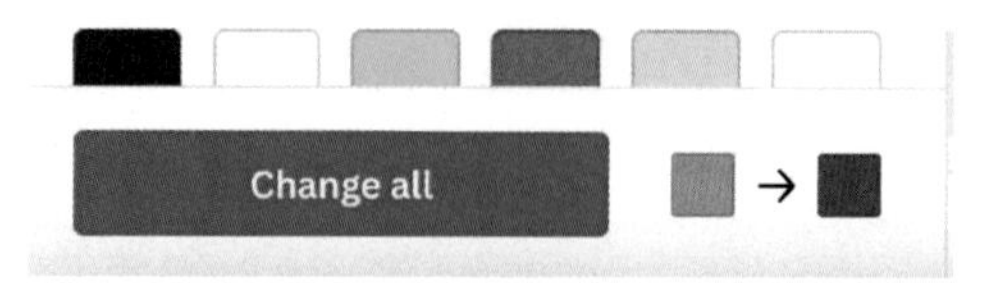

Figure 2.11 – The Change all color option

Let's now look at how to change the images on the template.

Changing images on a template

Changing the images is a good idea as you can use ones to suit your branding. Canva has hundreds of thousands of images available in their library for you to use. Many of these are available to both Free and Pro accounts. You can work out whether an image is available for your plan by hovering over the image; it will show a crown icon at the bottom of the image if it's available for Pro only, or nothing if it's available on both Free and Pro.

Most templates will use grids and frames to change the shapes of images (we will look at grids and frames in *Chapter 6, Expert Hacks to Create Your Own Professional-Looking Designs*).

Here are the steps needed for you to change the images on templates using relevant keywords

1. Select the **Photos** option in the menu and it will bring up all the available photos, including any recently used, recommended, and trending photos, so you can see which are most widely used.

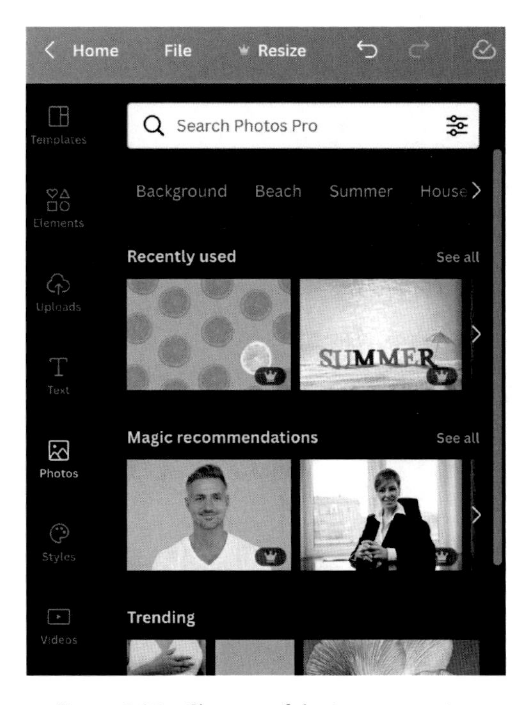

Figure 2.12 – Closeup of the images section

2. Here, we can search for a photo; we use keywords in the search box. Every image has been submitted to Canva with a selection of keywords attached that describe the image: what is in it, the colors, and its use. These are designed to help bring up a suitable selection to choose from. I'm creating a post for my fictional social media business, so I'll need photos of a computer or desk and someone working in the same environment, so I will search for the `Social media flat lay` keywords to get a range of images.

Figure 2.13 – Using a keyword to search for images

3. So, now all I need to do is select the one I like for my design. It will be added to the template and I can drag and drop it into the box on top of the existing image to replace it, repeating this for any other images I would like to replace.

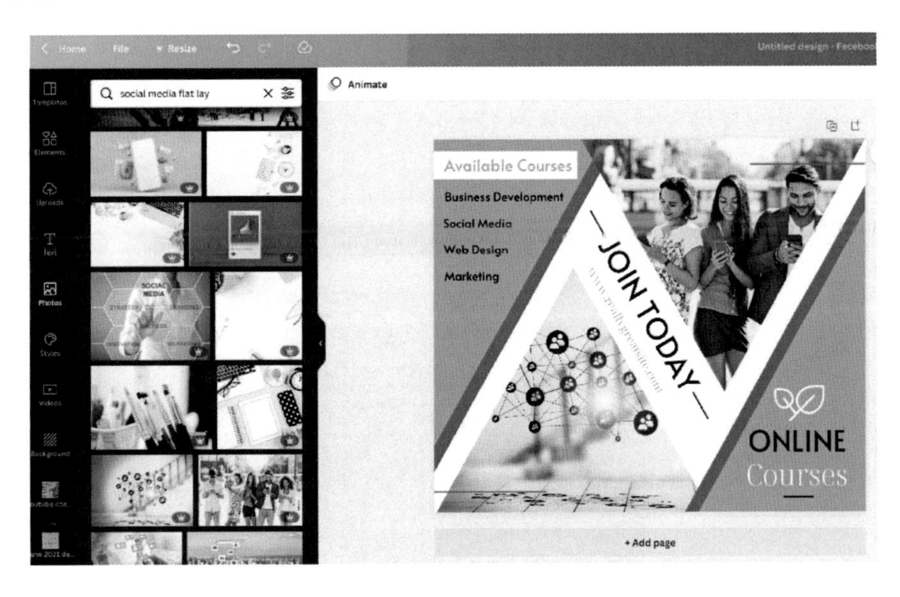

Figure 2.14 – Template with color and image changes

4. Now that I have my images and colors in place, I lastly want to change the text and font.

Changing the text and font

Canva has hundreds of fonts available. If you use a specific font that isn't in Canva, you can upload the font file to give you access to your fonts on every design you create. However, this feature is a Pro-only feature, so if you are using the Free version, you will need to stick with the available fonts. Take the following steps:

1. To change the information within a text box, just select the box in question, then click on it again and it will highlight the information in blue, meaning you can now directly type into the box.

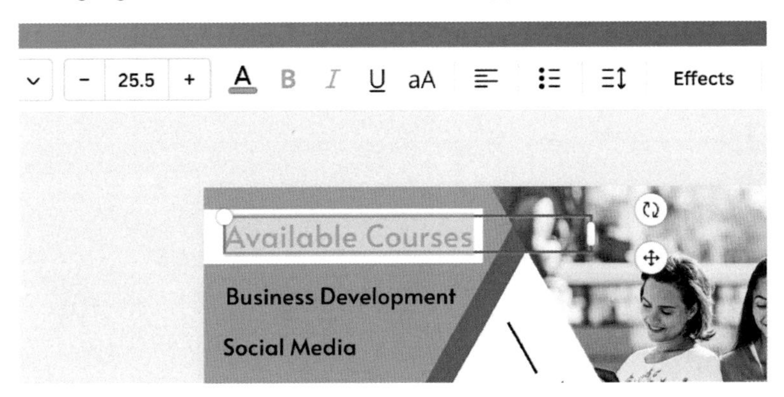

Figure 2.15 – Highlighted text box ready for editing

2. To add a completely new text box, you can either press the *T* key on your keyboard or select the **Text** tab from the left menu, which will give you the option to add header text, subheading text, or body text to your template, with some recently used text combinations displayed in the following screenshot.

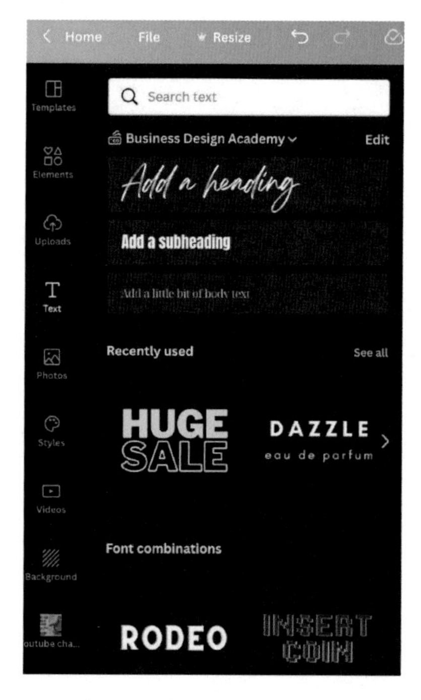

Figure 2.16 – Text menu, showing header, subheading, and body text options

3. To change the font, select the text box in question, then at the top, there is a bar with different options and boxes. The first one will give you a dropdown of all fonts available, the second lets you change the size of the font, and the third option lets you change the color of your font.

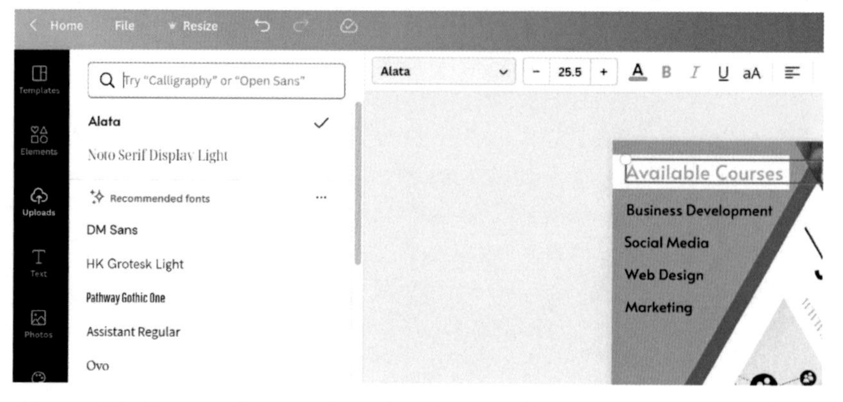

Figure 2.17 – Top bar of the text box, showing font, size, and color change options

If you know your font, you can search for it; otherwise, scroll through the options to find one that suits your design. I've gone for a more professional, corporate font, something that is clean, simple, and easy to read on this template.

We have now changed the color, images, and font. This is how the template looked before editing:

Figure 2.18 – Original template before editing

And after editing, it looks as follows:

Figure 2.19 – Finished edited template

So far in this chapter, we have covered how to find and edit pre-existing templates. We now know how to change the colors, images, text, and fonts. We've looked at where to find images and how to search for them using keywords, as well as where to find the color palettes and different fonts and how to add new text boxes. Next, let's look at how to create a design from scratch and how to find your templates once they are saved.

Starting and finding your designs

Using a template is often the quickest and easiest way to create quick graphics in Canva, but sometimes, it's necessary to create one from scratch, especially if we can't find a template that matches what we are looking for. Starting a blank template is very similar to using a pre-made template. Click on the **Create a design** tab and search for the size you require. A blank template of the selected size will open up for you. Alternatively, you can click on the **Custom size** tab and you are given the following size options:

- **px** (pixels)
- **in** (inches)
- **mm** (millimeters)
- **cm** (centimeters)

These are useful if you are creating a banner, poster, book, or something else that has a specific size you need to work to.

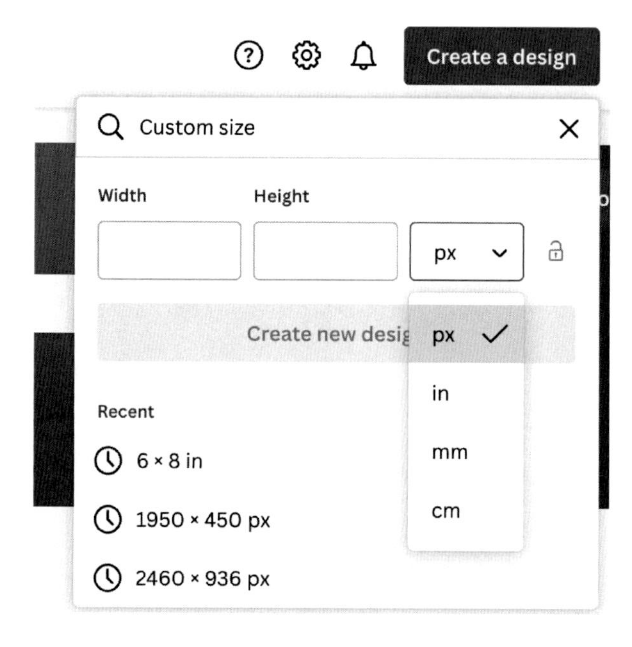

Figure 2.20 – Custom size options

Finding your designs

Every design in Canva is automatically saved as you go along, and they are all saved in your **Projects** tab in the left menu. Once you have finished creating your design, you can close the tab and come back to it later by navigating to the **Projects** tab and clicking on **Designs**, and everything will be there in order of when it was made, so the most recent will be displayed first.

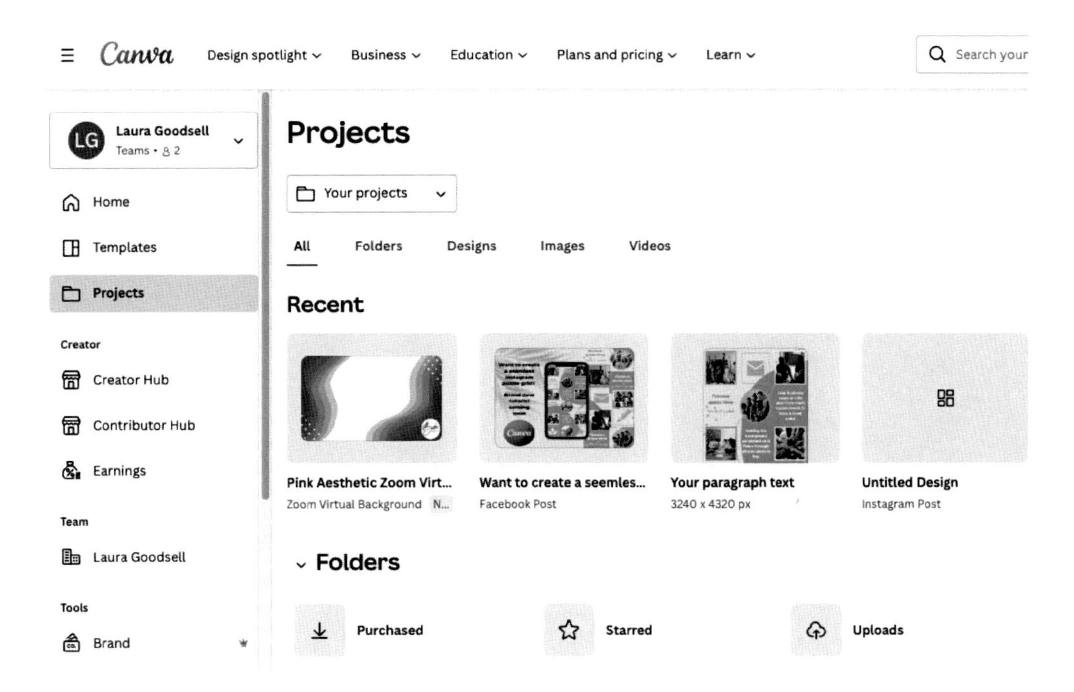

Figure 2.21 – Projects tab

You can also save designs into a folder for better organization, creating as many as you wish in both the Free and Pro accounts. We covered the use of folders in *Chapter 1*, *Setting Up Canva on Desktop and Mobile*.

Being able to start a design from scratch is something you can now do confidently. We've also looked at how to create a custom-sized template and where they are all stored, so you can find your designs quickly to use for your business. Let's now look at how to add and edit lines and shapes.

Using lines and shapes

Lines and shapes in Canva are instrumental to your designs. You will find that you use them a lot more than you ever planned to; that's because lines are brilliant at dividing and organizing information on a design and shapes are great at giving the design a sense of balance and can help to draw the viewer's eye to important aspects.

Lines

Lines can be found in two places. The first is the simplest: all you need to do is press the *L* key on your keyboard and a line element will appear on your template. The second is to search for `Lines` in the **Elements** tab, which gives you more line elements, as well as images that have used the `Lines` keyword. But for this section, we are looking for a normal line, which comes up first in the list.

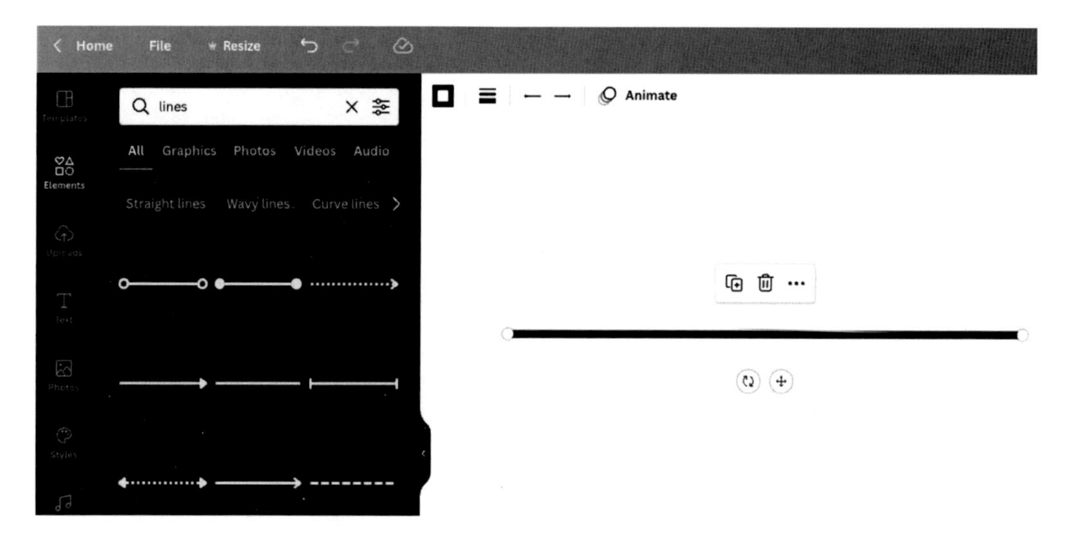

Figure 2.22 – The line element

We can now do more with lines in Canva. At the top of your template, you will see a selection of options. Hover over each one to see what it can do. They include the following:

- **Line Color**
- **Line Style**
- **Line Start**
- **Line End**
- **Animate**

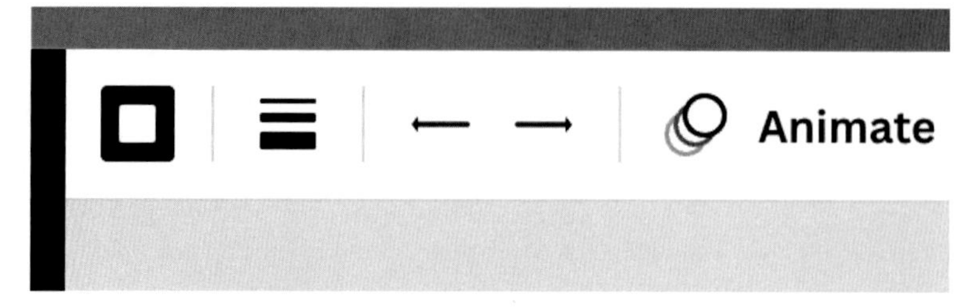

Figure 2.23 – Closeup of the line options

Line Color allows you to change the color of the line to any color you would like. It brings up all color palettes.

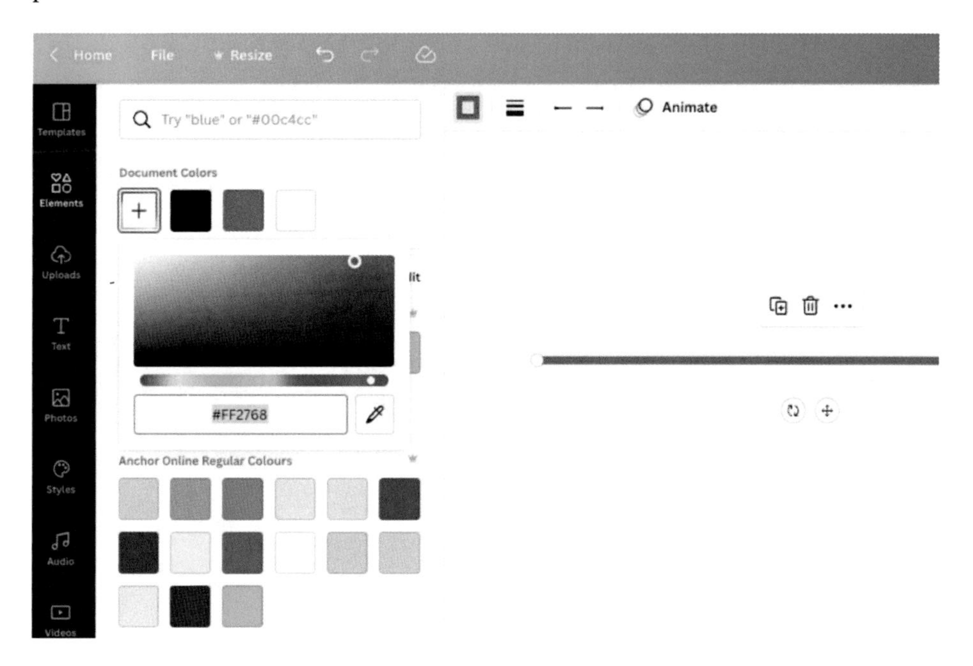

Figure 2.24 – Line Color closeup

The second option along is my favorite as it allows you to change the style of the line, so you can have a solid, dotted, or dashed line. It also has a checkbox for making the ends of the line rounded, and you can change the thickness of the line here.

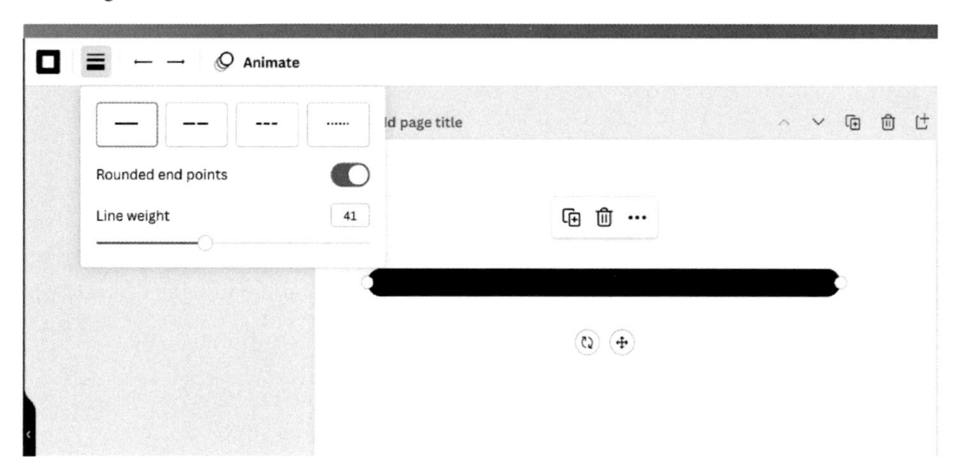

Figure 2.25 – Line Style

Next along, we have the option to change the ends of the line, giving it a more finished look. There is a separate dropdown for the start and end of the line, both of which have the same icons, but you can change either end, left and right independently, so you can mimic each end or have different ends.

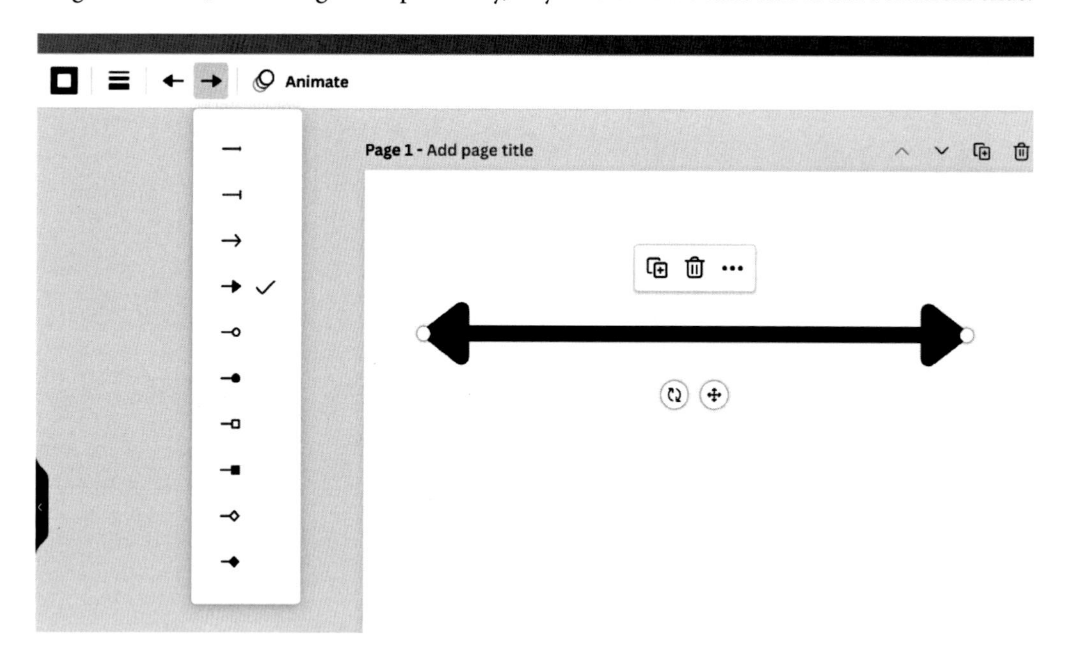

Figure 2.26 – Line End dropdowns

Lastly, you can animate your line as you can with every element, template, and image in Canva, but we will be looking at how to do this in *Chapter 10, Leveraging Video and Animation within Your Business Marketing.*

Shapes

Shapes in Canva are a staple part of most designs. You will find the majority of templates have made use of a shape or two, and there is more you can now do with shapes as Canva has added new features. You can find the shapes the same way you found the line element. There are two options: the first one is to use the *C* key on your keyboard for a circle, and the *R* key on your keyword will produce a rectangle. If you are looking for more or different shapes, you can find them in the **Elements** section by searching for the `shapes` keyword. Let's take a look at them.

There are many different shapes. Some are simple block color squares, triangles, and circles.

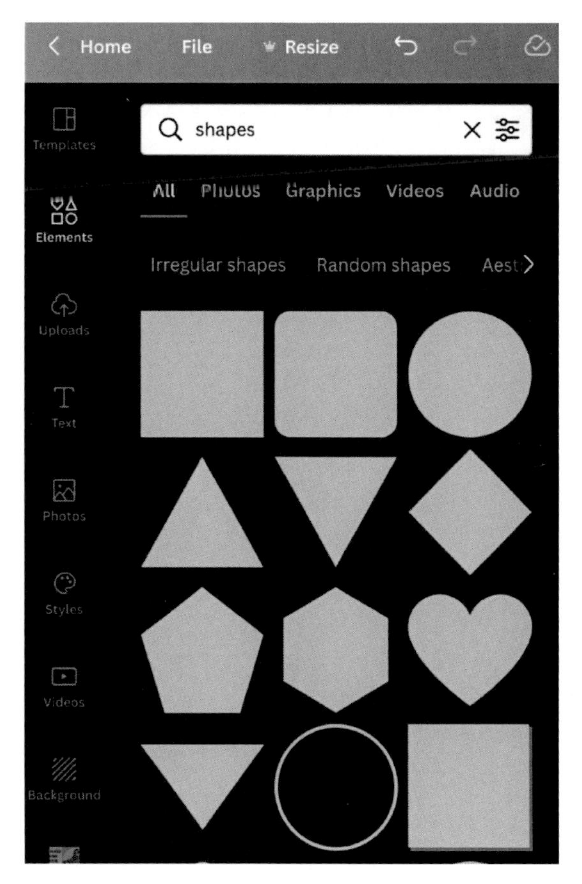

Figure 2.27 – Basic shape styles

Others are more complex, such as having fancy borders or multiple shades within them.

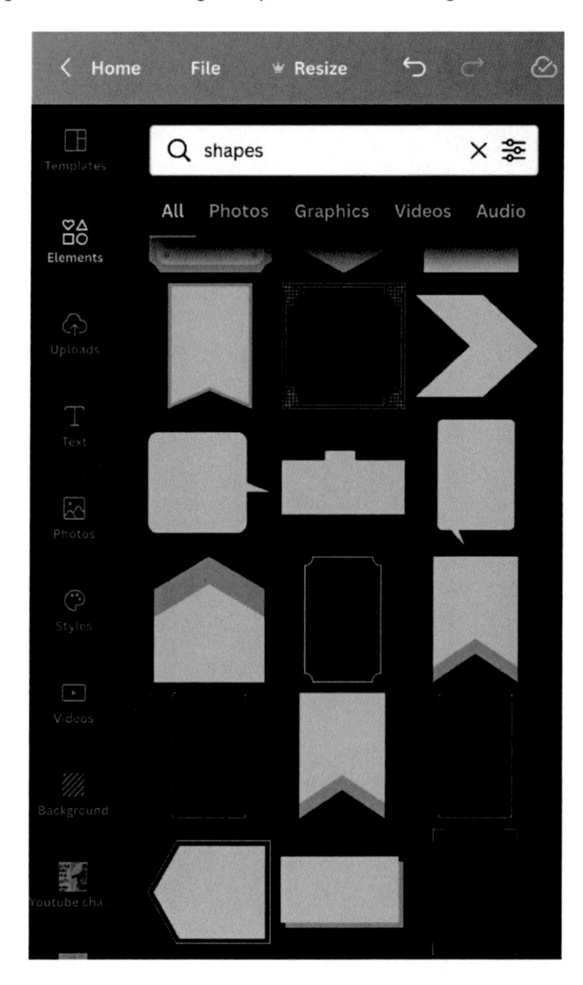

Figure 2.28 – Borders and different shape styles

The ones we are going to look at here have an extra level of features to them. They are the basic shapes, which include squares and circles. I have selected the plain square. When doing so, you may notice that a cursor appears in the center. We can now add text directly into the shape. If you don't want to add text, click away from the square and the cursor will disappear.

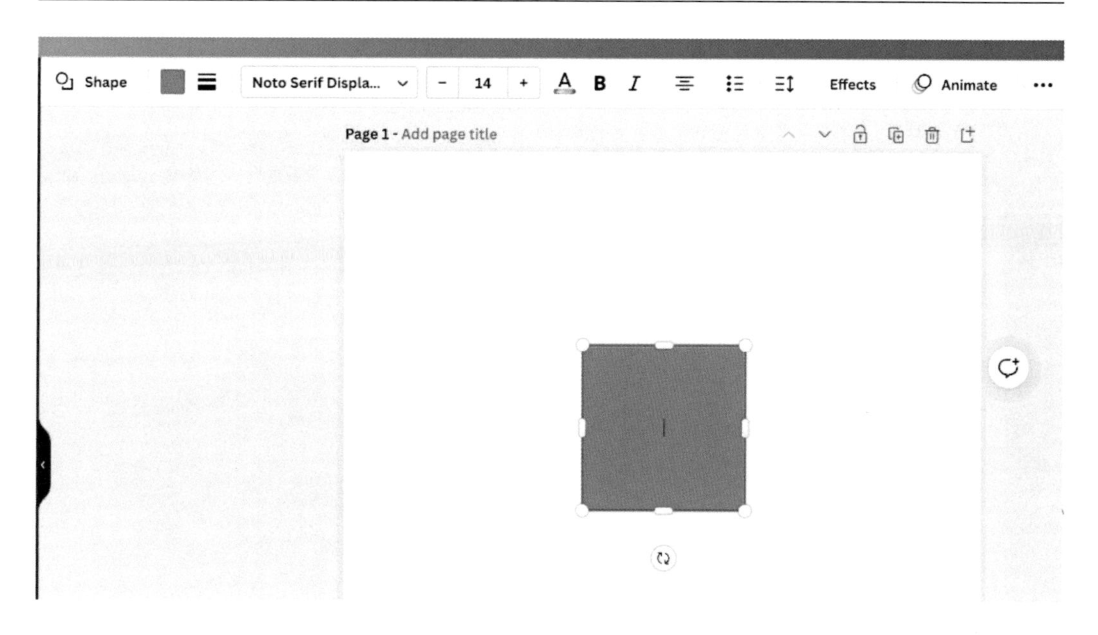

Figure 2.29 – Square shape added to template with cursor

As with the other elements we have looked at, the top bar shows us all the features of the shape. This bar will change depending on what element, text box, image, or shape you have selected. This shape now gives us a couple of features that are really useful. First of all, we can change the shape by selecting the first option on the bar, called **Shape**.

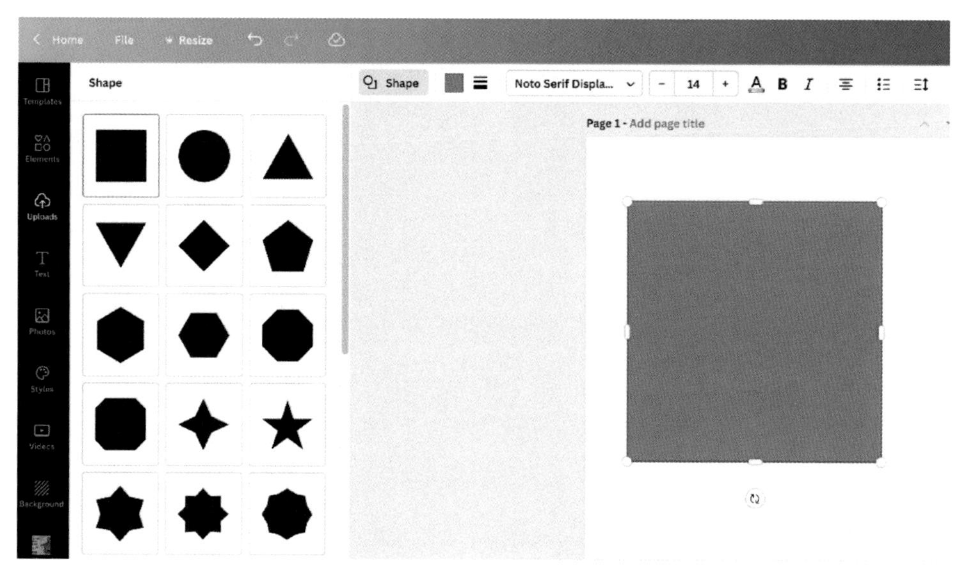

Figure 2.30 – Canva shapes

We can automatically change the shape to any of the suggested ones in the left column. I've changed the square to a star shape so I can show the next feature.

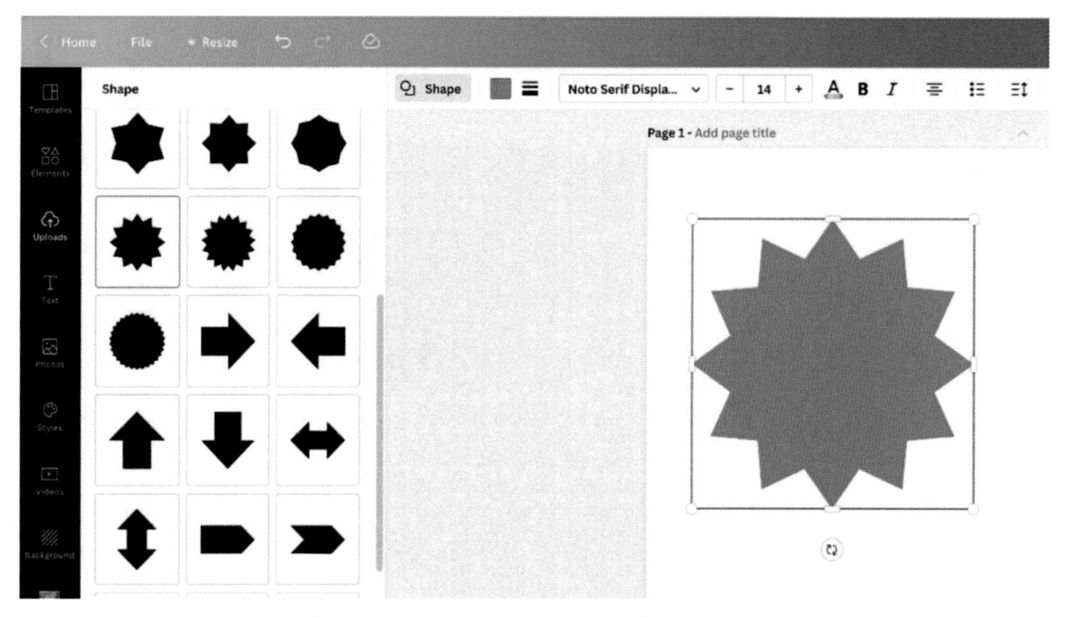

Figure 2.31 – Different shapes, including stars

This feature is the third icon along, the three lines next to the color block.

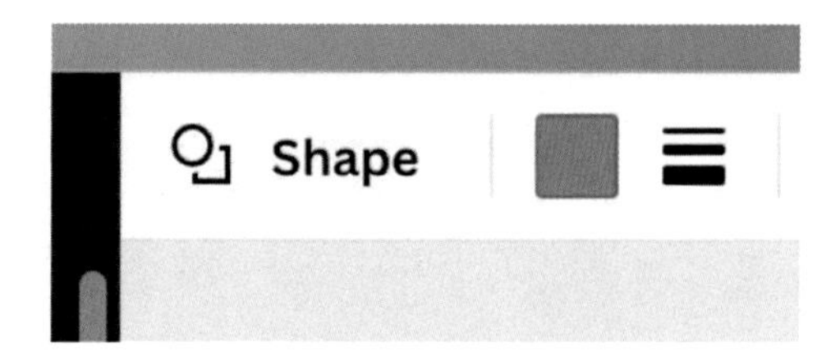

Figure 2.32 – Shape options

This is a great feature as you can give your shape a border. There are five options:

- No border
- Solid line border
- Large lined border
- Small lined border
- Dotted border

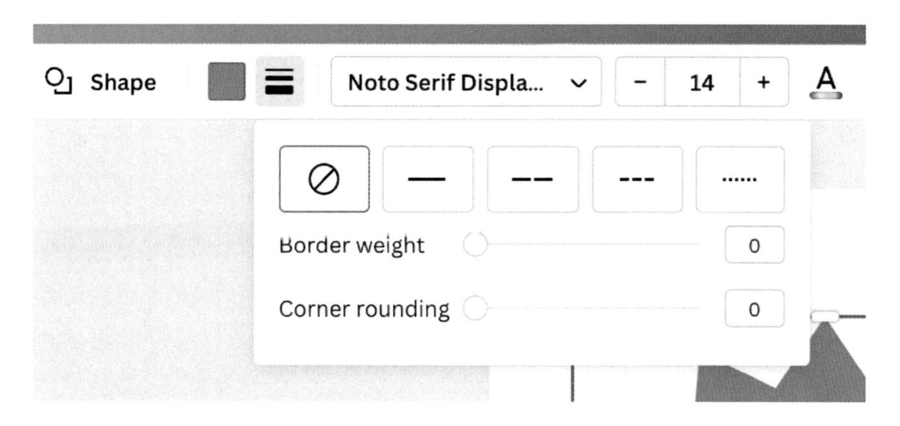

Figure 2.33 – Shape controls for border weight, style, and roundness

Once you select the border option, a new icon will appear in the top bar to allow you to change the color of your border.

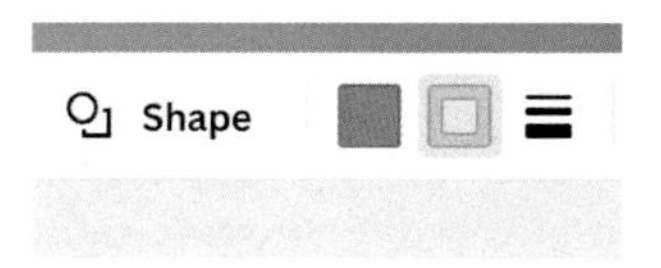

Figure 2.34 – Closeup of the top bar shape options, including border color

Below the line options, you have controls to allow you to change the thickness of your border and round the corners of your shape.

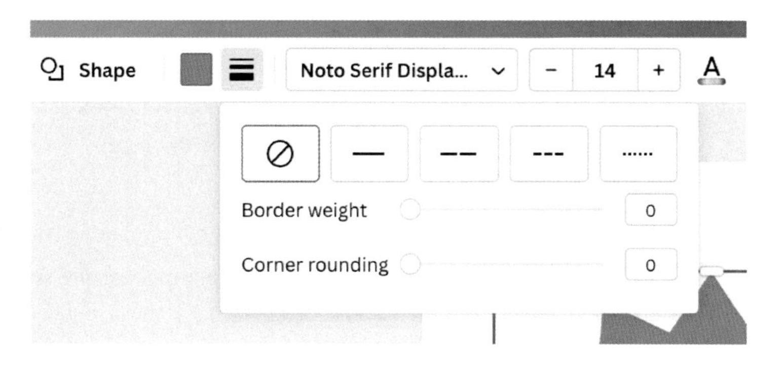

Figure 2.35 – Shape controls for border weight, style, and roundness

In a few short clicks, I have changed my plain square into a star, given it a lined border, and changed the thickness and colors, and I can now use this within my design.

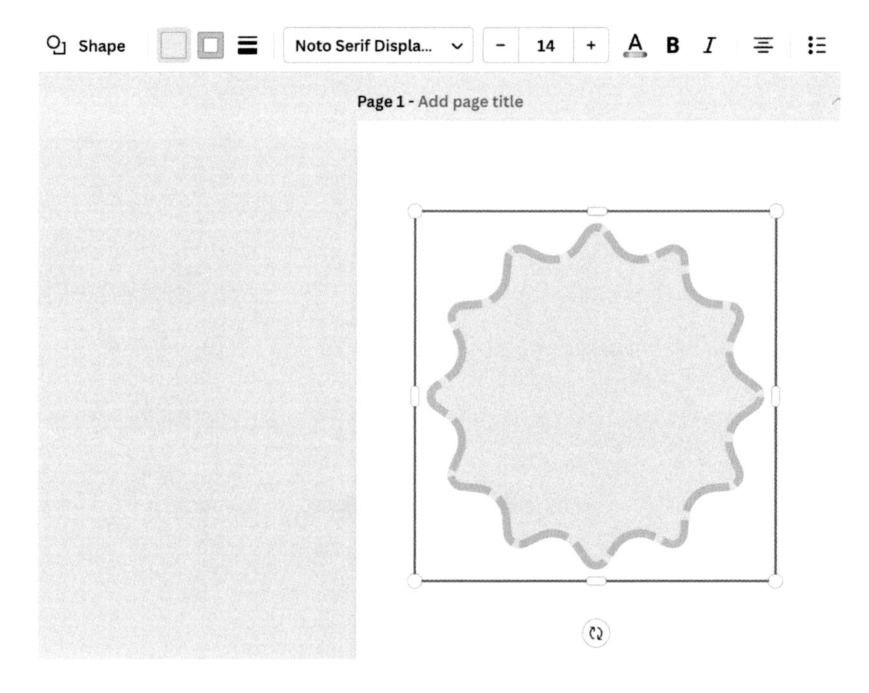

Figure 2.36 – Closeup of the final edited shape

Shapes may seem unexciting, but they are so versatile and useful in everyday design. Have a look around you and count how many shapes you can find. They work well in your business templates and it's useful to know how to edit them to suit your brand.

You can even use shapes as a background for your text boxes, so next, let's look at the different text effects and fonts.

Text effects and fonts

Canva is home to hundreds of different fonts, so whatever you are creating, you are sure to find a font to suit your design, but how do you find them and how can you make them stand out more? Well, that's what we are going to find out in this section.

The dropdown for fonts appears once you have added a text box to your template. It's the first option along the top bar. The fonts appear on the left side and you can choose one through search or scrolling as they're shown in alphabetic order with recommended, recently used, and your brand fonts appearing first.

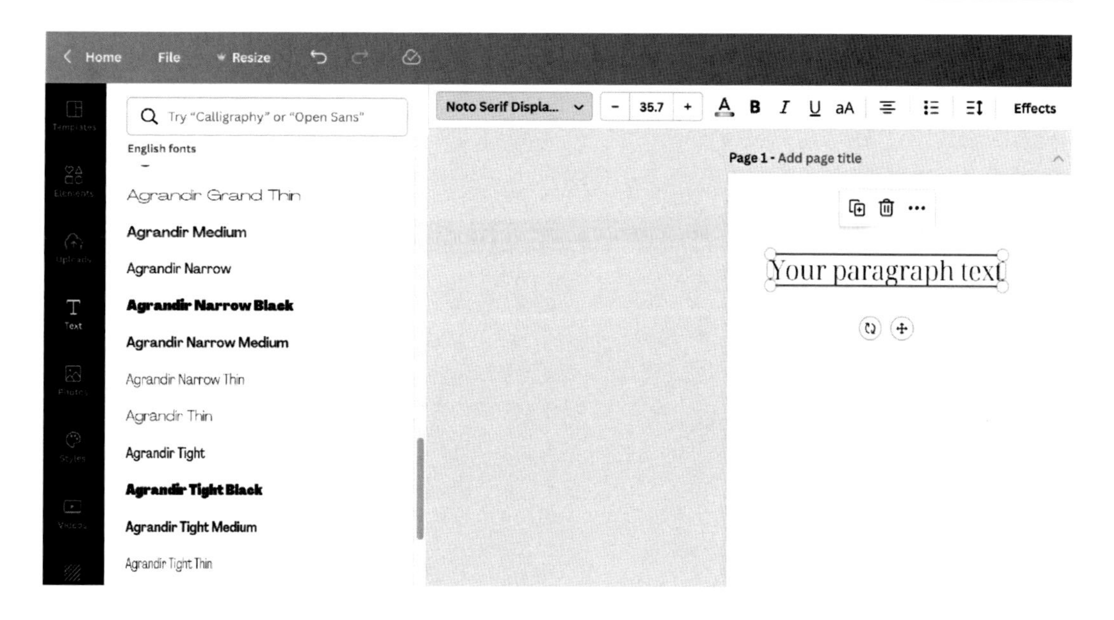

Figure 2.37 – Selection of fonts available in Canva

If by some chance you cannot find the font you want to use in Canva, you can also upload a font you have purchased or downloaded from the internet. As long as you have the OTF or TTF files, you can upload these to Canva. This is a Pro feature, and we will be looking at how to do this in *Chapter 5, Exploring the Awesome Creative Tools for Branding.*

But for now, we are going to find a font in Canva we can edit, I'm looking for a nice, easy-to-read font, as I may want to use this for a social media post, so using a sans serif font will help make it easier to read on screens.

The difference between sans serif and serif fonts

Sans serif fonts are fonts without the little feet or flicks at the end.

The following are examples of serif and sans serif fonts. Serif fonts have little feet at the end of each letter and are often used in print material, such as books, magazines, and newspapers:

Example Text - Serif

Example Text - Sans Serif

Figure 2.38 – Sample font styles

When you click on the search box, a selection of options will appear along the top. Here, you can choose a style of font. For example, if you require a fancy font for a business name, then you can select **Handwriting**, or if you need a more professional font for a CV, you could select **Corporate**.

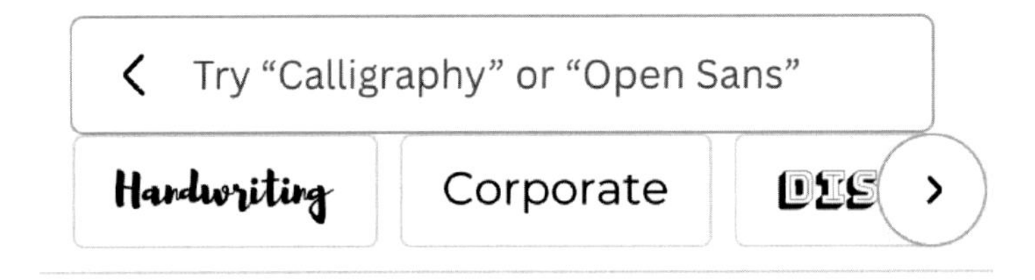

Figure 2.39 – Closeup of the font search bar

I've chosen the **Agrandir Wide Black** font, a nice, chunky, easy-to-read font.

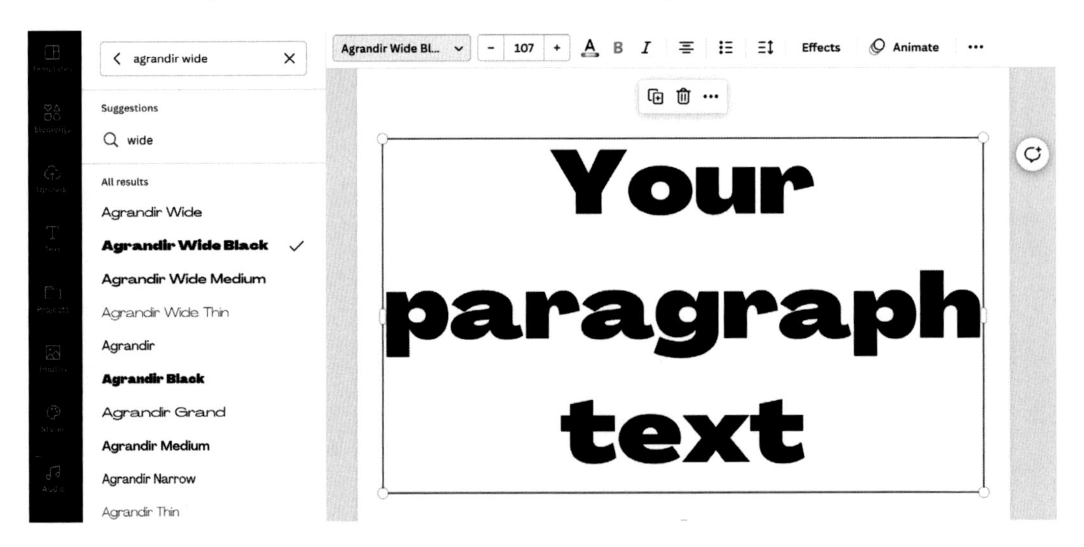

Figure 2.40 – Text box with chosen font

So, now we have a font we can use on our social post, let's add some styling to it. This can be done through the **Effects** tab. Here, you can give your font a neon glow, background shadow, hollow effect, and more.

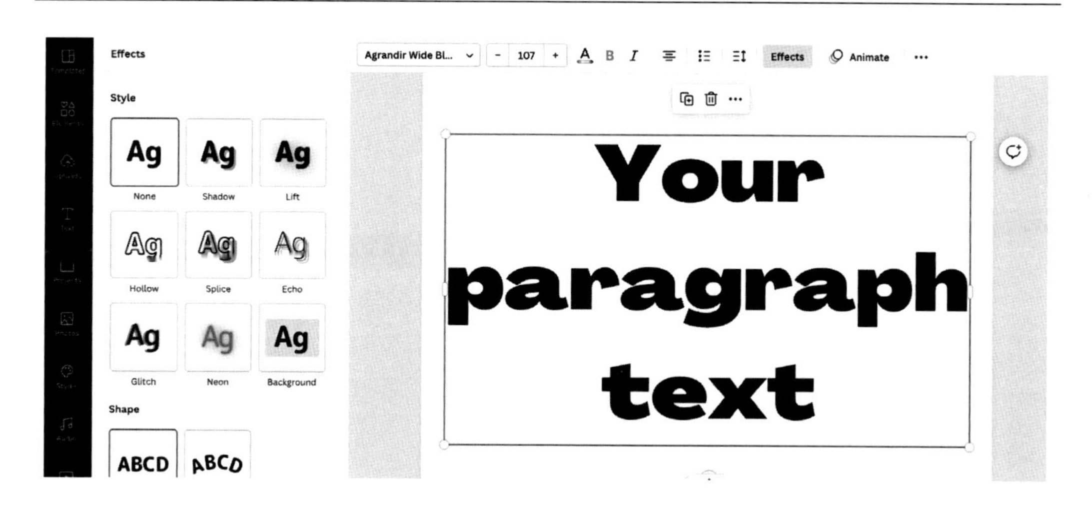

Figure 2.41 – Font effects

Each one of the effects has its own set of options, which you can adjust using the sliding bars. On the **Shadow** effect, we can change the offset of the shadow, the direction it flows, the blur and transparency, as well as the color of the shadow itself.

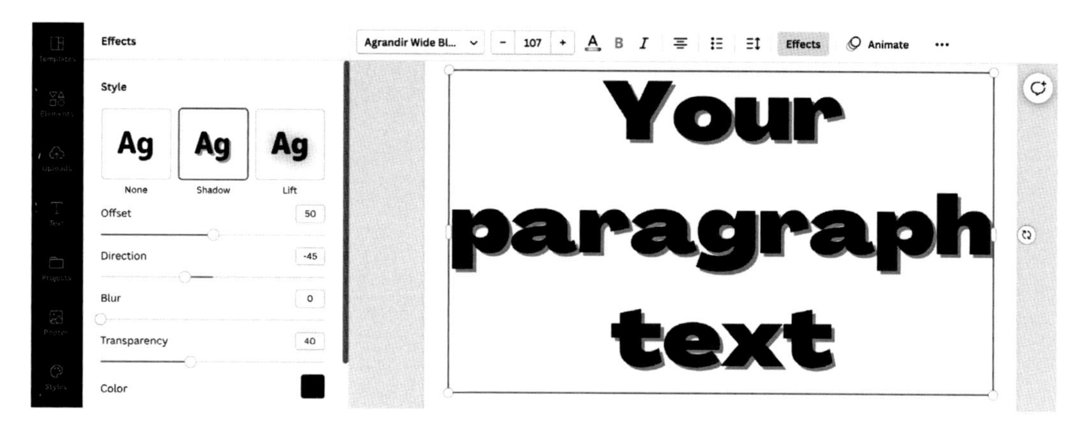

Figure 2.42 – Shadow font effect settings

In this example, I've increased the offset to make it appear like it's popping out of the screen, left the direction where it was, increased the blur to soften the shadow, slightly increased the transparency, and changed the color of the font, leaving the shadow black.

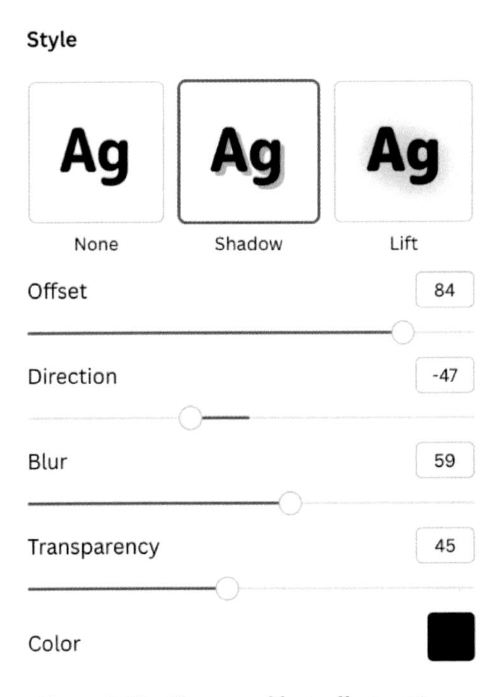

Figure 2.43 – Closeup of font effect settings

This is the finished effect, achieved in under a minute:

Figure 2.44 – Final version of fully edited text

Now, you can have text that will stand out more on your social posts.

Here are some of the other text effects:

- **Hollow**: Takes out the middle of your font and allows you to increase or decrease the thickness of the lines.

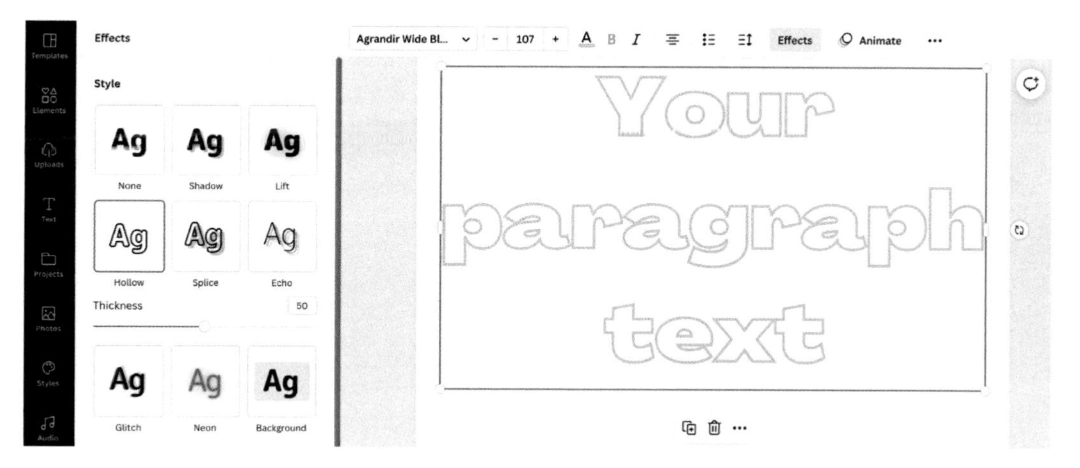

Figure 2.45 – Hollow text effect

- **Splice**: This is one of my favorites; it's the hollow effect with the background displaced. You can change the color of the background as well.

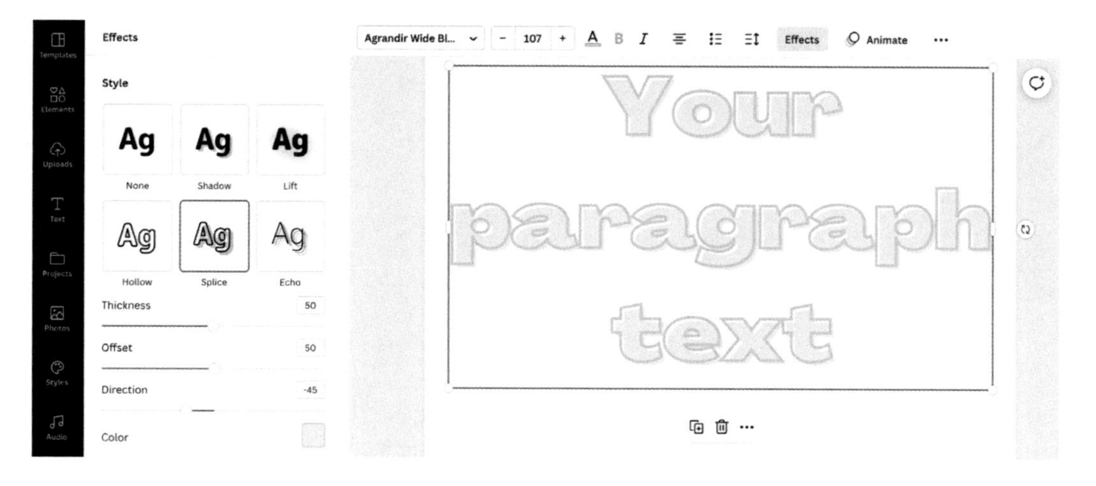

Figure 2.46 – Splice text effect

- **Neon**: This one gives your font a glow.

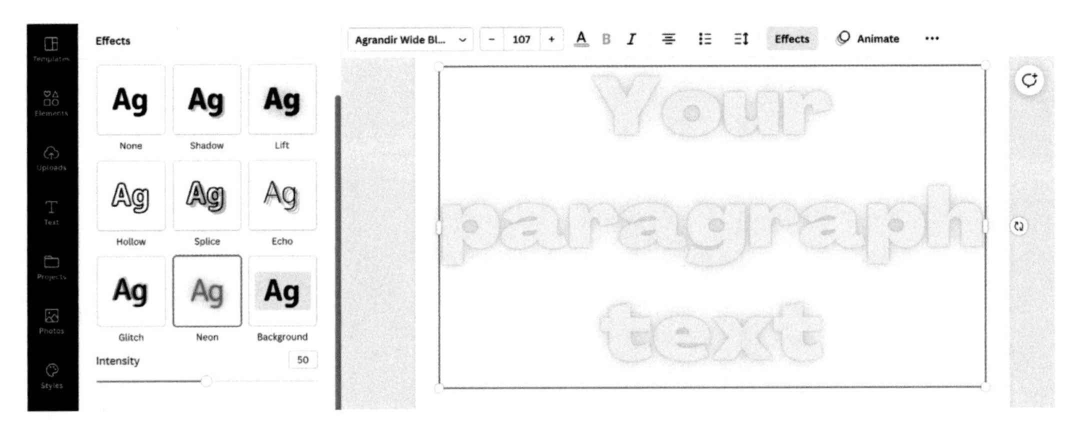

Figure 2.47 – Neon text effect

- **Background**: This effect follows the contour of your font and gives it a colored background.

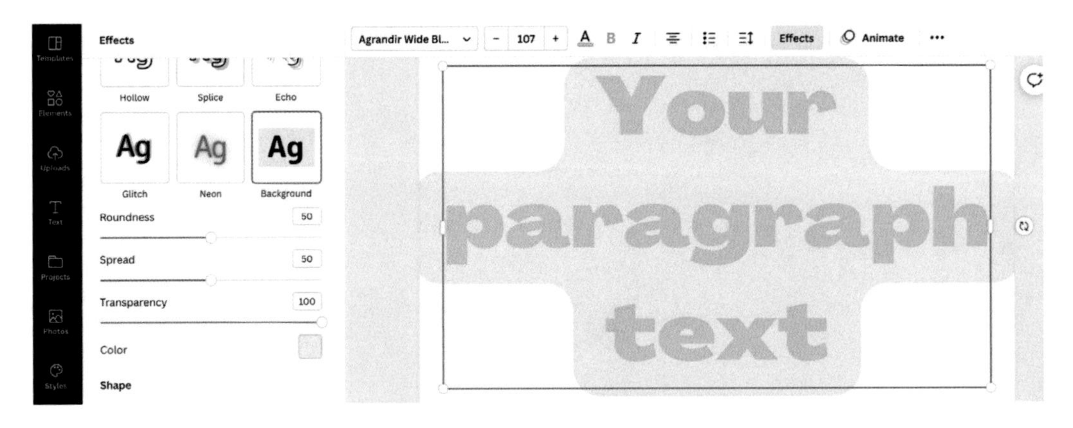

Figure 2.48 – Background text effect

The best way to discover what the effects can really do, and which one would work best for your design, is to have a look at all of them and have a play with each one and its different settings.

Curved text

Lastly, I'd like to show you a great feature that has saved me countless hours in Canva: the curved text feature. You can now curve your text with the click of a button. It can be found at the bottom of the font effects tab and allows you to curve the text either up or down, changing the ratio of the curve by using the scroll bar at the bottom.

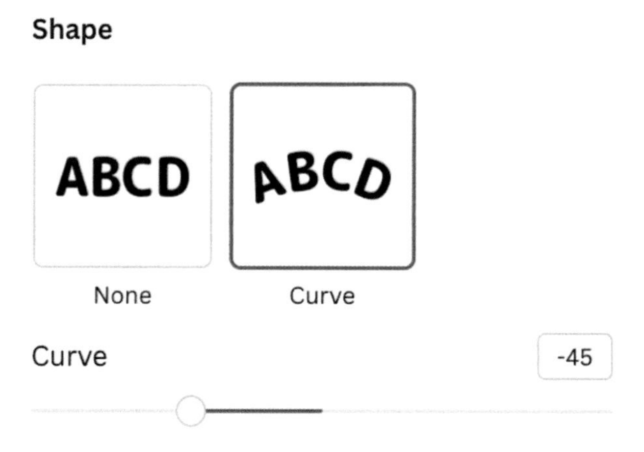

Figure 2.49 – Curved text feature

It's a simple but effective feature, perfect for logos or wrapping text around an icon or website button.

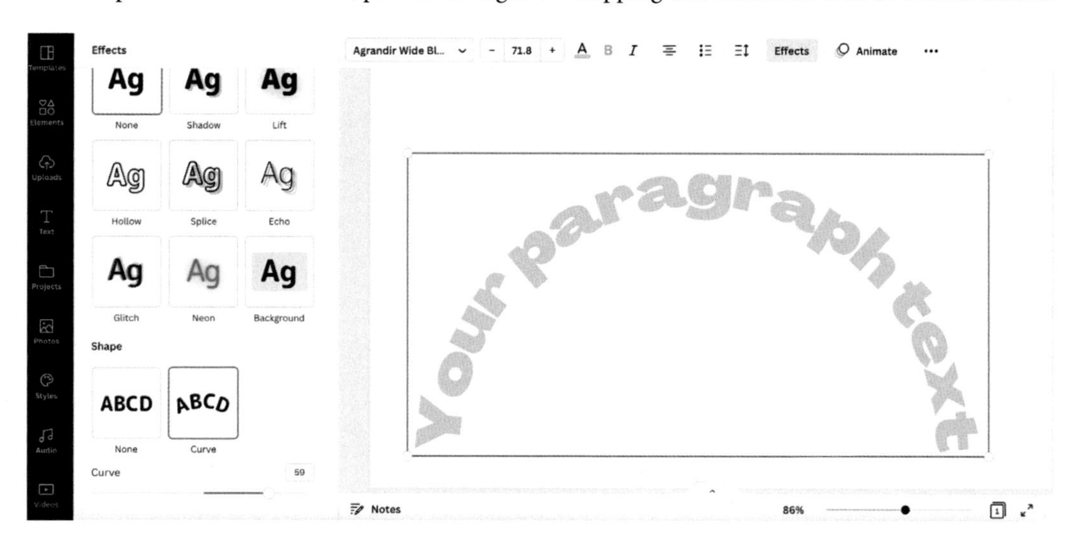

Figure 2.50 – Curved effect on text

I love the font effects in Canva and I hope you've found some you love too. They can really make your text pop on your design, drawing the eye of the viewer.

Summary

What have we learned in this chapter? Well, you'll now know how to find and edit a template to suit the theme of your business and change out the colors, imagery, and fonts. You've also learned how to find your designs after saving them and how to create one from a blank page. We've also learned how to use the line feature and change and edit shapes to give our designs a consistent look and feel.

So, that's it for this chapter. In the next chapter, we will be looking at how to search for and add different elements to your design, as well as how to find suitable images, the different image editing tools, and how to change backgrounds.

3

Tools and Features for Using Elements and Images

Elements and images in Canva can help to make your designs unique to your business; there are hundreds of thousands available for you to use. Images can be edited directly in Canva, and they have given us a large variety of tools to do so. Elements can also be edited but not to the extent of images. In this chapter, we will be looking at all the tools available to you and how to use them.

In this chapter, we are going to cover the following main topics:

- Adding elements into the mix
- Adding and editing images
- Changing the background

By the end of this chapter, you will have learned how to use the many editing tools for images, know how to change the background of a design to help it stand out, and the difference between element file types and which ones you can change.

Adding elements into the mix

Elements in Canva are the individual items that you use to create a design; they can be shapes, icons, animations, text, images, and video. Each one of these options has its place within your design. In this section, we are going to look at how you find and use these within Canva.

Let's look at static elements; these are elements that don't move. However, the following also applies to animated elements and stickers; you can't change the colors on these.

Once you have your template size open, head over to the **Elements** section in the top-left corner, and here you will see a search bar and lots of different sections below – **Recently used**, **Lines & Shapes**, **Graphics**, **Photos**, **Frames**, **Grids**, and so on:

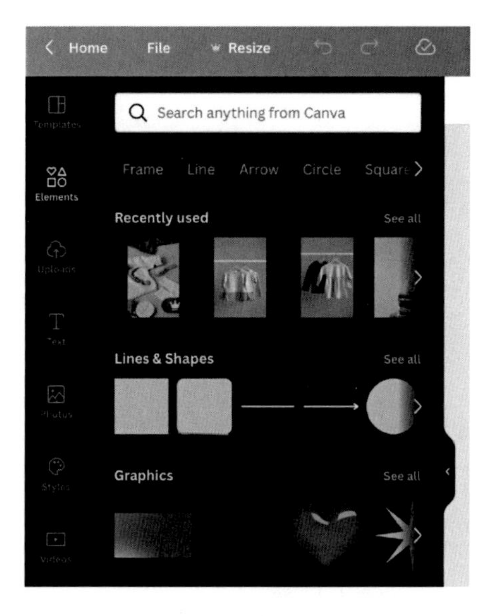

Figure 3.1 – A close-up of the Elements section

In the search bar, we are going to search for the keyword `blob`. This brings up a large selection of elements that are brilliant to use as borders for text and are a simple but effective style of design you can create quickly:

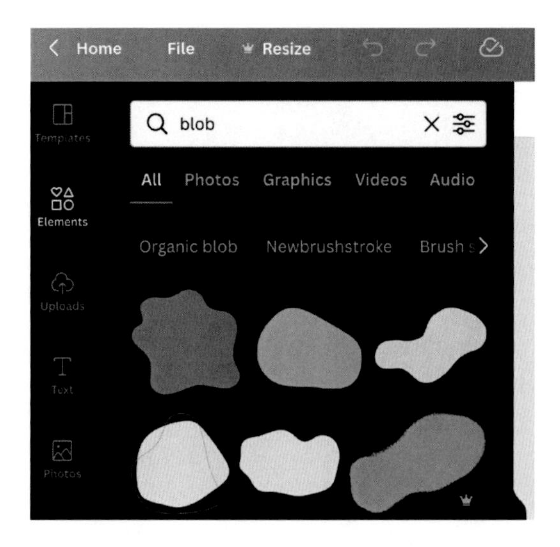

Figure 3.2 – Searching for the keyword blob

I've selected the one with the gold line, and it brings up a list of options at the top of the page. From here, I can change the colors of certain parts of the elements and crop, flip, and animate them:

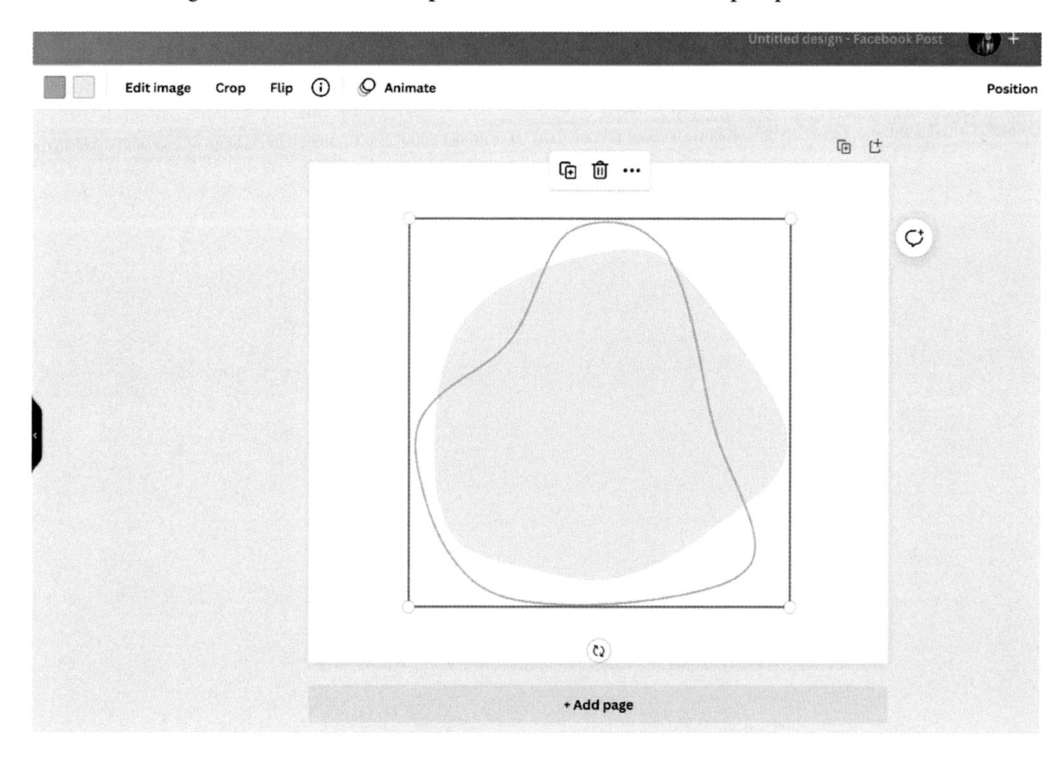

Figure 3.3 – The chosen blob element

> **Tip**
>
> When searching for elements in Canva you will find some give you the option to change colors. You can have up to five color change boxes on elements (the one in the preceding example has two), but some do not change at all. The reason you can change color on some and not others is dependent on the file type. The majority of elements in Canva are created by freelance designers, and they can choose the file type. Some are uploaded as SVG files (these are vector files – they can be adjusted in size without losing resolution), where you can create color-changing options. Others are uploaded as PNG files (these are images or raster files and they can't be resized significantly without losing some of their resolution quality) and are therefore unable to have their colors changed. This is just something to look out for when using elements that you may want to adjust the colors of.

Editing my chosen element

I have selected the element, so I can see the purple box around it, then click on one of the color options at the top. I can now change the colors of both parts to match my branding:

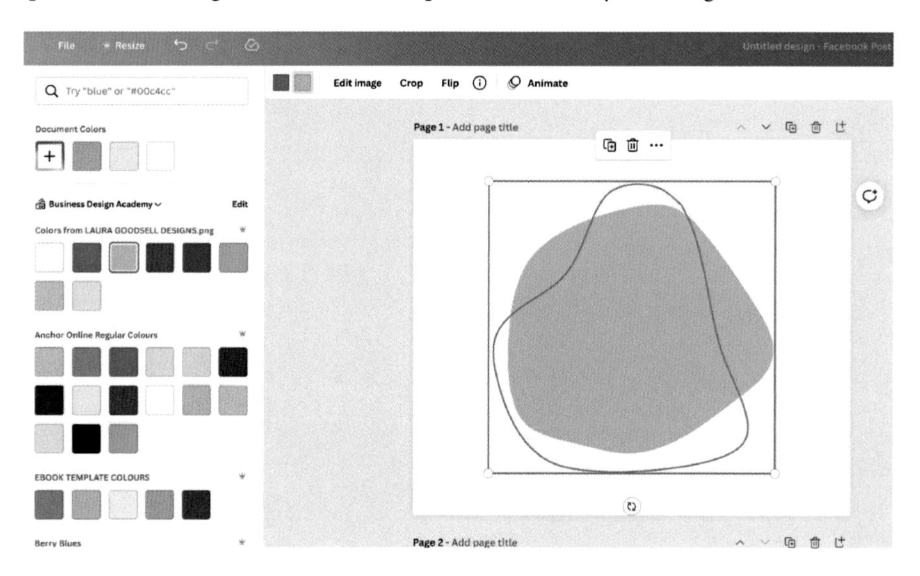

Figure 3.4 – Changing the color of an element

Next, I have the option to **Crop** the element; this is useful if there is a part that encroaches onto another element of your design or if you are removing a part that should not be there. You can crop by using the four corners of the purple circle. Once you are happy with the crop, select **Done**. You can then use the white circles in the corners to enlarge or reduce the size of your element without disrupting the shape:

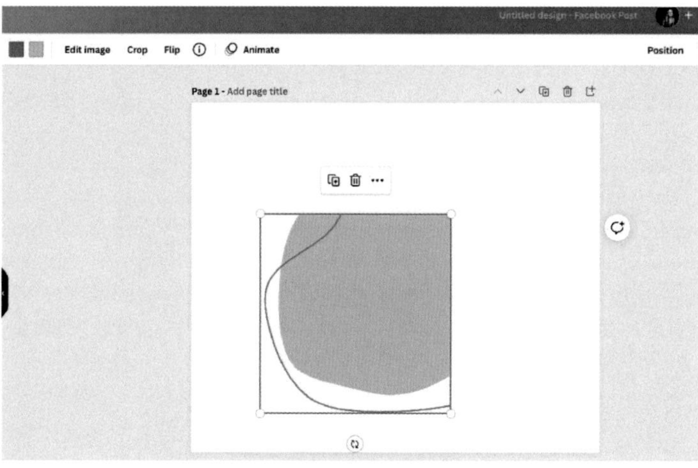

Figure 3.5 – A close-up of a cropped element

We can also flip or rotate an element. I love the rotate option as it allows you to place the element correctly within your design. The rotate option is one of the few that is not on the top bar; you will find it alongside the purple square, along with a few other options. They have been moved to stop the top bar from being overly cluttered.

Here you will find:

- **Duplicate**
- **Delete**
- **Copy**
- **Paste**
- **Delete**
- **Link**
- **Animate**
- **Comment**

Lastly, the circle with the two rotating arrows is the Rotate option, which you can drag around in a circle:

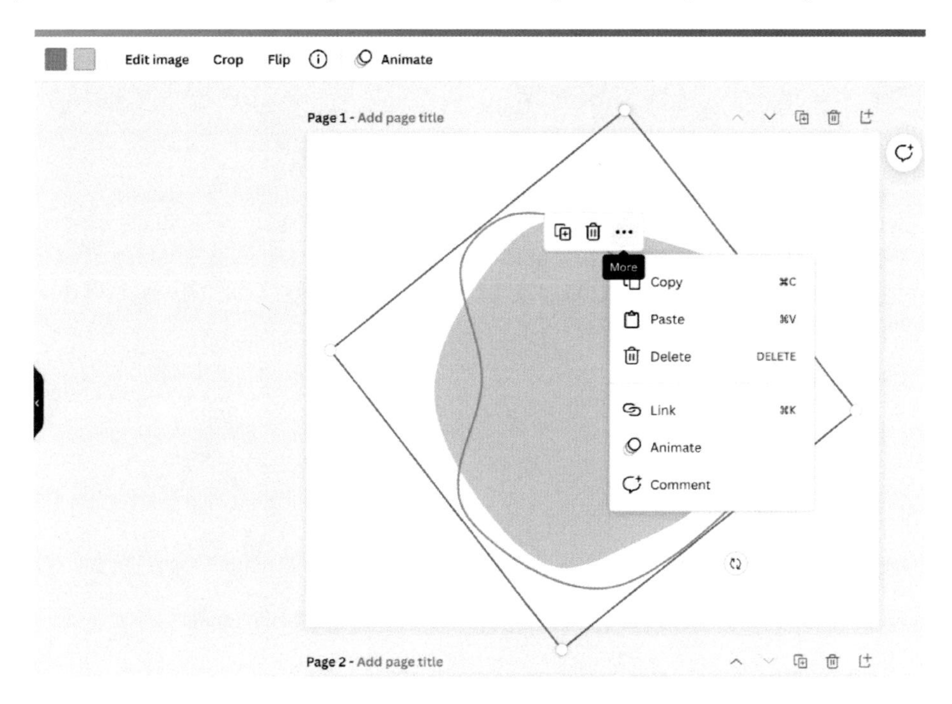

Figure 3.6 – Rotate and element menu options

The **Flip** button allows you to flip your element horizontally or vertically:

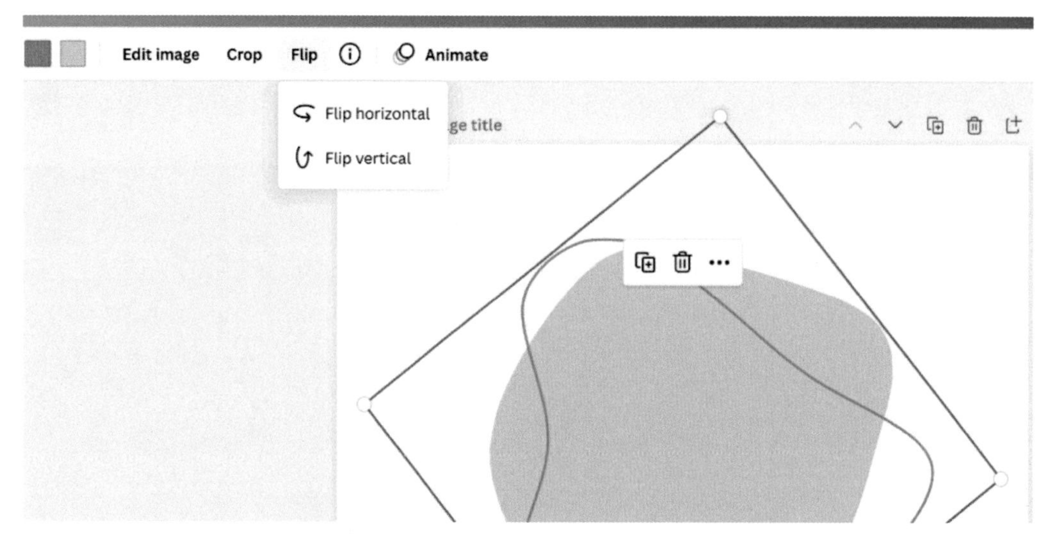

Figure 3.7 – Flip your element horizontally or vertically

There is also the **edit image** option here, but we're going to cover this further on in this chapter. You will also find the **Animate** option, which we will cover in more detail in *Chapter 10, Leveraging Video and Animation within Your Business Marketing*.

Being keyword specific

Thinking about what element you would like and then trying to be as specific with the keywords as possible will help you to find the right one quickly. For example, if you're looking for a big top tent for a circus-themed template, try searching for `circus big top tent`. Canva will then bring back a selection of images and elements that fit your keywords:

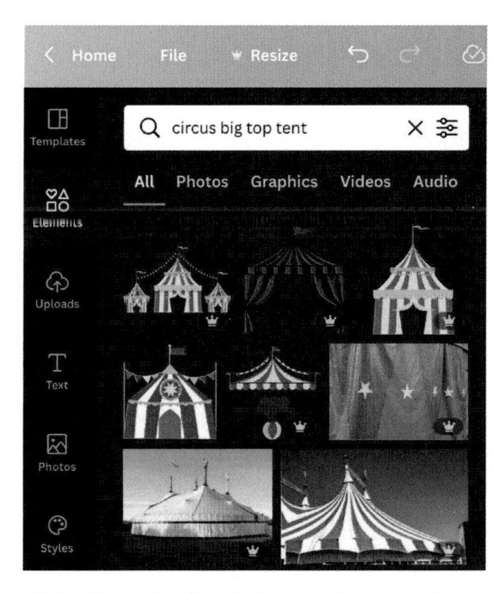

Figure 3.8 – Searching for the keywords circus big top tent

If you just want graphics and not images, select the **Graphics** tab at the top before hitting *Enter*:

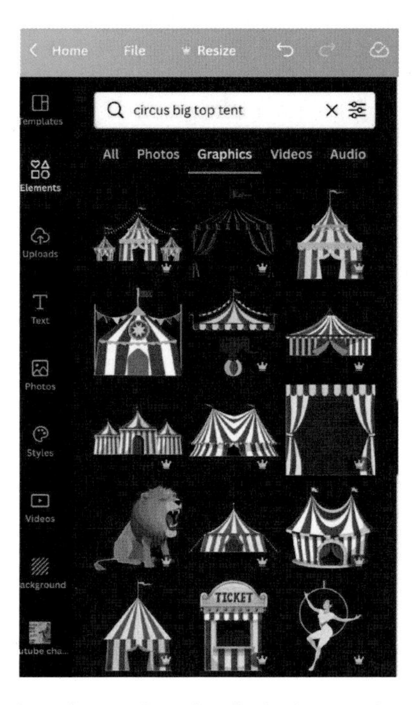

Figure 3.9 – Searching for graphics that fit the keywords circus big top tent

Element collections

Canva also has collections of elements where you can use a variety of elements that are all similar in style and theme, helping you to create multiple designs that are consistent. These can be found in the **Elements** tab by scrolling down to the bottom:

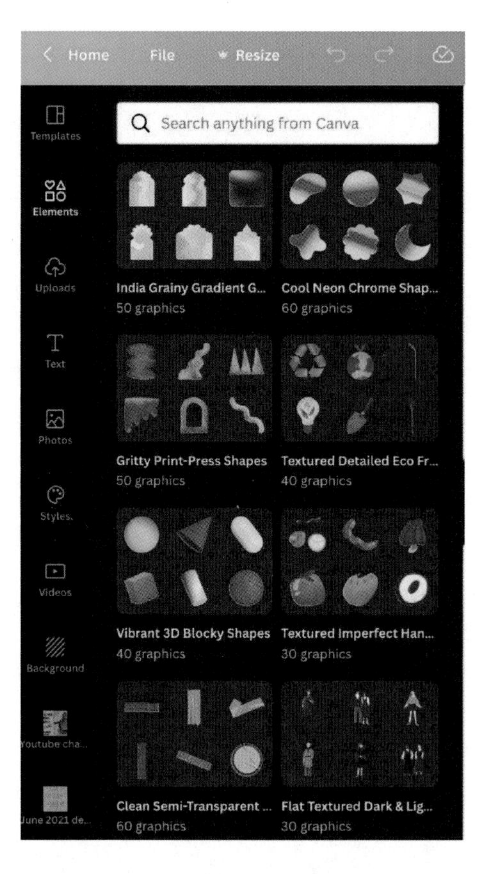

Figure 3.10 – Canva element collections

Select the set that appeals and it will give you access to the full collection for you to use in your designs and templates:

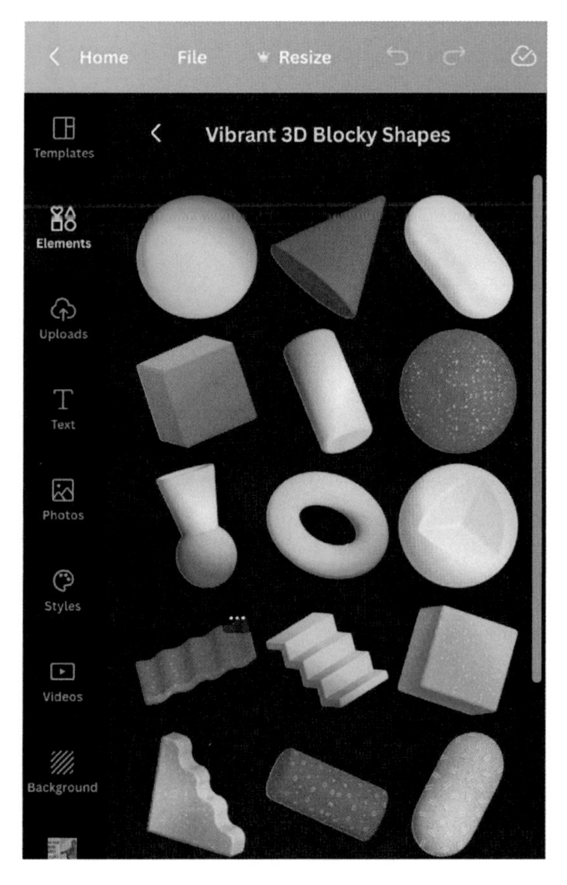

Figure 3.11 – Chosen element collection

We have looked at how to search and find your elements, change the color, crop, flip, and find collections of elements. Next, we'll look at adding lines and shapes.

Adding and editing images

Canva has amassed a huge library of images, hundreds of thousands, and it has vastly improved on the editing front as well. You can now do a lot of your editing directly on your template. Canva has teamed up with other image platforms such as **Pixabay** and **Pexels** to bring you even more amazing images.

If you can't find an image that you like or would prefer to use your own imagery, you can upload these to Canva, using the **Uploads** button. This can be found in the menu on the left of your template; from here you can upload images and videos you have saved on your device. There is also a great feature here where you can record yourself directly in your Canva template. We will be looking at this in greater detail in *Chapter 10, Leveraging Video and Animation within Your Business Marketing*.

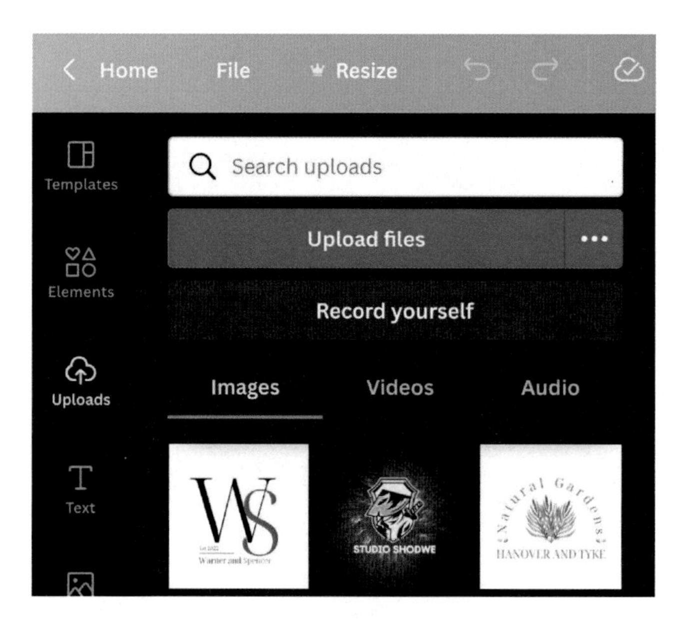

Figure 3.12 – Uploading your own images and video into Canva

The best way to check out all of the images in Canva is to open up a blank template and then head on over to the **Photos** section on the left.

From here, you can use any keyword as we have shown while searching for elements. You can find different images to suit your latest creation. I've chosen the keywords `colored pencils` to find a nice bright image, on which I can show you the features:

Figure 3.13 – A close-up of a colored pencils image

Select the **Edit Image** option in the top bar, and it opens up a whole world of options. Starting at the top, you have your recently used features, if you have used any image editing tools before. Then you have the background remover tool, which is a firm favorite among Pro users, and after that you have the **Adjust** settings:

Figure 3.14 – The image adjustment options

The three main ones are shown with the **See all** option opening up the rest:

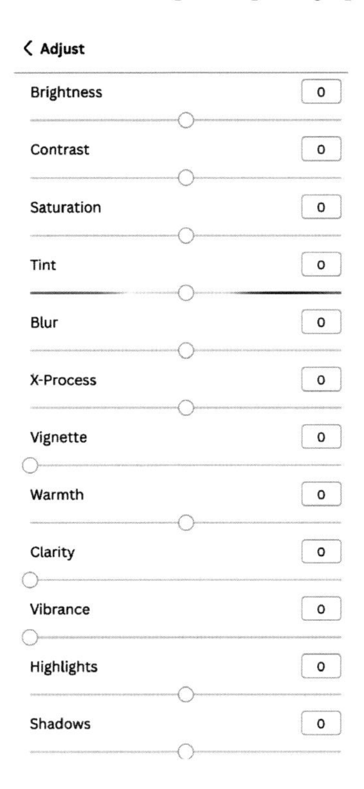

Figure 3.15 – The image adjustment drop-down menu

With these settings, you have full control over your image; you can make it darker and sharper, give it a slight blur, increase the contrast, or a combination of all of these to really change it. But it doesn't stop there. Next in the menu, you have multiple filters you can apply, Duotone effects, and the option to change the image into a letter mosaic, give it a trippy look, or liquefy it. Here is a selection of some of the effects; each one comes with its own section of options so you can edit them:

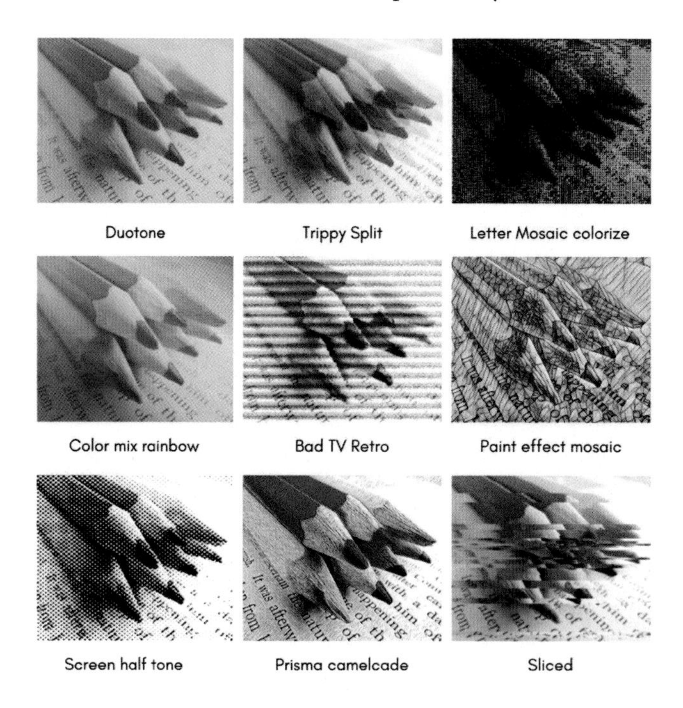

Figure 3.16 – Image effects

Smartmockups

Besides the effects, filters, and adjustment tools in the **Edit Image** feature, there are three other features that are worth mentioning. The first one is **Smartmockups**. Canva has teamed up with Smartmockups to bring you around 8,000 options, which are all available to Pro users, and about 20% are available to free account users. These are ready-made mock-ups that you can add to your design to make it look like it has been set up, perfect for product-based businesses, authors, fashion designers, app and website creators, and many more businesses.

There are two ways to access Smartmockups. The first is through the **Edit Image** feature when creating your template; this gives you a top level of the most popular mock-ups:

Figure 3.17 – Smartmockups

Clicking the **See all** option will give you access to all Smartmockups. For this example, I'm going to show you how to put a logo design onto a mug, and this process can be repeated for any design you would like to make with a smartmockup:

1. Have your logo ready on a template as a PNG file.
2. Click on **Edit Image** at the top.
3. Scroll down to the **Smartmockups** section.
4. Click the **See all** option and find the **Mugs** section.
5. Select the image you like.

Figure 3.18 – Smartmockup Mugs options

Once selected, Canva will then add your design to the mock-up for you:

Figure 3.19 – A logo on a mug

The other way to access **Smartmockups** is by selecting it from the main menu on the home screen. This brings up a new search bar where you have access to all 8,000+ mock-ups:

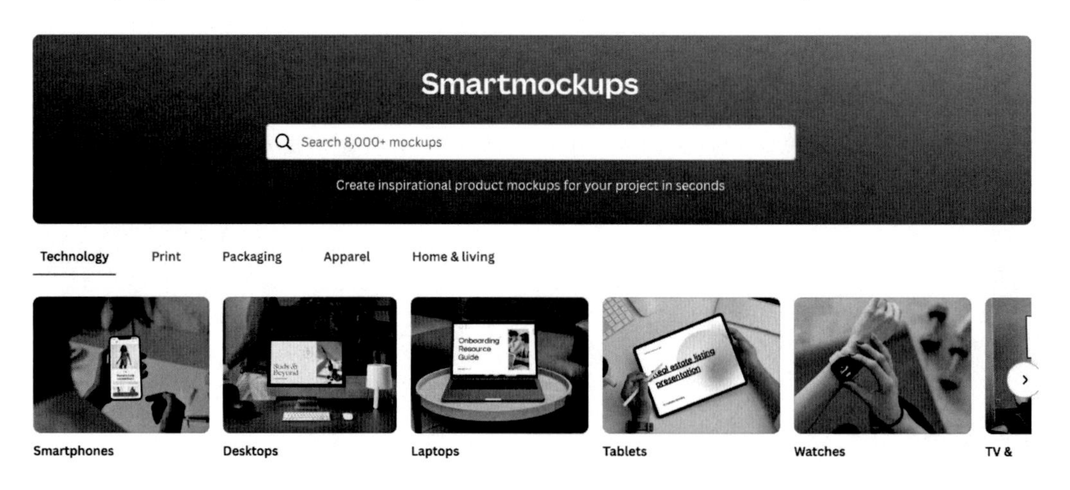

Figure 3.20 – Smartmockups search bar

Searching for the keyword Books, these are some of the results that appear:

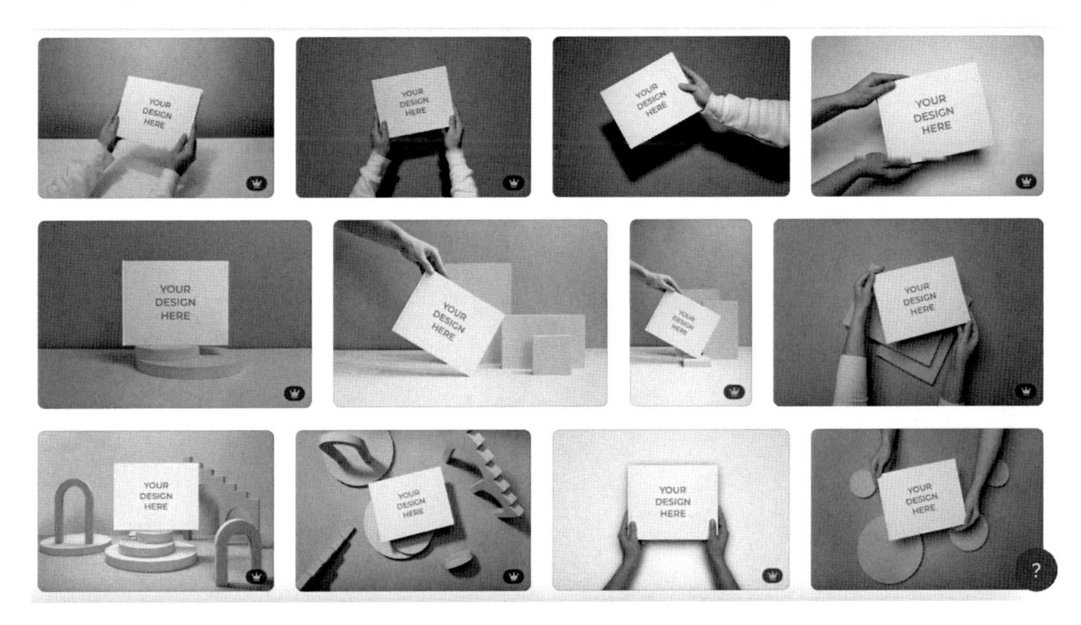

Figure 3.21 – Smartmockups book designs

After selecting one, it will ask if you would like to use it in a design:

‹ Back

YOUR
DESIGN
HERE

PRO One-design use license

Let's get started

Select an image or design to use in your mockup

Select

Figure 3.22 – Smartmockups book template

Once you have selected to use it, Canva then brings up a window with your recent uploads and design folders, so here you can now use a Canva design in the mock-up and not be restricted to just images:

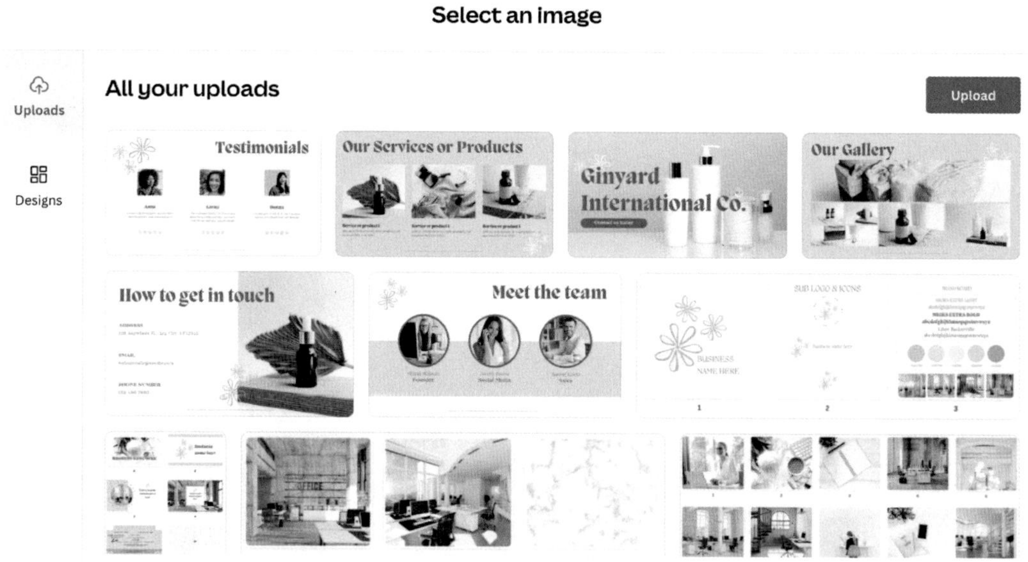

Select an image

Uploads

Designs

All your uploads

Upload

Testimonials

Our Services or Products

Ginyard International Co.

Our Gallery

How to get in touch

Meet the team

Figure 3.23 – Designs and Uploads folders

Scroll through your designs, select the one to use, and Canva will add it to the mock-up for you:

Figure 3.24 – The final mock-up

Once happy with the design, you can save it for future use or choose to adjust the image:

Figure 3.25 – Saving or adjusting the mock-up

Canva will give you one last option to either use the mock-up in a design or to download it as is:

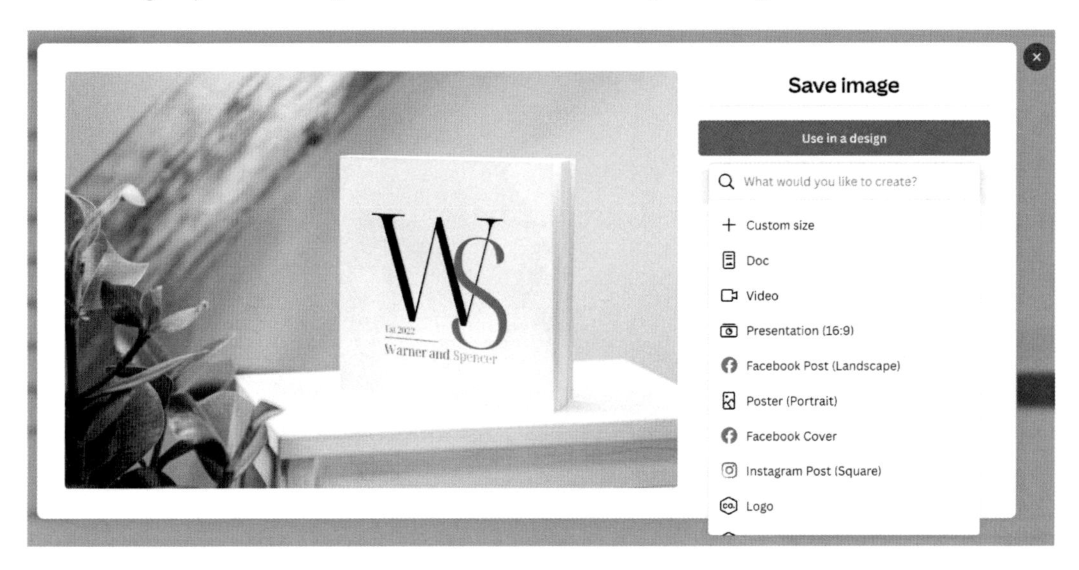

Figure 3.26 – Using the mock-up in a design

If you choose to use it in a design, you can then select the size template you would like to create and use your mock-up.

Shadows

The shadow feature gives your images extra depth; they bring your image to life, making it look like you could pick it up off the page. I will use the same logo image that I used in the previous example to show you:

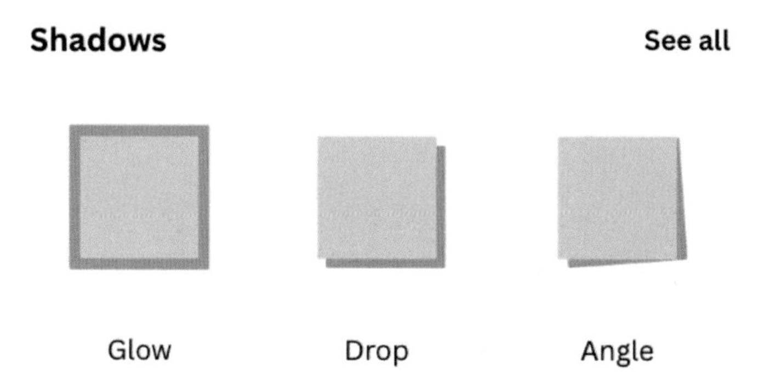

Figure 3.27 – The shadow feature

There are only a few options, but each one comes with its own settings to edit:

Figure 3.28 – Different shadow options for a logo design

In this example, I used the **Angle** shadow and slightly increased the blur:

Figure 3.29 – The Angle shadow

This one uses the **Curved** shadow with no additional edits:

Figure 3.30 – The Curved shadow

Using shadows for your images gives a very striking effect; these work really well on logos, vision boards, product images, family photos, and more.

Frames

Lastly, in this section, I wanted to show you the **Frames** section. This is a selection of frames that will automatically resize to fit your image. You can find a lot of frames in the **Elements** section but you will need to manually resize them to fit, whereas these are done for you. They are found under the **Edit Image** feature when you are on a template and have your image ready to use:

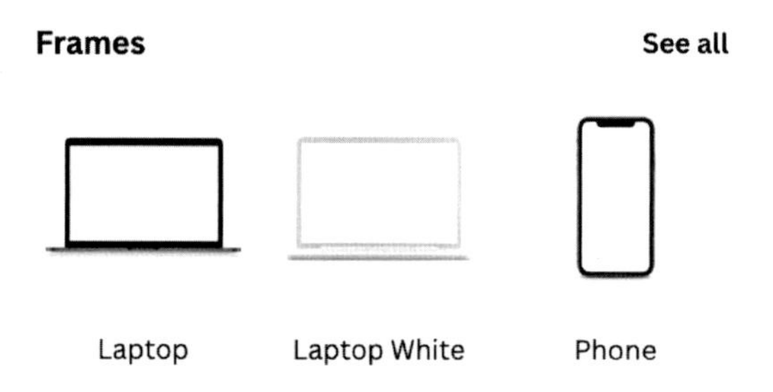

Figure 3.31 – The frames feature

At the top, you have a mobile, laptop, and tablet frame, and then under these, there are polaroid, neon, gold glitter, floral, and vintage frames:

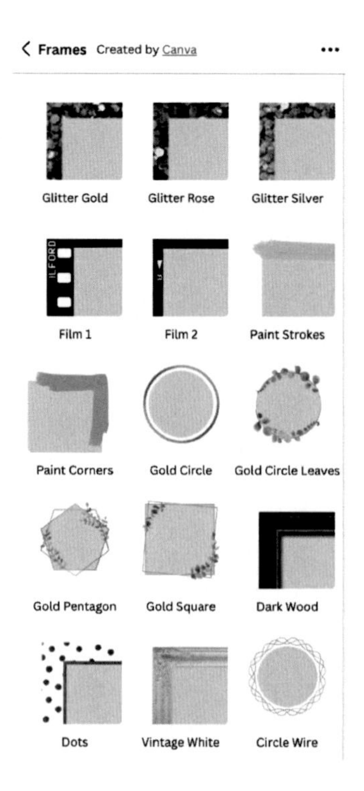

Figure 3.32 – The Frames drop-down menu

Selecting one of these will automatically add it to your image:

Figure 3.33 – A selection of different frames

Frames are a great way to add a quick border to an image that may otherwise get lost in your design. So, with that in mind, let's look at backgrounds and how you can make information stand out more on your social posts.

Changing the background

Backgrounds in Canva help to give our design more depth, and Canva has given us access to a tab specifically for backgrounds. We can also use patterns, images, and elements for a background.

First of all, let's look at the **Background** tab. It's in the main left menu when you're in a template.

I have this clear basic design here, but a background will help the message stand out so much more. I have searched for a modern geometric pattern, as I like the idea of something that suits the message of a new website, keeping the design theme. Adding a floral background, for example, wouldn't look right, unless the business is a florist (we need to have every part of a design doing a job; if it isn't, it needs removing).

Figure 3.34 – A basic text template

Now, the design looks better. It has a patterned background and the message is still clear and uncluttered:

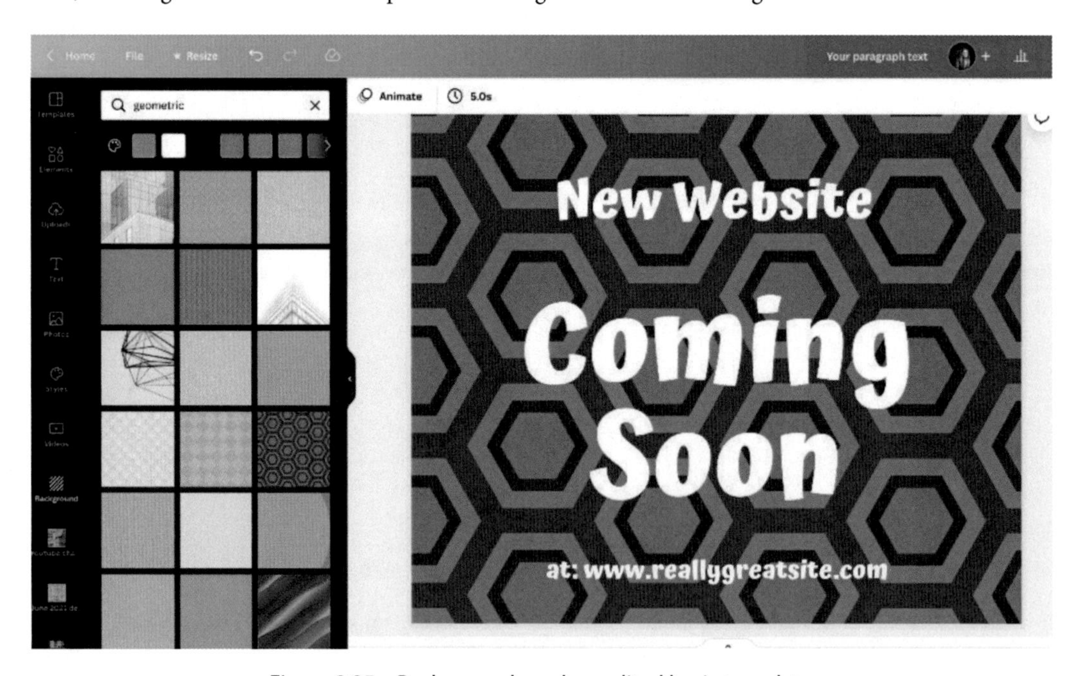

Figure 3.35 – Backgrounds and an edited basic template

Often a simple gradient can achieve the same effect. It reduces the plainness of a design but doesn't over-clutter it:

Figure 3.36 – A selection of gradient backgrounds on a basic template

A photo or pattern from the **Photos** section can work well; just make sure it's not too light, doesn't cover your information, and is in keeping with your message. For this one, I searched for the keyword `website`.

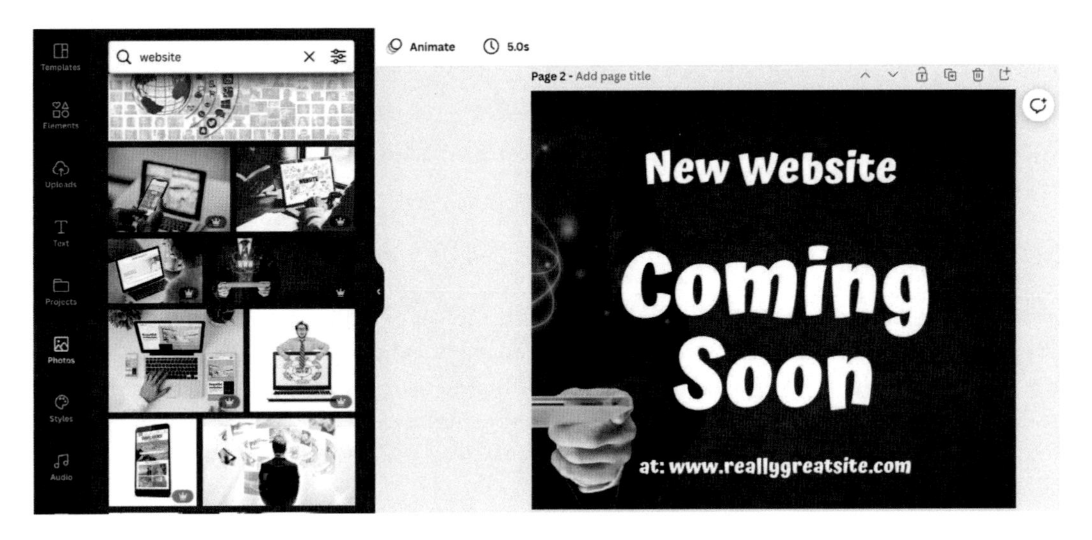

Figure 3.37 – Images used as a background

Lastly, you can use an element. There are some great patterns and shapes you can use; comic, cartoon, floral, and blobs all can look great as a background for a simple design:

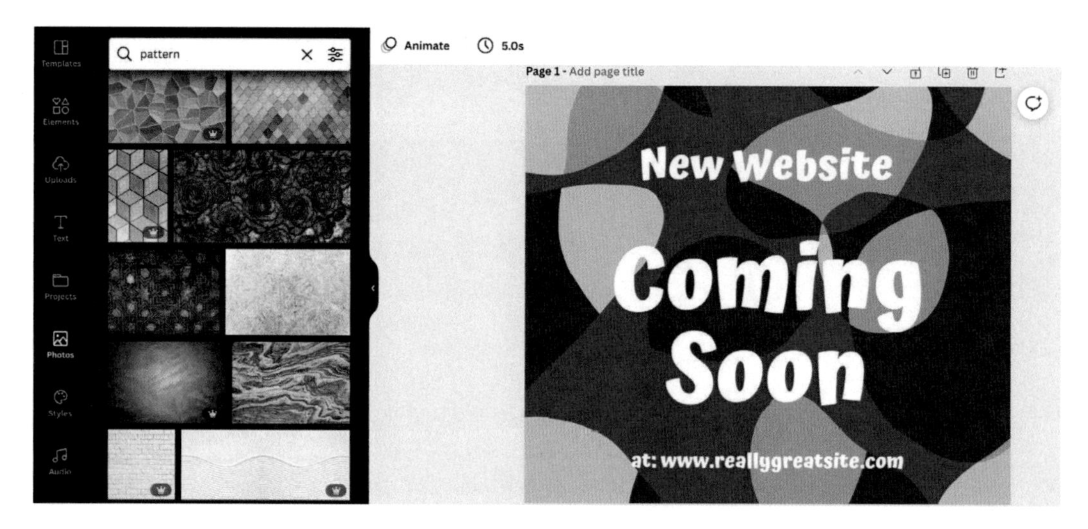

Figure 3.38 – Patterns used as a background

Now we have a great design that we can use on social media to help with the visibility of our business, just by using a simple pattern or image as a background.

We've come to the end, so let's take a look at what we've learned in this chapter, which is packed full of information.

Summary

Imagery and elements are some of the main parts of any design in Canva. Understanding how these work will help you on your way to creating amazing designs. So, what have we learned in this chapter? You have discovered the importance of elements, and how to search, select, and edit them. You have also learned how to find and fully edit an image in Canva, using all of the different tools available to you, as well as how to edit a background, giving a blank color block a pattern or image to help your information stand out more.

So that's it for this chapter. In the next chapter, we will be looking at some of the Canva features that you can use, alongside the knowledge you have learned in this chapter, to create eye-catching graphics.

4

Designing Eye-Catching Graphics through Useful Features

Canva has many great features, but some of the best are the simple ones that you may miss when creating your graphics. They help with consistency, saving time, resizing quickly, and positioning your elements correctly. Many of them are along the top bar of a template, so in this chapter, we're going to look at each one in more detail.

In this chapter, we are going to cover the following main topics:

- Grouping elements
- Align and spacing text
- Rulers and margins for print
- Locking elements
- Changing the transparency
- Resizing your designs
- Positioning elements front to back
- The Background Remover tool

By the end of this chapter, you will be able to use all of the template features, understand what each one does, and know how to use the Background Remover tool.

Grouping elements

Grouping multiple elements together allows you to move and position them quickly, keeping them all in the same place. The grouping option appears once you have selected an element, text box, or image. You can move individual images around or group them, but if you've placed images into a grid, then you cannot group grids together.

In this example, I have highlighted the **Available courses** text box and the text boxes underneath. Canva will automatically group them together for you, but once you click off, they ungroup. To leave them grouped, highlight all required text boxes and select the **Group** option in the top bar, to the right, next to the **Position** option.

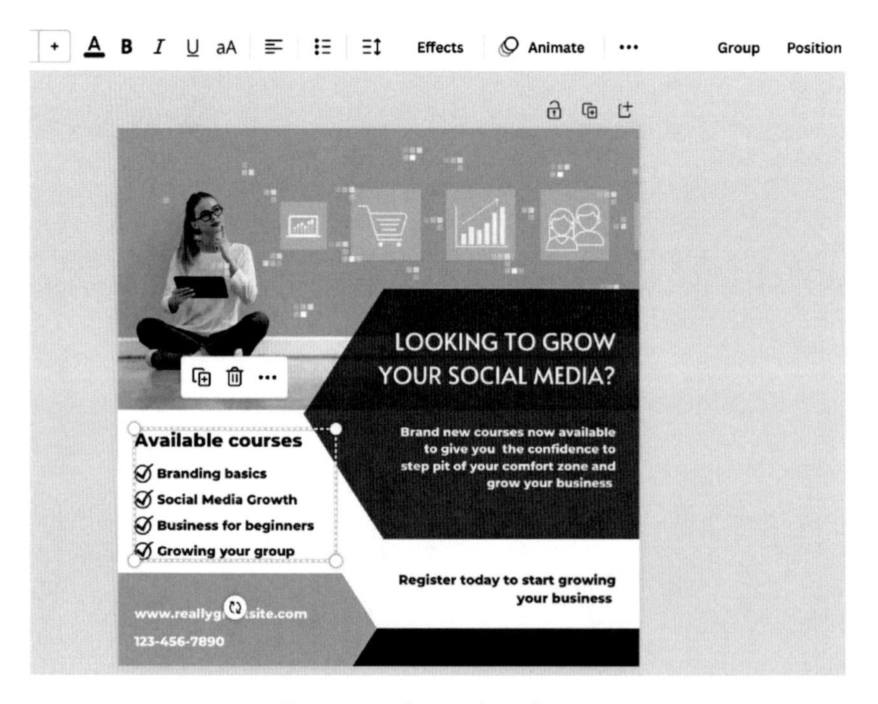

Figure 4.1 – Grouped text boxes

They will now stay grouped until you select to ungroup them by selecting the same option on the top bar, as seen in the following screenshot:

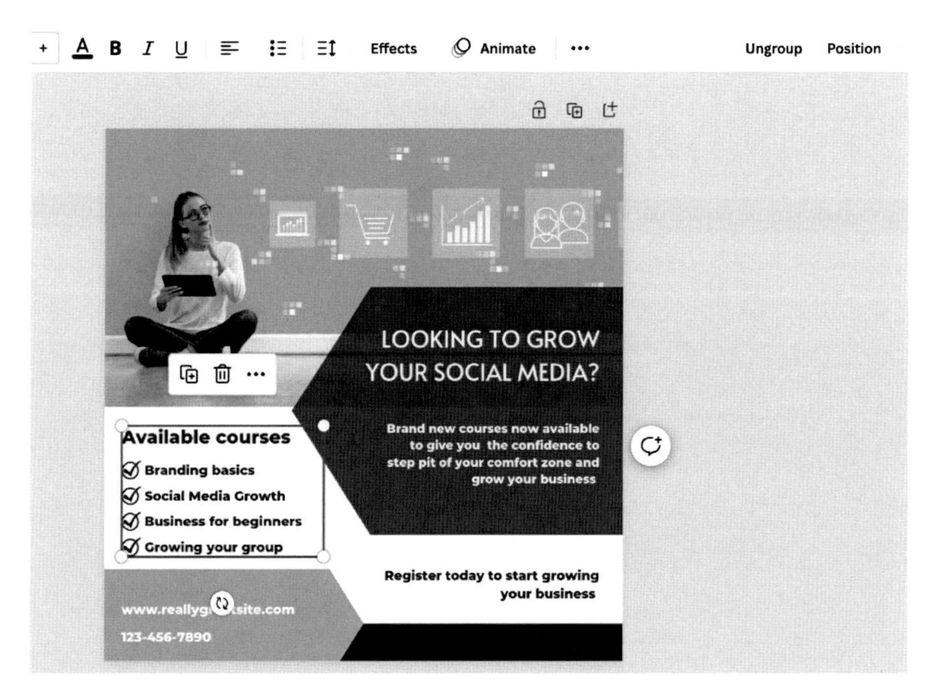

Figure 4.2 – Text boxes grouped with the Ungroup option now available

Grouping elements, text boxes, and images in a Canva design works well when you have multiple pages and want to copy select parts of the design without transferring the entire page.

Grouping elements is a useful feature that works well alongside aligning and spacing your text, so let's look at that next.

Aligning and spacing text

Using the Alignment and Spacing features will help give your designs a uniform look, increase consistency, and make them visually pleasing.

To align anything within your design, and this works with all elements, images, and text boxes, you need to drag your mouse across them to highlight the elements and text boxes as a group, then select the **Position** tab in the top bar. This will give you lots of options for alignment, as shown in the following example:

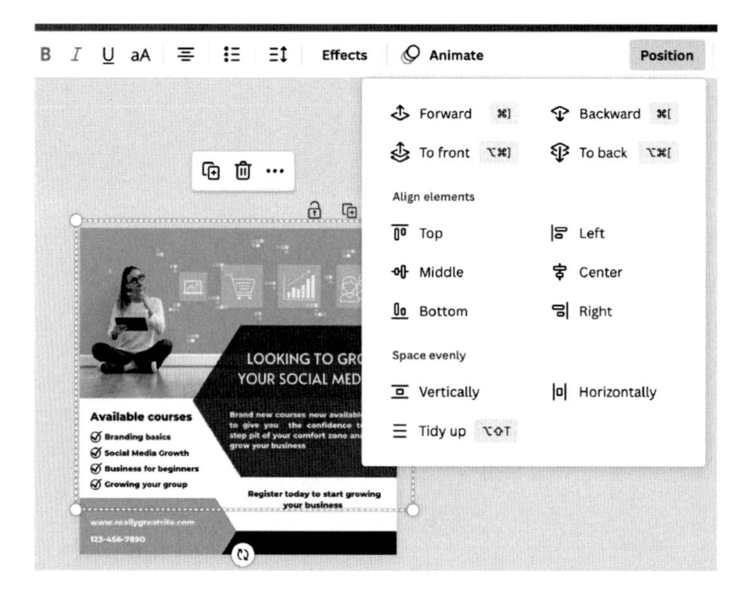

Figure 4.3 – Alignment options drop-down menu

In this section, we are looking at the bottom two groups of options.

You can now align the various elements selected, by selecting the **Top**, **Middle**, **Bottom**, **Left**, **Center**, and **Right** options; it will align every element that has been highlighted. You can also give each element equal spacing using the bottom options **Vertically** and **Horizontally**, and the **Tidy up** feature will give everything equal spacing all around. This is brilliant for individual elements, but what if you wanted to align or give the text within a text box more space?

To align text, you need to select the text box in question and then the **Spacing** option in the top bar, as shown in the following example:

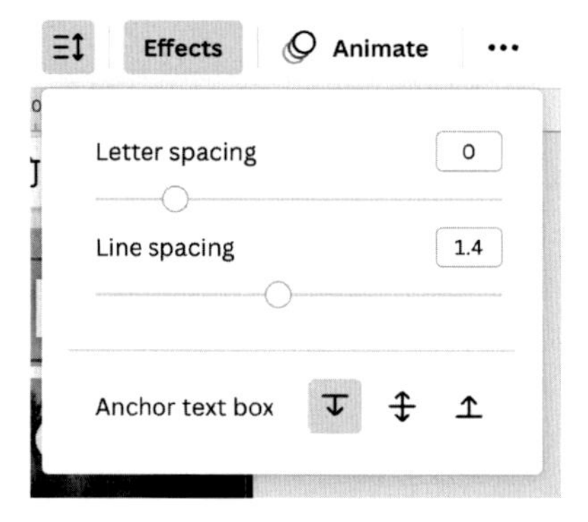

Figure 4.4 – Letter and line spacing options

The **Spacing** option gives you three choices: you can adjust the space between letters, which is perfect for smaller fonts or fonts that have the letters naturally close together; **Line spacing** gives you more or less space between the lines of text; and lastly, **Anchor text box** allows you to choose in which direction the text flows while adding more text to the box. This helps make sure other parts of your design are not covered with the new text.

There is a feature on the top bar to change the alignment of your text; it looks like four lines and changes with the alignment of the current text, as shown in the following screenshot:

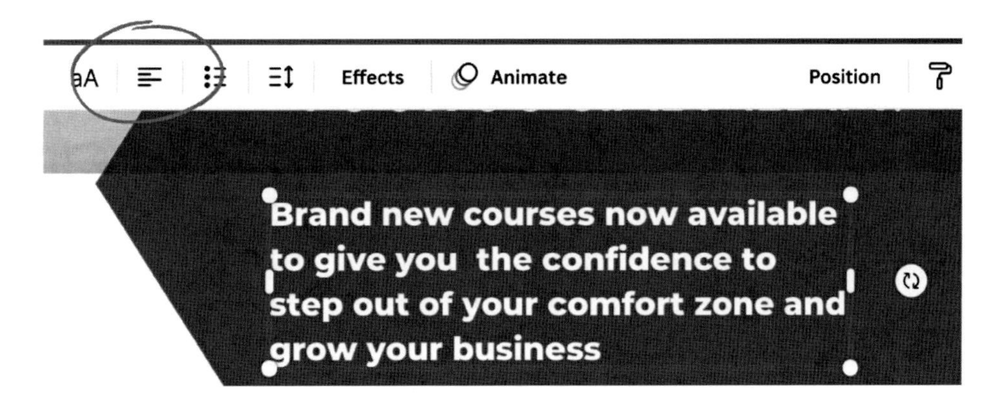

Figure 4.5 – Alignment tool

For example, the text box in the preceding screenshot has the text aligned to the left and the alignment feature also has the four lines aligned to the left; keep clicking the button and the alignment will change.

So, now that we can align and space our lines of text correctly, let's look at rulers and margins. They work well with the preceding elements, so they are important features to cover.

Rulers and margins for print

Rulers and margins are great for printable designs, such as books, magazines, and leaflets, but they are also helpful in getting things in the right place. For example, if you want everything on your design 100 px in from the edge, you can add a ruler line to guide your elements into the right positions. The rulers, margins, and print bleed can be found in the **File** option at the top of the page.

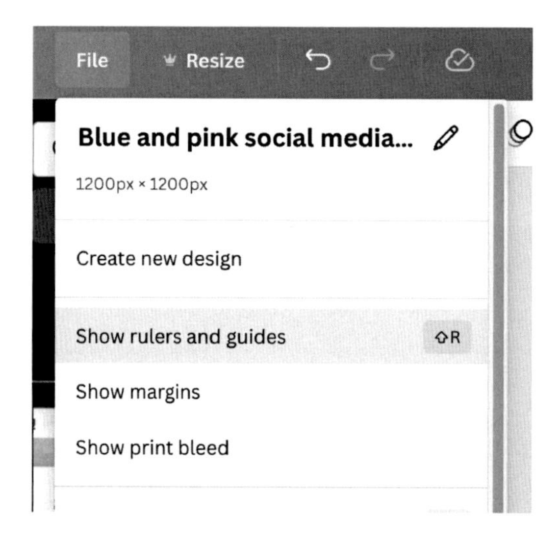

Figure 4.6 – Rulers, margins, and print bleed options

By selecting each of these options, they activate automatically on your design. Rulers allow you to create as many lines as you would like on your design. These lines are related to the type of template you have created. So, for example, if you have created an A4 document in millimeters, the ruler will measure in millimeters, or for a social media template in pixels, the ruler will measure in pixels. To create a ruler line, click on the ruler along the far edge and drag it inwards; it will show you the measurement in the purple box so that you can place it correctly, as shown in the following example:

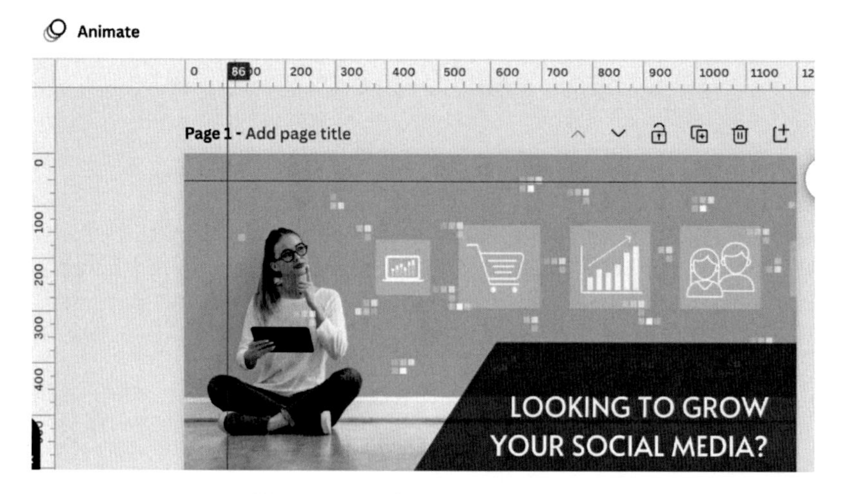

Figure 4.7 – Ruler lines on a design

Activating margins will give you a border to work within. This helps you to keep all the important information safe from being cut off during printing, as shown in the following figure:

Figure 4.8 – The margin feature

This is a good feature to activate if you are creating a book, as you don't want the text too close to the book's spine.

Lastly in this section is the print bleed, again another feature needed for printing. It gives you an extra border around the outer edge. This is the area that is trimmed off when printed, so it makes sure that any color that needs to go to the edges does so. This feature is shown in the following example:

Figure 4.9 – 3 mm print bleed

Print bleed is generally, as a rule of thumb, 3 mm wide, but please check this with your printing company to make sure you have their correct requirements first. Once you've set up your margins and rulers and started adding elements in place, it may be useful to know how to lock them so they don't move. Let's look at this next.

Locking elements

The **Lock** feature allows you to create more complex designs and move things around without displacing elements you don't want to move. Lock them in place, and they won't move until you unlock them. To lock an element or multiple elements, select it or highlight the group and select the padlock in the top-right corner.

Here I have selected the blue background arrow shape and locked it in place. You can see it's locked as a small padlock appears in the bottom corner, as shown in the following screenshot:

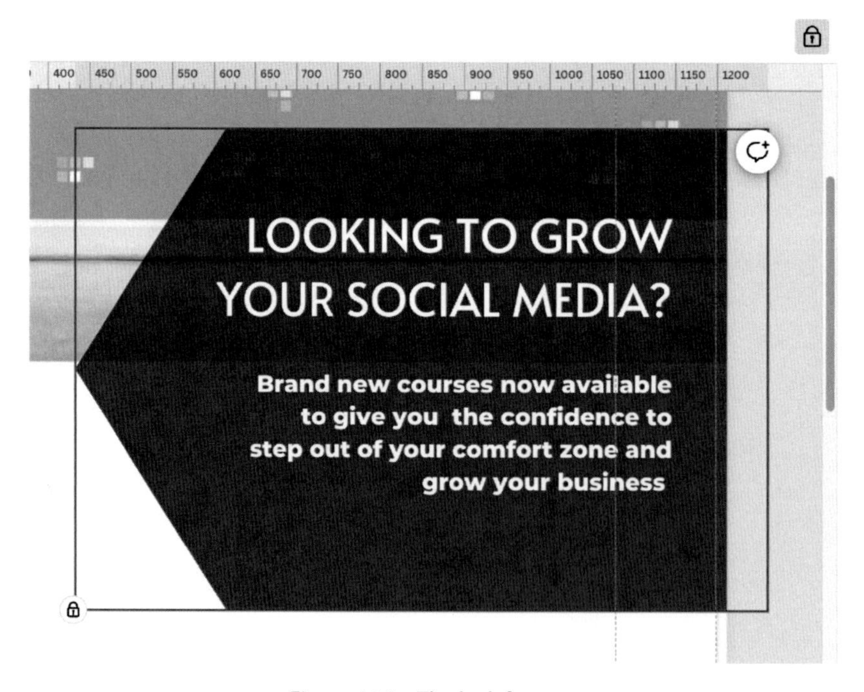

Figure 4.10 – The lock feature

With text boxes, you have the additional feature of the padlock. When it's clicked once, it locks the text box in place but gives you the option to edit the text. Click the padlock again and it will be fully locked, meaning you cannot edit the text until it's unlocked. The following example shows this feature:

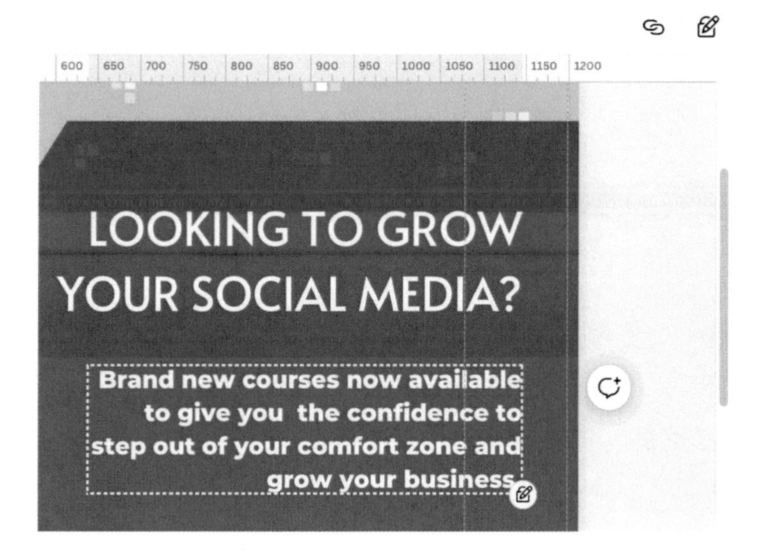

Figure 4.11 – The lock feature with additional text editing

This is shown by the icon changing to a padlock and pencil. Click again and it changes to just a padlock. This is a great feature when you have a lot going on in your design, but what about when you want to add text to an image or a block of color? Let's look at how to adjust the transparency in Canva.

Changing the transparency

Transparency is one of the features I think I use the most; it's great for social media posts where you have an image and would like to overlay text. So often, text on an image becomes unreadable due to the heavy use of color, but adding a shape with the transparency adjusted really brings out the text.

In this example, I have an image underneath and have adjusted the transparency of the arrow so that you can read the information on top but also still see the image beneath:

Figure 4.12 – Transparency

To adjust the transparency in Canva, select the small box that looks like a chess board in the top-right corner, as the following screenshot shows:

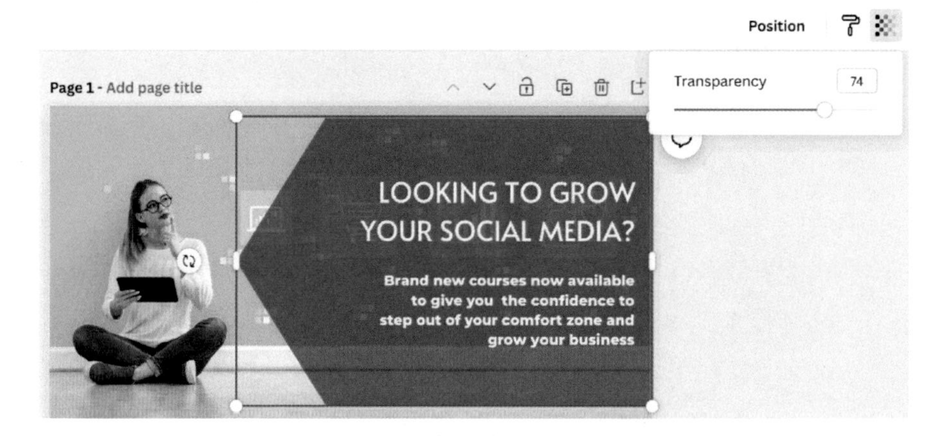

Figure 4.13 – The transparency slide bar

This gives you a slide bar to adjust the transparency on any element, image, or text box – a really useful feature for great-looking designs. So, let's look at how you can resize that design to suit a different social platform; Canva has a PRO tool just for this.

Resizing your designs

Being able to resize a design means staying consistent across all social channels, your website, posters, and adverts – in fact, any materials within your business.

Canva has provided the magic **Resize** tool, which is a Pro feature, and very much worth having Pro for. At the click of a button, you have your design in any other template size, as shown in the following example:

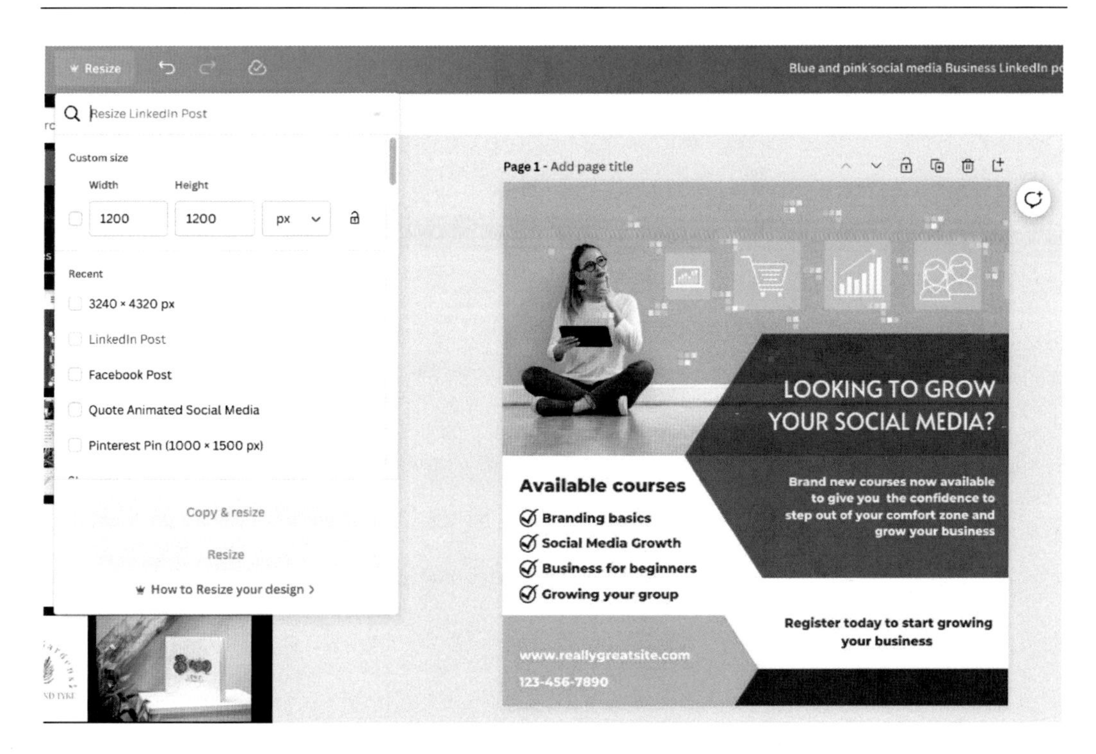

Figure 4.14 – The magic Resize drop-down feature

The **Resize** button is on the top blue bar. You can search for the type of template, add in your own custom dimensions, or scroll through the options, then click either **Copy & resize**, which will keep your original, or **Resize**, and it will change the size of your current design.

Depending on the template type you choose, you will need to adjust your design elements, text, and images to fit, as the **Resize** tool only changes the template size, not the information on it.

All of the features we have covered so far are great on their own, but only if you can place your elements correctly. If you can't access an element you've added because it's hidden behind another, you will struggle using features such as transparency or locking. Let's look at how to overcome this next.

Positioning elements front to back

Canva works with layers; all elements, text boxes, and images are layered upon one another within the template. These layers can be adjusted so that you can add backgrounds, text boxes on top, and elements in between, building up your design.

To change the layering, select the **Position** tab and the top options will allow you to bring your element forward or backward one layer at a time or straight to the front or back, as shown in the following example:

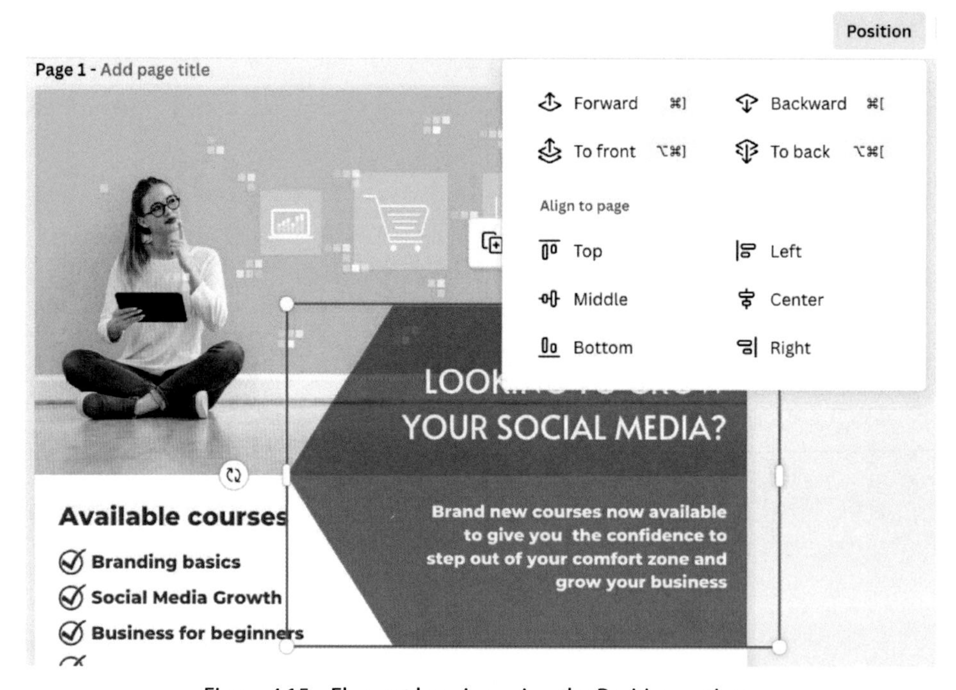

Figure 4.15 – Element layering using the Position options

Have a go with these options, as often, just moving an element by one or two layers can have a great effect on a design.

Lastly, we're going to look at what is probably the most popular feature on Canva, the **Background Remover** tool.

The Background Remover tool

The **Background Remover** tool has got to be, hands down, the most popular feature of Canva Pro; it always comes up as a favorite. It allows you to remove the background of any image within your designs. It also gives you the option to add or remove parts that have been missed in the background removal process.

It can be found in the **Edit image** section, as shown in the following screenshot:

Figure 4.16 – The Background Remover tool

As seen in the following example, it takes everything out of the background, leaving your main focal point:

Figure 4.17 – An image with the background removed

Sometimes, if the background colors are similar to the main subject, parts can get left in or removed in error, so you have the **Erase** and **Restore** tools, which give you an adjustable brush size to paint back or remove parts of your image, as shown in the following screenshot:

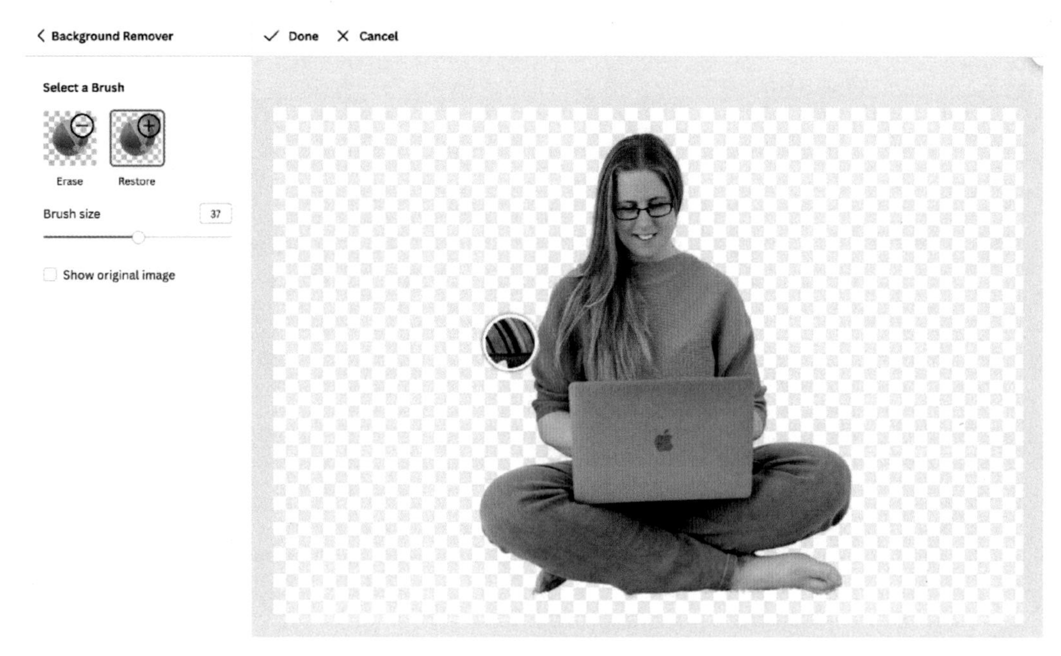

Figure 4.18 – Background Remover Restore and Erase brushes

Once you are happy with the removal process and have adjusted any parts that need adding back in or taking out, select **Done** at the top, and you are ready to use it within your design.

Lastly, if you would like to use an image within Canva rather than your own, have a look at the **Cut-out** section, as this gives you a lot of imagery that already has the background removed. The option for this is in the **Photos** tab and then the **advanced options** section, which is the three lines with circles in the right corner, as seen in the following screenshot:

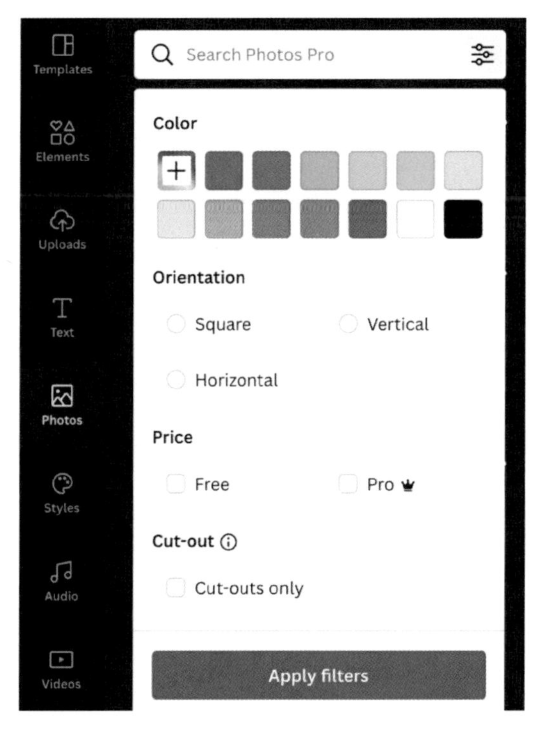

Figure 4.19 – Cut-out option for Canva images

We've now come to an end, so let's take a look at what we've learned in this chapter, packed full of useful features.

Summary

In this chapter, you have learned about several small features fundamental to designing in Canva. We've looked at how to group and move multiple elements and learned how to align and space out your text. You can now adjust the transparency, lock elements in place, and know how to use the **Background Remover** tool. You've also learned how to resize your design for different social channels and now have a good understanding of how Canva works in layers, and how to move these layers to create an effective design.

So far, you have learned a lot about creating designs in Canva, so now it's time to look at the all-important topic of branding and get you set up in the next chapter.

Part 2: Creating Your Brand and Design Tips

Now you know how to get your account set up, can create your own designs, and can also edit and use any templates available in the Canva library. The next step is getting your branding right, that is, creating a brand that is consistent and true to what you do. In this section, we will look at every aspect of branding and building a brand in Canva so that you can ensure all of the designs you create for your business have a consistent brand. We'll also dive a little deeper into some of the popular Canva features to help you create graphics for your business, and you will find tutorials in this section that you can follow along with to help you add that little something extra to a design that will make it eye-catching. Lastly, we can't forget our design principles, which are a set of guidelines designers use to create designs that look complete and attract the right audience, so we're going to learn how to apply them to our own designs.

This part includes the following chapters:

- *Chapter 5, Exploring the Awesome Creative Tools for Branding*
- *Chapter 6, Expert Hacks to Create Your Own Professional-Looking Designs*
- *Chapter 7, Five Graphic Design Principles You Need to Know*

5

Exploring the Awesome Creative Tools for Branding

Getting your brand kit set up in Canva is always one of the things I recommend every business completes first before getting on with its designs. Once you have your brand in place in Canva, it's so much easier and quicker to create consistent, branded graphics. It will save you time and also keep you on brand. You may use the color blue, for example, but there are thousands of shades and tints of blue, so having the exact one in your kit keeps you on brand.

In this chapter, we are going to cover the following topics:

- Understanding the basics of a brand
- The importance of consistency
- Canva's awesome color generator tool
- Discovering Canva's fonts
- How to create your brand kit
- Understanding copyrights and trademarks

By the end of this chapter, you will fully understand what makes up a brand and how to create your own brand kit in Canva, along with color and font combinations, plus the basic copyright and trademark rules when it comes to using Canva.

Understanding the basics of a brand

A brand is your business story that you share with your audience, clients, and anyone who may come across what you do. It helps to define relationships and appeal to your ideal customer.

The building of a brand is something that needs some serious thought. Before embarking on creating your brand, it's best to clearly define your business, who your target market is, and how you can help them.

Branding in itself is a big enough topic for a separate book, so in this chapter, we are going to assume you already have a basic idea of what your brand looks like or what you would like it to look like.

Broken down into sections, a brand includes the following:

- **Business Name**

  Try to pick a simple, easy-to-remember name that says what you do, look for words and phrases not used by other businesses in your sector, and then check to see whether the website domain name is available for it. If you can get the domain name, then this helps with consistency and authority.

  Here, I'm using my business as an example. I teach design, so I went for the name **Business Design Academy** and I also have a matching domain name:

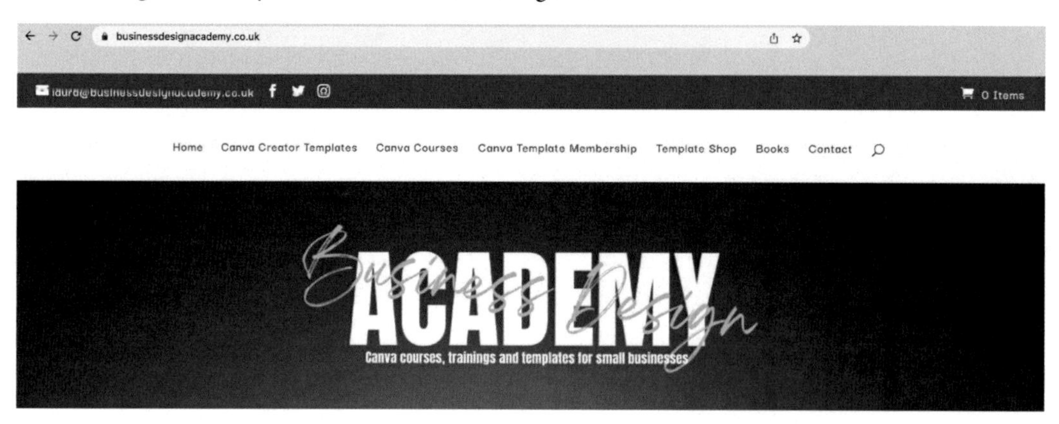

Figure 5.1 – Business name and matching domain name

- **Logo**

  Logos can be created in Canva, but there are some restrictions on what you can do. We will be looking closer at this in *Chapter 8*, *Creating Your Perfect Logo*, but for now, have a look through some of the templates available and it will give you an idea of the types of logos you can use. Often, simple is best – check out some famous brand logos and you'll see what I mean. For my own, I created this:

Figure 5.2 – Simple business logo design

Then, as a sub-logo, I wanted something that could be added to social media, as these are often smaller and they need to be simple with fewer words:

Figure 5.3 – Sub-logo design

Clean, clear, and simple is best when it comes to your logo – it's easier to remember and recognize.

- **Imagery**

  The images you use should represent your business, what you do, and how you want to be perceived by your clients. Often, using bright, clean, neutral images work well for online service businesses and floral, pretty pastel-colored images are suitable for the flower industry, as are professional office-based shots for banks, finance, and professional service-based businesses.

  What do your images say about you and your business? Here's an array of images I often use:

Figure 5.4 – Flat lay images

I tend to use flat lay images that are clean, neutral, and professional, such as these here.

- **Fonts**

  With fonts, I would say less is more – keep your fonts consistent, simple, and easy to read, and stick to just three or four fonts that you will use on a regular basis. If you're not sure what style would suit, then have a look through the fonts on Canva.

  When on a template, click on the **Text** link at the side and it will show you different font combinations that work well together:

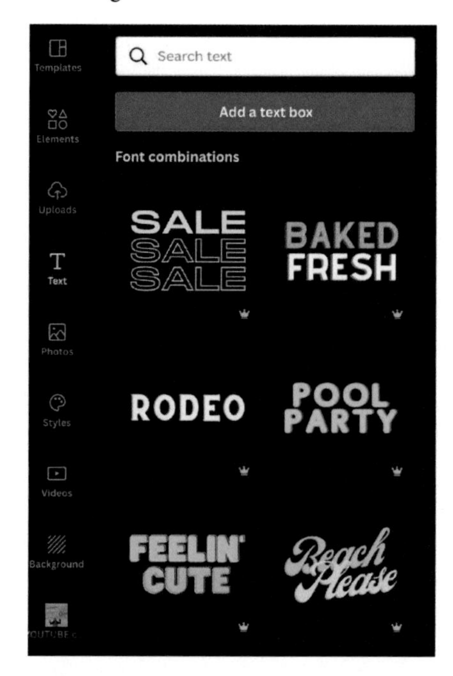

Figure 5.5 – Examples of font combinations

Once you have added a text box to your design, you can then select the font box, which will bring up all of the available fonts in Canva:

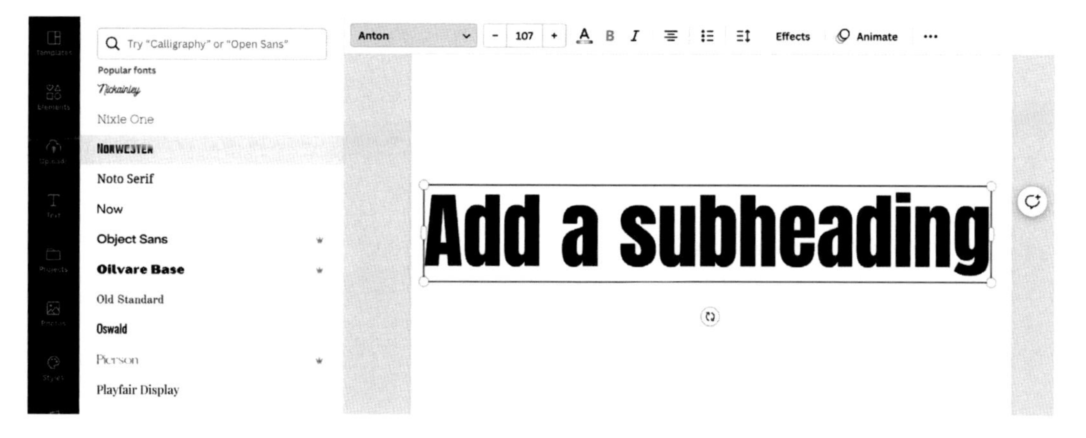

Figure 5.6 – Different fonts available in Canva

From here, you can search through them in alphabetical order, making note of any that could work for your branding.

You may or may not have noticed that in Canva, you only get the option to add three fonts to your brand kit. That's because we don't really need more than three for our branding. It can get messy if we use lots of different fonts.

The three fonts are as follows:

- **Header font**: Used for your business name or main information on social media posts, so this could be something fancy or a little bit different to make it stand out.
- **Sub-header font**: This needs to be a clear font that is easy to read, works well with the header font, and is used for titles and section headers.
- **Body font**: Again, this needs to be simple, clear, and easy to read, as it will be used for the main body of your information and passages of text and often has a small size.

Header font

Sub-header font

Body font

Figure 5.7 – Three font styles required for your brand

If you're unsure of what font would work best, stick with the more common fonts to begin with. You can always adapt and change your branding as your business grows.

- **Colors**

  Lastly in this section, we have color, my favorite part of branding – this is where you can really shine and show off who you are.

  All colors have different meanings and can bring out different emotions in people. We want to bring out the right emotion in our ideal client, so getting the right color palette is important. For example, if you were to run a funeral directory, you probably wouldn't want to use yellow as the main color. Black or gray would be more suitable for the business.

  You do need to love the colors you pick as well.

  Selecting three to four main colors that complement each other will help form your brand. That may not seem like a lot, but you also have the use of all the different shades and tints of these colors to use as well. The rule of thumb here is very similar to the number of fonts we need – too many colors can look messy and people will find it difficult to recognize our brand.

  Canva has some great resources on colors, palettes, and the meanings behind the colors, which we will be looking at later in this chapter:

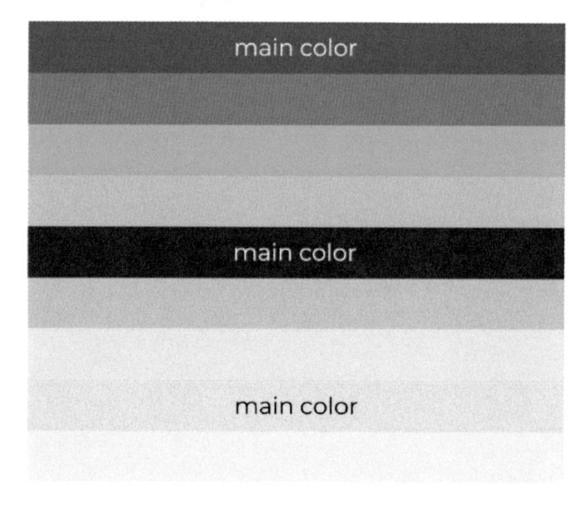

Figure 5.8 – Color palette combination with tints

Here, we have an example of my color palette – it includes three main colors and then different tints for each one, keeping my brand on point but allowing me to have a wider color range to use.

Your imagery, fonts, and colors all need to work well together and remain consistent, so let's explore this a little further.

The importance of consistency

Consistency is very important when it comes to your brand. I'm not going to go into a huge amount of detail on this subject, but I wanted to add a section just to give you an overview.

A consistent brand – that means you consistently use the same color palettes, imagery, logo, and fonts everywhere within your business – will help elevate your brand's status.

People who follow you on social media will start to recognize your posts because you are always using your brand, your business will become familiar quicker, and people will stop scrolling to read your content because they have seen something they know, like, and trust.

We are very visual as human beings – colors, imagery and fonts jump out at us if we see them all the time and recognize them. This is important, especially on our social media channels, which are such fast-moving platforms and full of competitive content. We need to grab someone's attention straight away and make them pause to look at what we are offering or saying.

Consistency in our brand is one way to do this and keeping consistent with our color palette helps with recognition as well, but where can you find different color palettes that would suit your brand? Canva has you covered here with their color generator tool, which we are going to look at next.

Canva's awesome color generator tool

Think about your business sector – are you in finance? Floristry? Do you run a cleaning business? A retail shop? Each type of business will draw a different color palette.

Look at the below for examples of different color meanings:

- **Blue**: Loyalty, trust, and safety – which is why banks and finance companies often use blue.
- **Orange**: Creativity, warmth, and confidence
- **Red**: Passion, power, and energy
- **Pink**: Love, care, and kindness
- **Black**: Professionalism, power, and security
- **Yellow**: Energy, brightness, and happiness
- **Green**: Nature, health, and freedom

Canva has a color generator page on its website: `https://www.canva.com/colors/`. I love using this page to find new color palettes and there is even a color meaning section, so it's a great page to use for your branding color research.

There are four different ways to generate colors on the Canva color website page:

1. The first part gives you the option to pick the colors from an image. I've used this one as an example. I took this photo myself in our garden:

Figure 5.9 – A photo of a pink flower

These are the colors it has picked out for me. If you use this section for your brand colors, keep a list of the HEX codes underneath, as you will need these to create your brand kit:

Figure 5.10 – Color palette

I can now use these colors within any design by adding in the HEX code, which is the # underneath the color's name.

2. The second part gives you different color palette ideas:

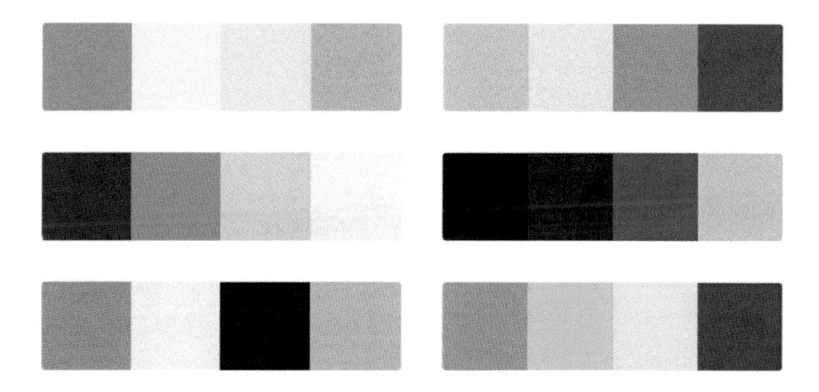

Figure 5.11– Selection of color palettes

You can select any palette and it will take you to a page with more options and all of the HEX codes.

3. The third part is the color wheel. You can choose colors that complement each other here, so they are opposite each other on the wheel, or you can choose triadic colors, which are equally spaced around the color wheel:

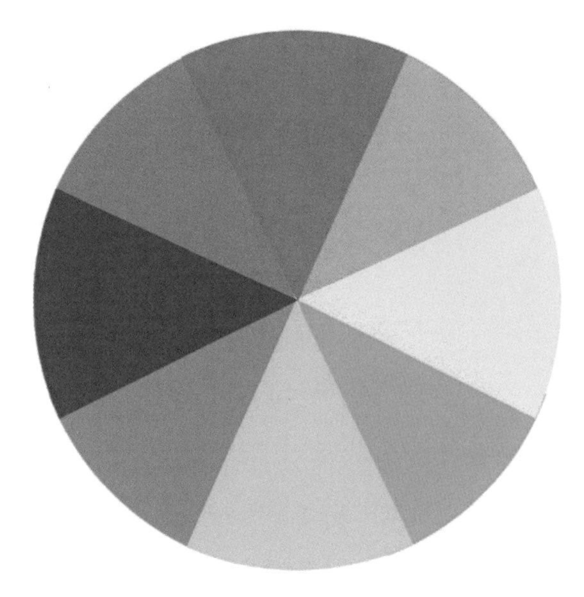

Figure 5.12 – A basic color wheel

This is a great feature to have a look at, especially if you're unsure and would like to have the option to pick colors that work well together.

4. Lastly, we have color meanings. Here, you can learn more about what each color represents, the history and symbolism of the color, and how to use it:

Figure 5.13 – Color blocks

You can click on each colored block and it will take you to an information page. It's an interesting page for any budding business owner to really great to grips with their brand colors and make sure they have the correct palette set for their business.

We've covered a lot of information about colors so let's have a look at fonts next.

Discovering Canva's fonts

Canva has hundreds of fonts available to you. Some are creative handwritten fonts, others are more corporate or modern, and some are vintage-style or bold. You can pick any that you would like. Those with a crown icon next to them are only available on Pro – those without are free to use.

Choosing a font for your brand is tricky due to the vast amount of different style fonts; what do you go for?

This is where you need to look at your business sector again – depending on what you do, this can help you pick a font style. Businesses in corporate, financial, or big industries often work better with straight-lined, bolder fonts, but if you run a women's fitness group or children's craft classes, you may want a softer, rounder font.

The best way to get started is to look through the fonts in Canva and write down the names of any you like the look of. Use the headers at the top of the font dropdown to get an idea of where you want to be and then pick out three that work – one for a business name main font, one for your sub-headers, and one for your body fonts.

There are lots of different font sections including but not limited to the following: **Handwritten**, **Modern**, **Cool**, **Retro**, **Brush**, **Comic**, **Curly**, **Graffiti**, **Cartoon**, and **Wide**, all within the font dropdown:

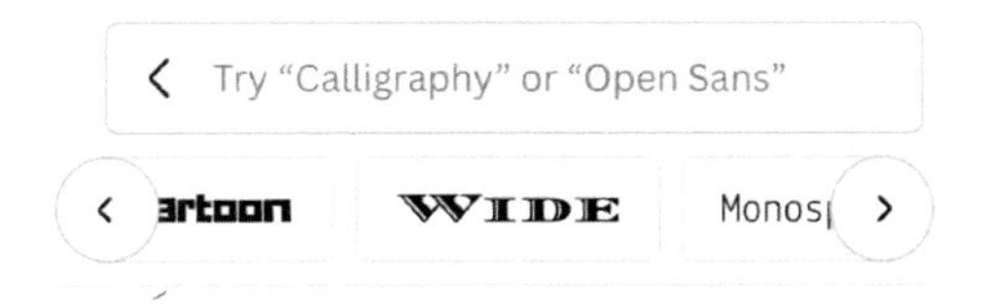

Figure 5.14 – Font sections

Use the left and right arrows to search the different sections. As mentioned in the first part of the chapter, stick to just three or four fonts to keep your brand consistent. Too many can look cluttered and will dilute your brand.

Another place to find fonts in Canva is in the **Styles** section on the left. Here, Canva has given you lots of mini branding boards; you get three fonts and a color palette. These are great for changing the look of a template quickly and also for getting an idea of what fonts work well together:

Figure 5.15 – Using styles to change a template

Here are two examples of the same template, but using two different style boards. The only parts that remain the same are the placement of elements and images:

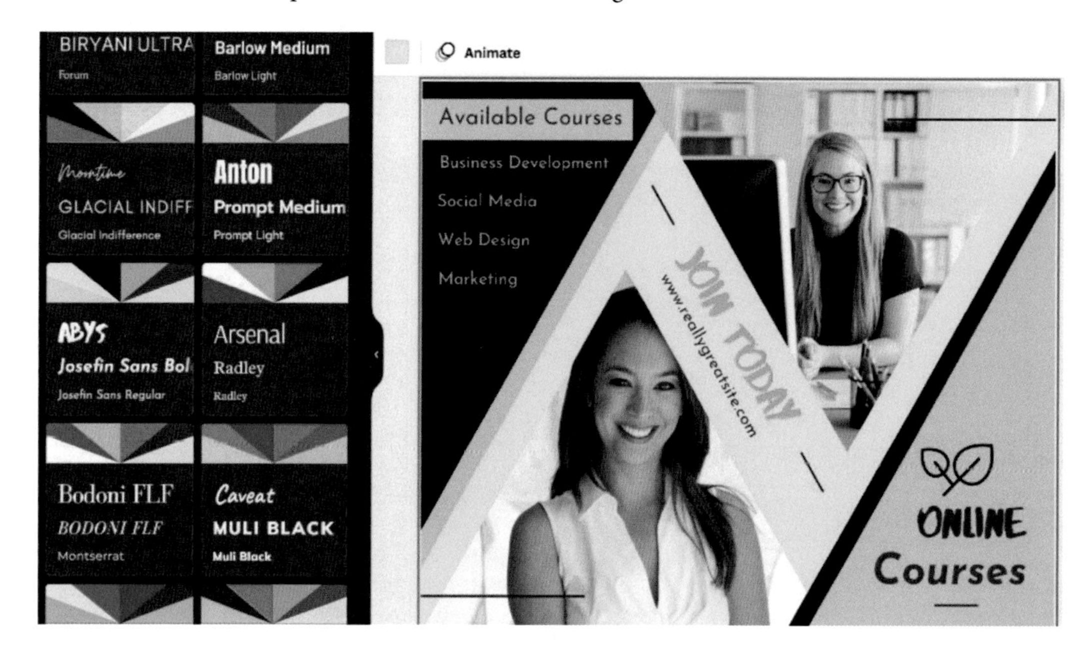

Figure 5.16 – Using styles to change a template

We're at the end of the breakdown on branding. We've covered, logos, color palettes, fonts, and imagery. Now, it's time to put it all together and create our brand kit.

How to create your brand kit

At this point, you should hopefully have an idea of what will be going into your brand kit. The next step is to create the kit ready for you to use when creating designs in Canva.

There are two ways to do this because we have two account types: Pro and Free. I'm going to start with the Pro account, as you get a brand kit to populate within your account.

Creating your brand kit with Pro

To find the brand kit, head over to your Canva account, and in the left-hand menu is a **Brand** link. This will open up the branding page and from here, you can select the **Add new** button on the top right to create a new kit or select an existing one once you have created it.

Here, I have created two brand kits:

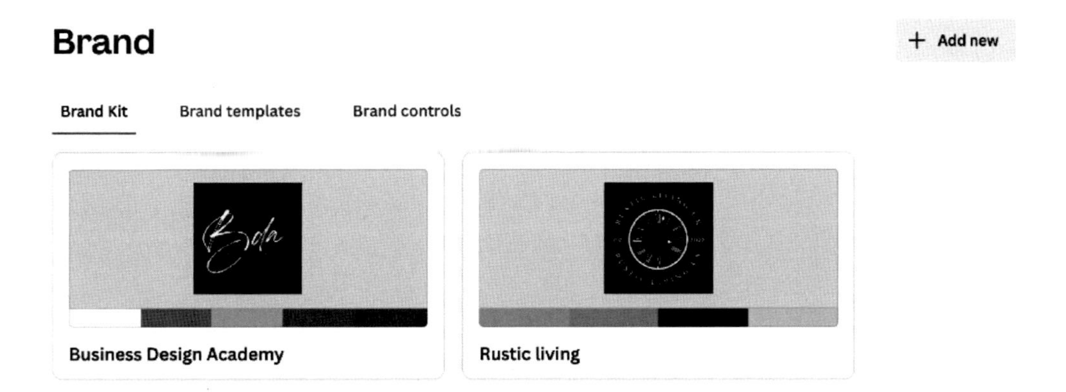

Figure 5.17 – Brand kit page

To create a new kit, we are going to select the **Add new** button, and then click **Brand Kit** (it also gives you the option to create brand templates here as well – that can be saved for later use, making it easier to stay on brand):

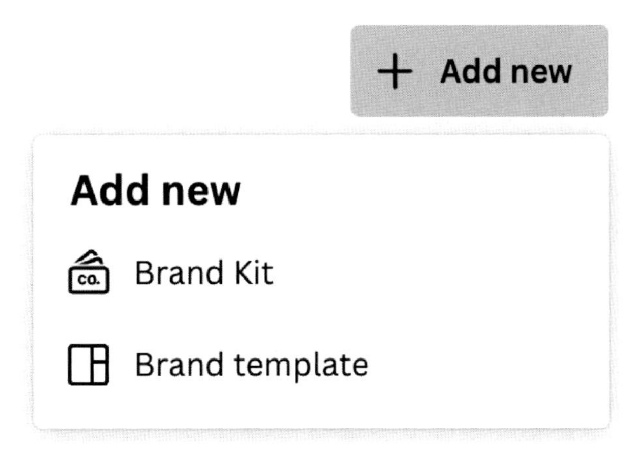

Figure 5.18 – Adding or creating a new brand kit

Name your kit – don't worry, this can be changed at a later date – and click **Create**. We now have a blank kit for us to populate:

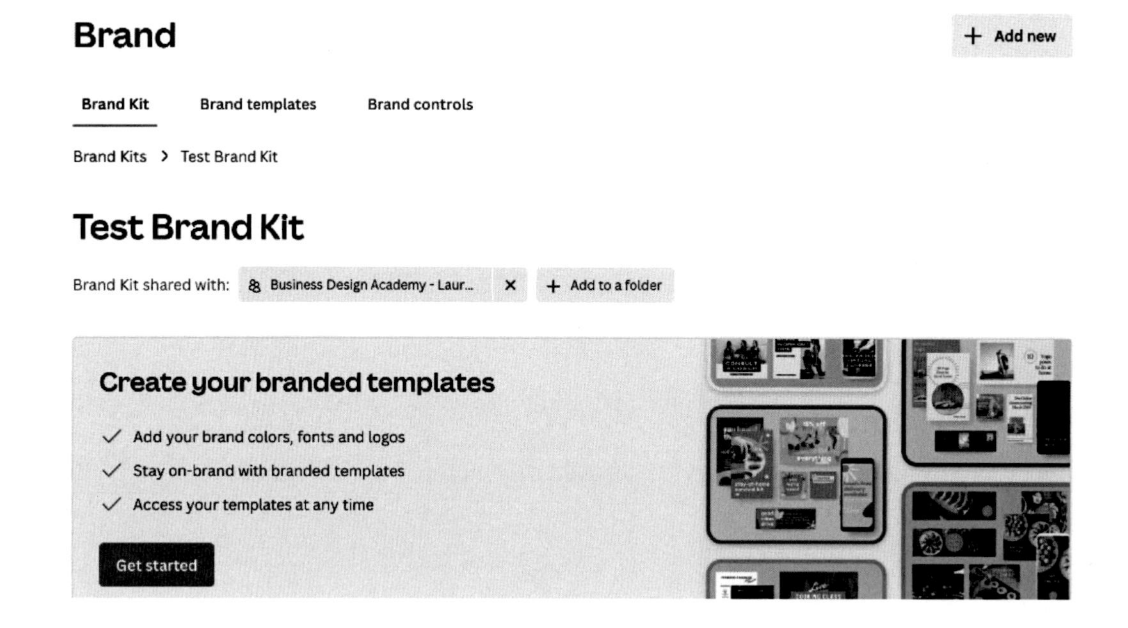

Figure 5.19 – Blank branding kit

If you click on the **Get Started** button, it will take you to the **Quick create** feature to create your first set of branded templates. We will be looking at this feature in *Chapter 6*, *Expert Hacks to Create Your Own Professional-Looking Designs*.

Scroll on down to the logo section and let's add our logo. If you have designed your own, that's wonderful, but using a template is ideal in the beginning.

To add a logo, it needs to be in an image format. If you haven't already, you will need to download your logo. Using the **Share** button at the top of the design, select **Download** – it will be set to **PNG** for you – and then save it to your computer or mobile:

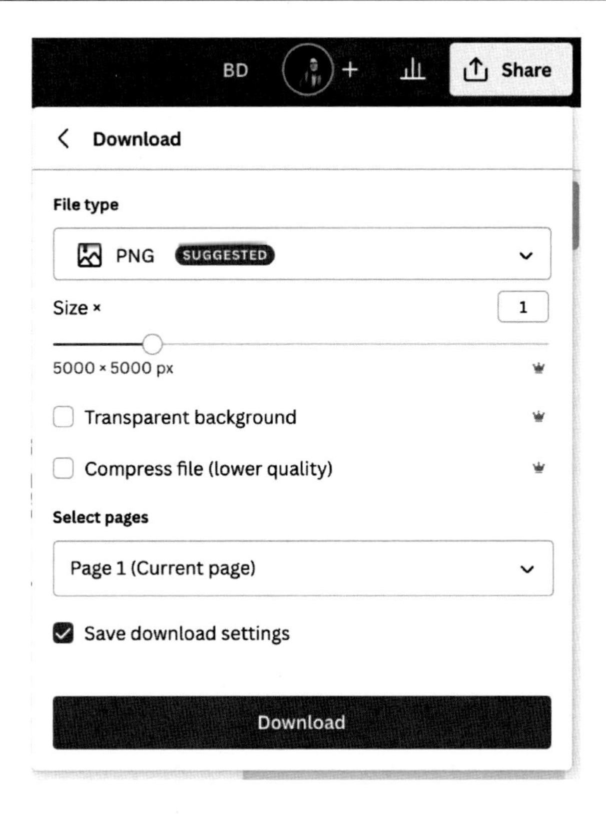

Figure 5.20 – Downloading your logo as a PNG

We now need to go back to the brand kit we set up, and under the part where it says **Brand Logos**, select the plus symbol and find our logo image. It will now show in place of the plus symbol. You have successfully added your logo to the brand kit and you can now repeat this process for any other logos or sub-logos you have:

Figure 5.21 – Brand kit logo upload

Now, we're going to add our brand colors. Did you keep a list of your HEX codes from the color section? You're going to need them now. I will be using the color palette I created from the image of a pink flower:

Figure 5.22 – Color palette from the pink flower image

To start a new color palette, click on the plus symbol under **Color palette** to get started:

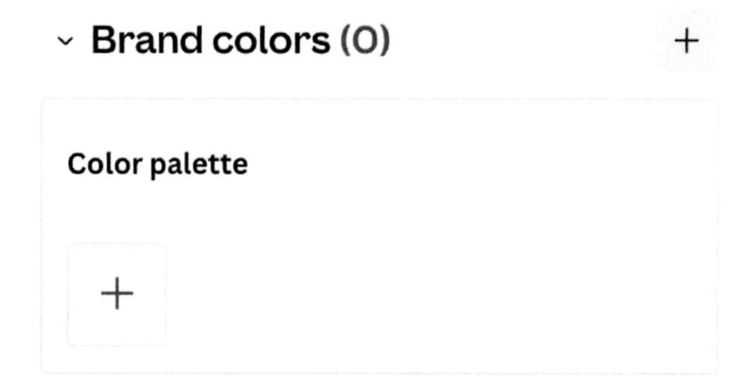

Figure 5.23 – Adding colors to the brand kit

This opens up the option to now add in any color we like. You can select a new color by moving the white circle around or you can copy and paste in your HEX code to generate the exact color you are using for your branding:

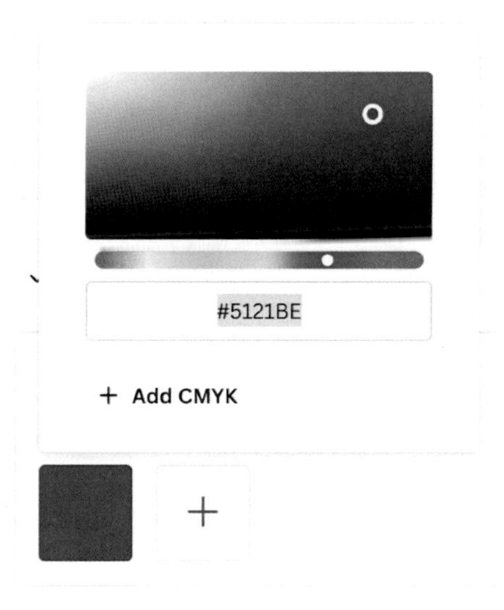

Figure 5.24 – Branding color options

I have copied and pasted over all four of the hex codes from my color palette, repeating the same process of clicking on the plus symbol to add each color. This is my new color palette:

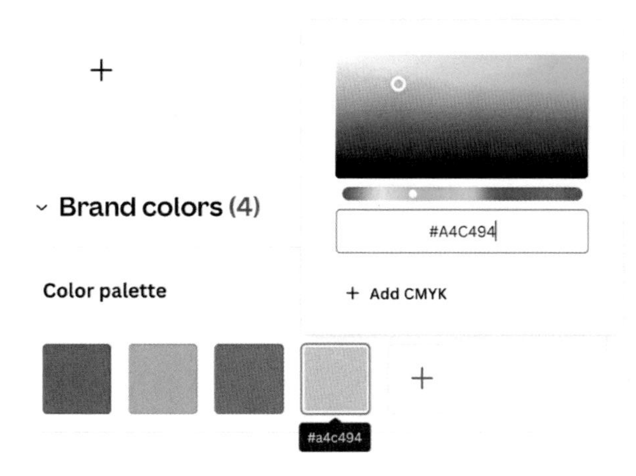

Figure 5.25 – Branding color palette

You can add in multiple color palettes – for example, if you have different projects that use different colors, by clicking the plus symbol at the top of the color palette section, adding in as many as you need:

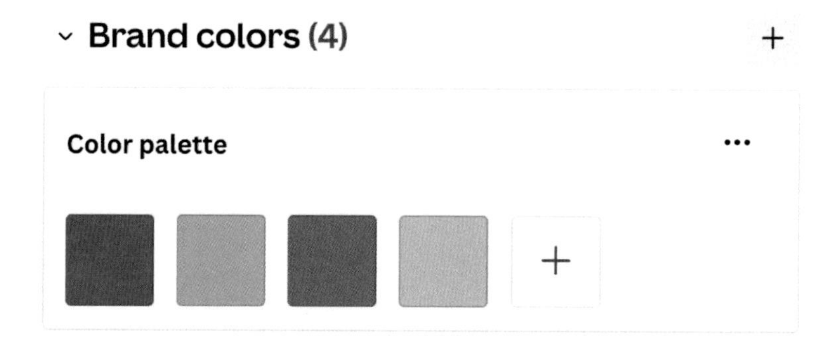

Figure 5.26 – Color palettes

Lastly in this section, we are looking at adding our fonts. To do this, you can see there are three sections where you can add your heading, subheading, and body fonts. Click on each one and you can choose your font from the Canva dropdown:

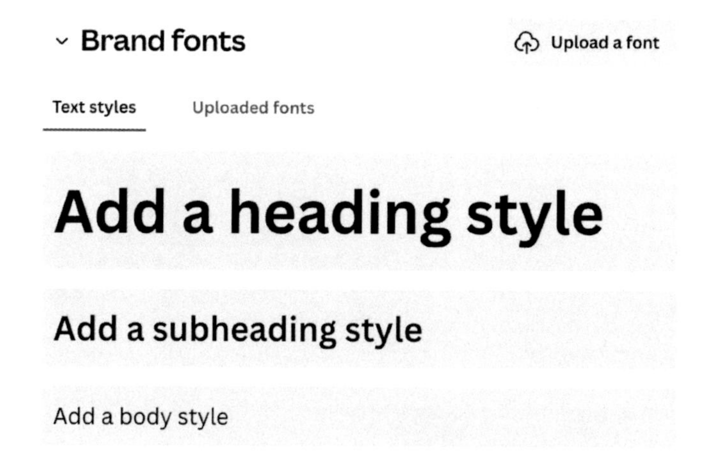

Figure 5.27 – Canva font boxes

Follow the same process for all three boxes that you add your brand fonts into. However, if you cannot find the font you would like to use, you do have the option to upload external fonts to Canva with a Pro account:

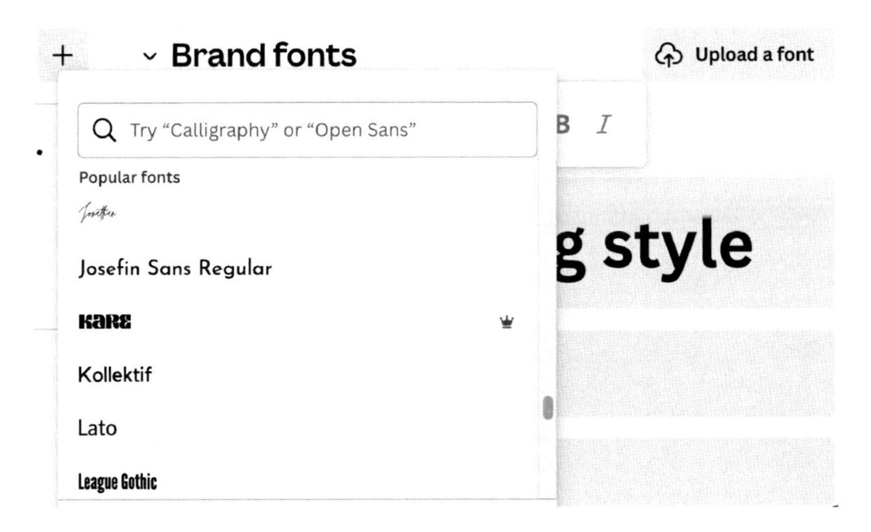

Figure 5.28 – Selecting your fonts for the brand kit

To upload a font, you will need to have downloaded the correct file format for it, which is usually an OTF or TTF file. These will be sent to you when you purchase or download the original font. Click on the **Upload a font** button and find the file. This will then upload here for you to use and it will also appear in the font list when you are in the middle of creating your designs.

Create your brand kit with a free account

That's it for creating a brand kit in Pro, but these options are not available with a Free account. You can, however, add three colors to a color palette using the HEX codes. Beyond that, you can use a template from Canva to create your kit.

Search for terms such as `Moodboard`, `Brand board`, or `Brand kit` and you will see a huge amount of templates that can help. Select one that resonates with you but keep in mind that everything on it can be edited:

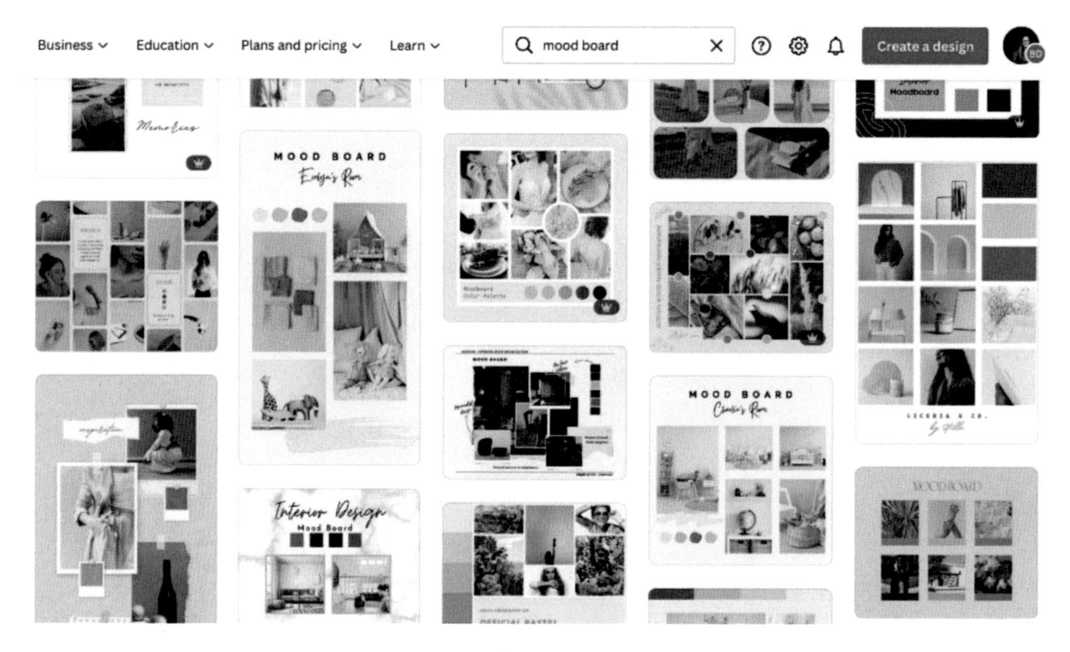

Figure 5.29 – Moodboard example templates

Moodboards and brand boards do have different elements to them, so have a good look at each one. Brand board templates will also have font options and sometimes submark spaces:

Figure 5.30 – Brand board example templates

I've chosen this template to show you as an example:

Figure 5.31 – Blue moodboard

Within this template, you have multiple image blocks, color circles, and different fonts. You can replace any of the images by uploading your own to Canva or using the existing images and then dragging and dropping the image into the space – it will replace any current images.

Click on one of the color circles and you can add your own HEX codes. By selecting the plus symbol in the color section, you can also paste in your HEX code as well:

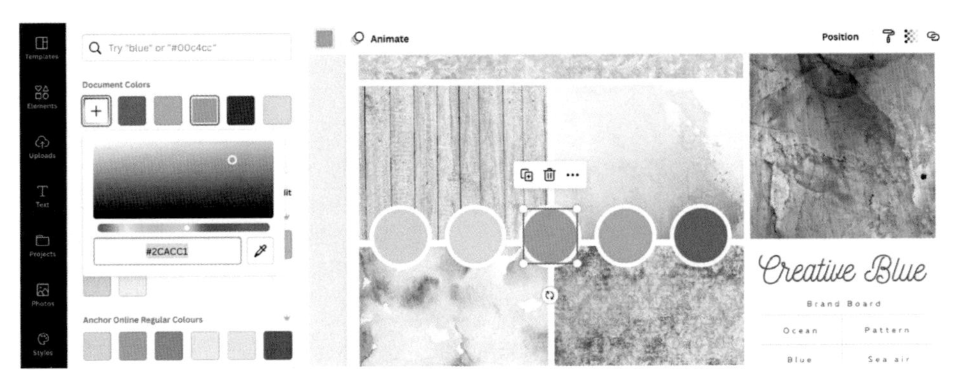

Figure 5.32 – Changing colors on templates

Lastly, you can change the existing font to match your brand font. Select the text box and then use the drop-down menu to change the font. there are a lot of free fonts available. You can also edit the text to the name of the font:

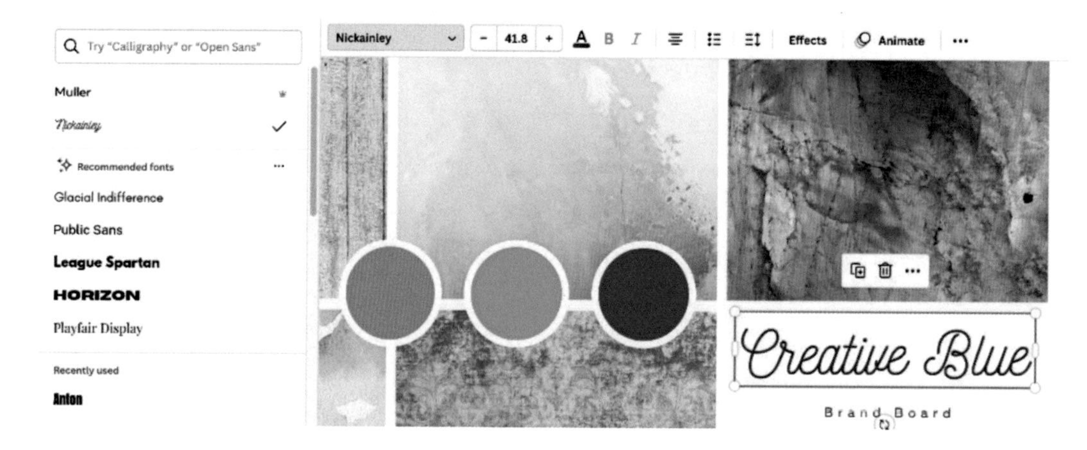

Figure 5.33 – Changing the text on templates

This is the easiest way to put your brand kit together. You can print it out and display it somewhere. As you grow and your brand changes, you can edit the template and reprint it, but keep in mind these options on the left don't appear when creating designs for your business. These will only be there if you have Pro and have set up the brand kit within your account.

We are nearing the end of this chapter, so now you have your brand kit in place, there are a few extra things you need to know in regard to copyright and trademarks within Canva.

Understanding copyrights and trademarks

At this point, I wanted to go through a few things on what can and can't be done with content in Canva. Before we really dive into creating content, it's good to understand the platform better and how it works.

Licenses and copyright

Canva is a free-to-use platform with a lot of free-to-use content, but every time you use a template, image, or element a license is created in the background giving you permission to use it. This is granted automatically for everything in Pro on the export of the design, and you can purchase a license individually in a Free account for any Pro content. Free content may still require a license depending on its source. You can hover over the **(i)** symbol within Canva for more information.

The reason a license is granted is that a large proportion of the content has been created by designers outside of Canva – they and Canva have the rights to the content, and hence, you need a license to use it.

The copyright of the content belongs to Canva or the designer.

Templates

Templates are perfect for most business uses. You can use a template, edit the colors, change the font, and use it on your social media. However, there are restrictions on its commercial use. I would not recommend using an existing template in a product or item you plan on selling, as the template belongs to someone else. Always create your designs from scratch if they are to be sold.

If you are looking to create designs to sell on physical products, please make sure you use free Canva content only, do not use Pro content, this is against Canva terms and conditions. If you are creating content to sell that brings to end user back to Canva, so they can edit the templates themselves; an example of this would be a social media template pack, you can use both Free and Pro content, but please be aware the majority of Canva users are on the Free account and if you add in Pro content they will need to then purchase additional licenses to use the Pro content, this may not be ideal for the end user as these are unexpected costs.

Trademarks

Trademarking is generally only referred to in Canva with regard to logos, but this actually applies to all content. As I've mentioned previously, you do not own the content in Canva, so you cannot trademark a logo (or any other content in Canva), as the elements or template that make up the logo design belong to someone else. It is available to be used by other people, meaning it is not unique and trademarking is not possible. If you want to trademark your business logo, you will need to have it created by a designer outside of Canva. You can still upload and use it within your designs even if it was not created using content in Canva.

If you don't mind not being able to trademark your logo, it's just a temporary logo, or you are just looking for inspiration, then by all means use a template. There are lots of amazing logo templates in Canva to help you and your brand get started.

This is by no means everything on this subject. I wanted to give you a brief overview. Here's a link for more information and the full details on the Canva licenses, `https://www.canva.com/policies/license-agreements`, so that you are informed from the beginning of your Canva journey.

We've now come to the end, so let's take a look at what we've learned in this chapter on creating your business brand.

Summary

This has been a big chapter with a lot of information on branding and creating your brand kit. You have learned about the basics of branding and what makes up a brand. You have learned about colors and how they complement each other and have discovered more about their meanings; you have looked at different fonts and styles and where to find them within Canva; you have seen the importance of imagery, consistency, and how to use log templates; and you have also learned how to create your brand kit, putting everything together to have a finished brand you can use within your business. We've even touched on copyright and trademarks, so you now know what you can and can't do with the content in Canva.

So far, you've learned a lot about creating designs in Canva and setting up your brand, so let's do something a bit more fun. We're looking at five Canva tutorials you can follow along with next.

6

Expert Hacks to Create Your Own Professional-Looking Designs

In this chapter, we're going to delve a little deeper into some of the features that will really help you understand how to quickly create graphics in Canva that look great, are branded, and include some great elements such as grids and frames. These are both fantastic features of Canva and ones I love to use myself.

In this chapter, we are going to cover the following main topics:

- Adding gradients to achieve depth
- Using the Quick Create feature
- Using grids for quick, effective designs
- Creating with frames
- Creating graphs for your documents

By the end of this chapter, you will be able to add gradients, grids, frames, and graphs to your designs, as well as knowing how to use the **Quick Create** feature to create branded graphics for multiple platforms.

Adding gradients to achieve depth

Gradients within a design can really help to make the information stand out. It gives a design that little something extra. Adding a gradient to the background will help to increase your visibility on social media channels, potentially catching someone's eye and stopping them from scrolling on by. Adding a gradient in Canva is a really simple and quick thing to do. Let's look at how.

First of all, we need to open up a template. It could be a blank one or an existing template that you would like to edit and use. Here, I'm going to use one I've created:

Figure 6.1 – Floral graphics with a block color background

The template here is perfectly fine as is. It has a plain block color for the background and pretty floral elements that match, but we can make this better by adding a gradient. To find the gradient, just type `Gradient` into the search bar for the elements. You will find hundreds of different styles appear, all different shapes and sizes. The one we need is further down. It's a free element and is a square with two colors that you can change. Both are shades of blue within the original element:

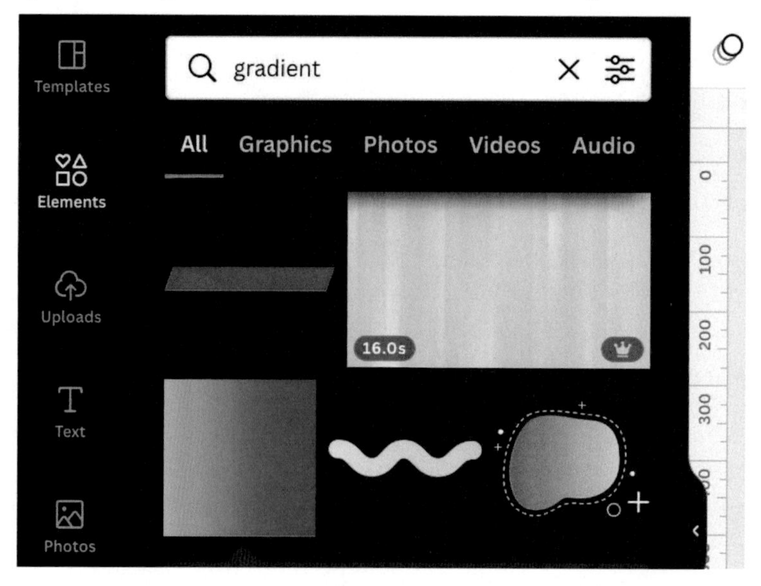

Figure 6.2 – Searching for gradients in the Elements section

Once you have selected the gradient and added it to your design, use the white circles in the corners to drag it out to cover the full size of your design:

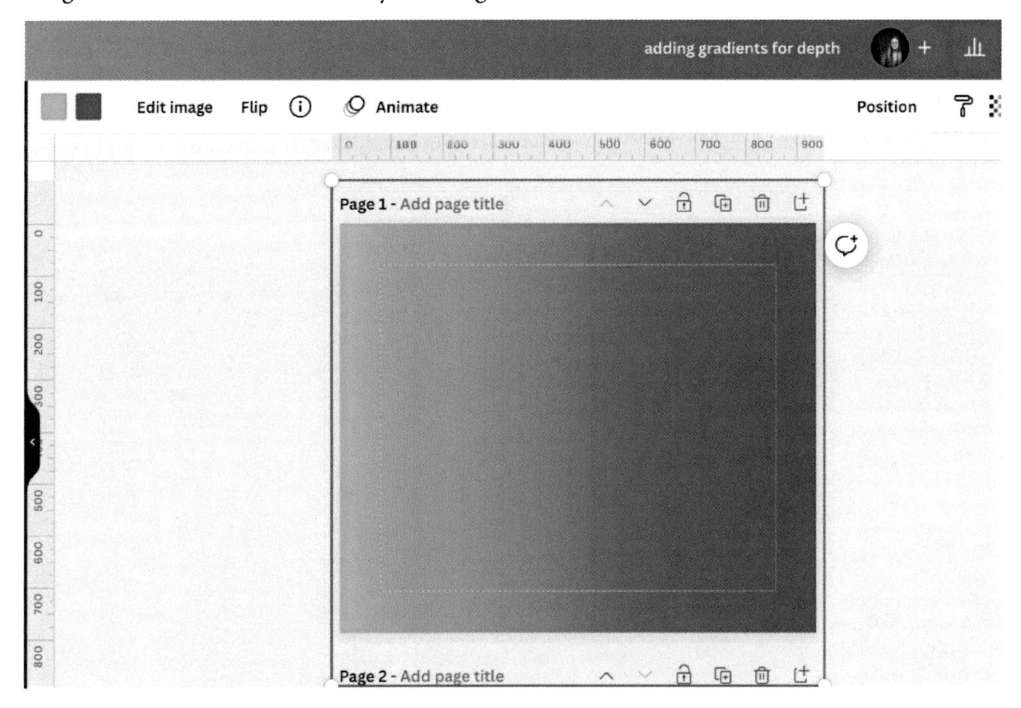

Figure 6.3 – Adding a gradient to your design

Select **Position** in the top-right corner and then click the **Backward** option in the dropdown. It will then place itself as the background to your design:

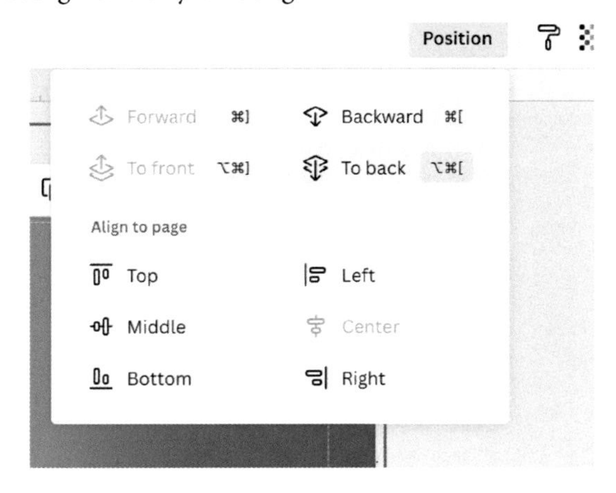

Figure 6.4 – To back option

Next, we need to change the colors, we can use our branding colors or use the colors within the design. So in this case, I will use the colors from the elements themselves. First I must select one of the two color options in the top-left corner and the color palette will open. Here, Canva has a color picker tool – the paint dropper icon shown in the following screenshot. It allows you to hover over any part of the page and select the color to use within your design:

Figure 6.5 – Changing the color of gradients

I have selected the light pink color from the petals and the green from the leaves for my two background gradient colors. Here is the finished effect:

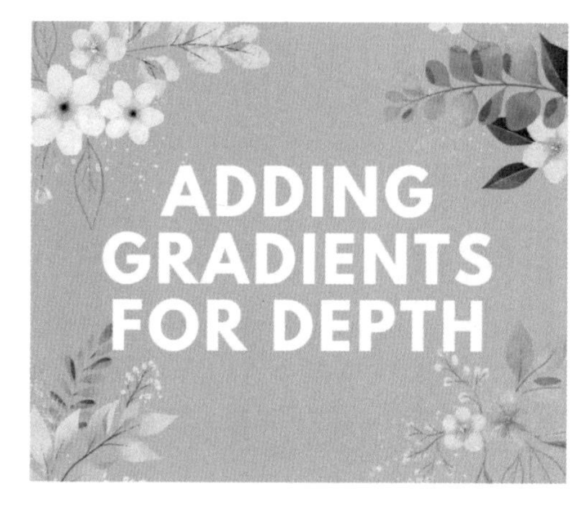

Figure 6.6 – Finished design with gradient background

Compare this image to the original one and you can see the difference a simple background gradient can make to a design. Try adding a gradient to one of your own designs and experiment with different colors to see what you can create.

Next, we will look at another great feature of Canva, which can save you time.

Using the Quick Create feature

The **Quick Create** feature is a relatively new one to Canva. I've found it so useful for creating graphics for multiple platforms when I need something quick but I also need them to match in terms of style. So if you have a project, e-book, course, or something else you would like to promote, have a look at this feature.

To open the **Quick Create** feature, you need to go over to the **Social media** section on the Canva home page – it's the fourth icon along:

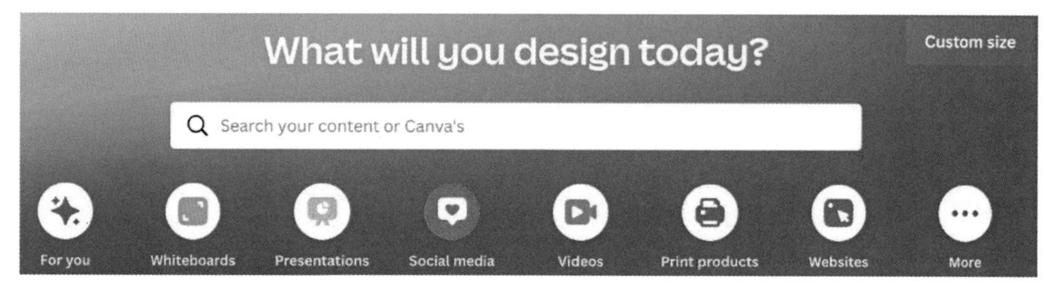

Figure 6.7 – Canva option icons on the home page

Here you will find lots of social media templates, images, and content ideas, but we're looking for the very first section, **Quick Create Collection**. Click on the image of the four pink and blue graphics and it will open up the step-by-step page to create with this feature.

Quick Create Collection

The quickest way to create a collection of designs for social media.

Figure 6.8 – The Quick Create feature

The first thing we need to decide is which platforms we would like to create graphics for. Choose a platform by selecting the white boxes next to each one:

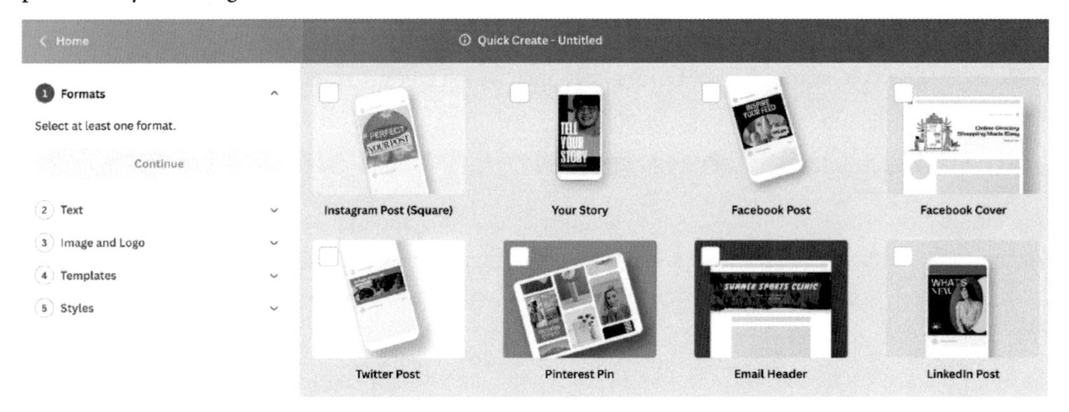

Figure 6.9 – Step 1 of the Quick Create feature – picking the formats

I've chosen, Instagram, Facebook, Twitter, Pinterest, and LinkedIn. Once you have selected your platforms, click **Continue** and it will take you to the next step.

Figure 6.10 – Step 2 of the Quick Create feature – adding text

On this page, you will find lots of different template styles on the right and two textboxes on the left. Add your main information to the first one and then any additional information to the second:

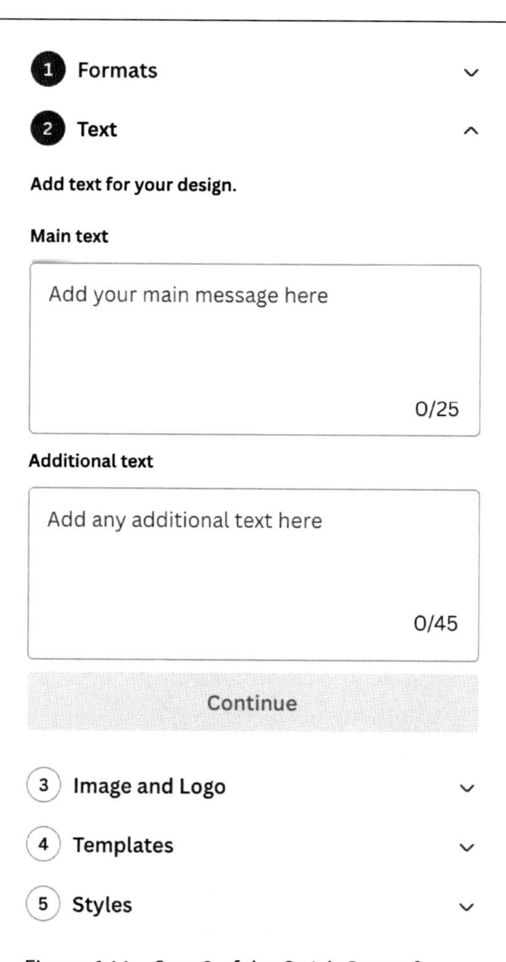

Figure 6.11 – Step 2 of the Quick Create feature

When you add in your information, it automatically shows it on the templates to the right, so you can see how it will look. Once you have finished, press **Continue** and it will take you to the next step.

This is where you can now add your images and logo to the design. It will bring up your uploaded file so you can select an image you already have available, or you can upload one directly. Select an image and it will populate the template for you; the same happens with your logo. Once done, press **Continue**:

Figure 6.12 – Step 3 of the Quick Create feature – adding images and a logo

Now it's the fun part – selecting which template style you would like to use. Have a look through and find one that suits your project. Don't worry about colors or fonts yet as that is the next stage.

Once you've selected your style and pressed **Continue**, it will show you each template laid out:

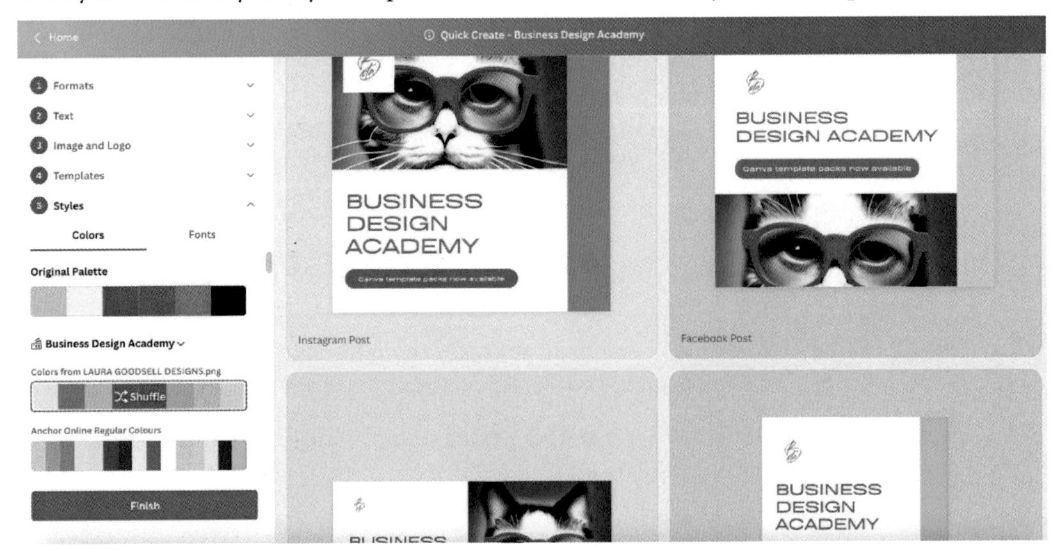

Figure 6.13 – Step 4 of the Quick Create feature – picking a template

You can now select your colors. You have a few choices here: you can use your branded colors or any color palettes that you have saved, and if you scroll down, Canva gives you multiple color palettes to choose from. I've gone with my branded colors in this example, so it matches everything else I have. Once you are happy with the colors, select the **Fonts** option:

Figure 6.14 – Step 5 of the Quick Create feature – styles

Canva offers multiple font choices. You can use the ones from the template, your branded fonts, or a combination of other fonts. I've gone for a large bold font that suits the template style. Once done, select **Finish**, and your templates will be created:

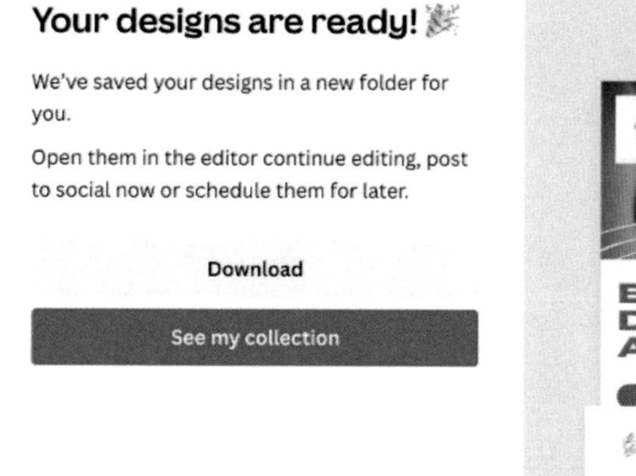

Figure 6.15 – Downloading your finished designs

You can now download the collection to use, or select **See my collection** and the templates will open within your Canva account. From here, you can make any edits to them individually if needed:

Figure 6.16 – Your designs are now saved in your Canva account

Now you have a collection of templates that you can use, but you only had to create the content once and you don't have to then resize any of them. This is a brilliantly useful feature. Another feature that helps save time is using grids, so let's have a look at them next.

Using grids for quick, effective designs

I love grids. For those of you that have ever been to one of my training courses or watched my tutorials, I always mention grids. They can help you to create a lovely-looking graphic in mere minutes, giving you space for your images, business name, branding, and information. So, let's dive straight into how to add a grid to your template.

Grids can be found in the **Elements** section on Canva, so once you have your blank template open, head over to the **Elements** section and type in `grids`:

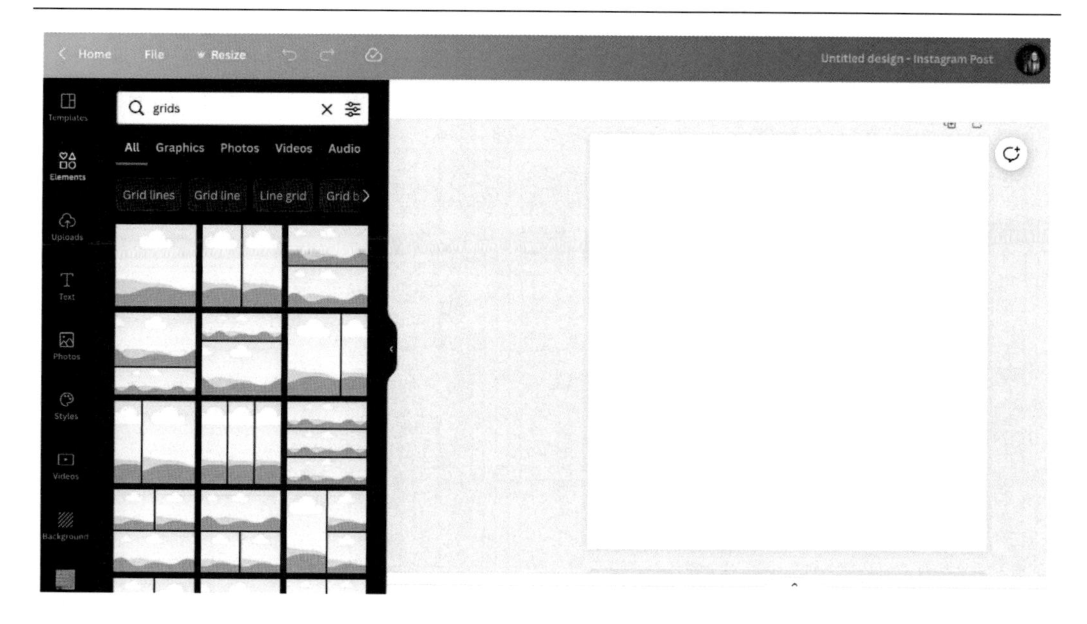

Figure 6.17 – Finding grids in the Elements section

You will notice that you now have a long list of straight-edged elements that include a green hill, a blue sky, and a white cloud – any element in Canva that has the white cloud, green hill, and blue sky within, can have either a color, image, or video added to it. Scroll down and select one that has a few different size squares. I've selected the one that has seven different sections for this example:

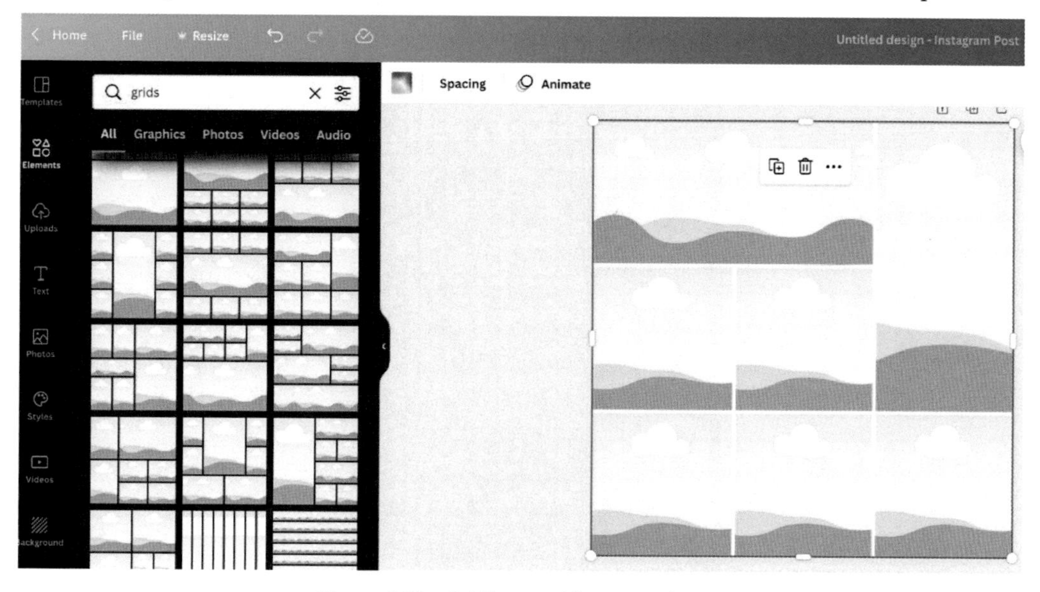

Figure 6.18 – Adding a grid to your design

Now, bring in the corners using the white circles to give your grid a border, and start dragging and dropping in your images. These can be from the **Uploads** section or the Canva image library. I've added some autumn shopping-based images to create a sales post:

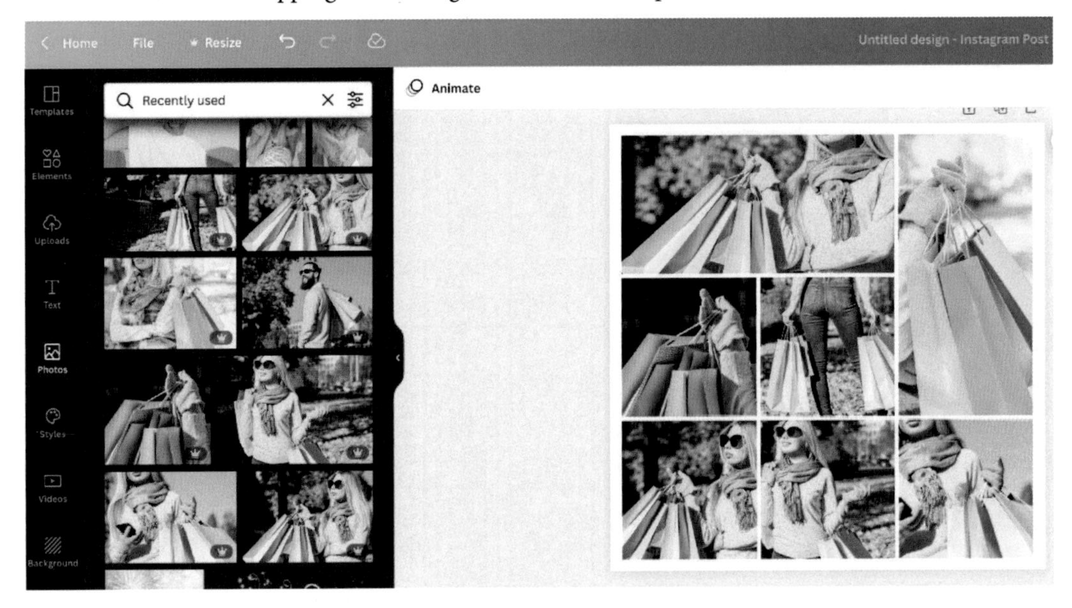

Figure 6.19 – Adding images to your grid

After filling your grid with images, you may like to add some information, perhaps a business name, logo, or sale location. Select the central image and hit **Delete**, then go to the color palette and change the square to the same color as the background.

This has created a lovely space to now add any extra information:

Figure 6.20 – Finished design with space for information

In this example, I have added three textboxes and a leaf icon to the central box, keeping within the space. This is my finished design:

Figure 6.21 – Finished design

With just a few clicks, you have a great image that you can now use on your social media profile. In this example, I now have an image to promote my autumn sale, created using a grid and textboxes.

Let's look at creating a graphic using frames next – a very similar process to grids but a bit more fun.

Creating with frames

Frames are similar to grids in that you can add an image, color, or video to them, but they are different shapes rather than just square. These can be great to create fun graphics. They can be found in the same place as grids, but you can use the `frames` keyword instead.

I've added a scribble-style frame as the basis of my design example:

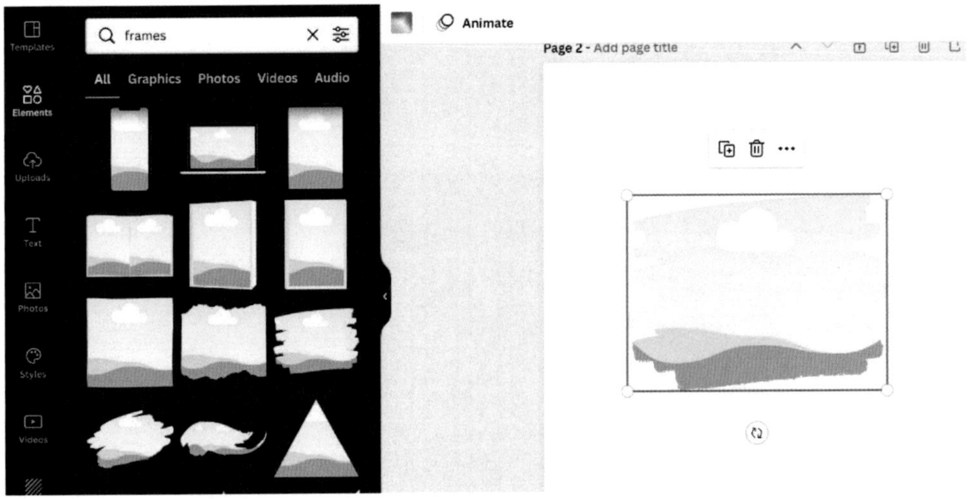

Figure 6.22 – Adding frames to templates

I will be creating a video blog-based template for this example, but you can create any style of your choice. Add a flat lay image, which is a photo taken from directly above, this could be of a notebook, pens, and a tablet arranged on a desk in a pleasing way. These can be found in the **Photos** section of Canva. Also, add a textbox at the top. At the bottom, add a square shape that can be stretched across the template. Then, add another template box for your information and website details at the bottom:

Figure 6.23 – Nearly complete frame-based design

You're beginning to build up a usable design for your business, but it feels like there is something missing from this design. As we now know, we can add colors to grids. We can also do the same with frames, so duplicate the frame and select the color option. Then, change the frame to a color that matches your design:

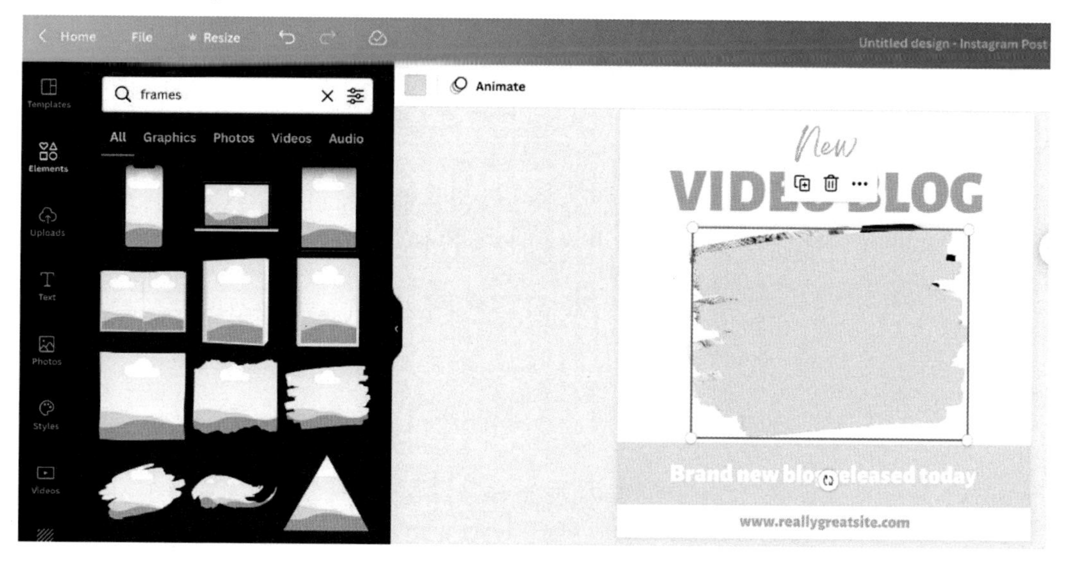

Figure 6.24 – Changing a frame's color

Lastly, use the **Position** option to send the colored frame to the back, giving the frame with the image in place a background shadow. Now, the design looks finished:

Figure 6.25 – The finished design

This is the finished design. You can see the effect the frame shape with the image has, as well as the effect of the background color and shape on the overall design. It stands out so much more than a plain square or oblong image would.

Frames and grids are great for creating quick social media graphics, but sometimes we want to add in a bit more information. This can be done using graphs in Canva, so let's look at how we can add these in next.

Creating graphs for your documents

Graphs can be used for a variety of graphics, including calendars, planner pages, and infographics, so knowing how to add a graph to your design will allow you to offer more information in a well-presented way.

Graphs and tables are both found in the **Elements** section. Type in `graph` and you will see lots of different styles.

Graphs

Let's select one of these graphs. Canva will give you different options to help you edit your chosen graph :

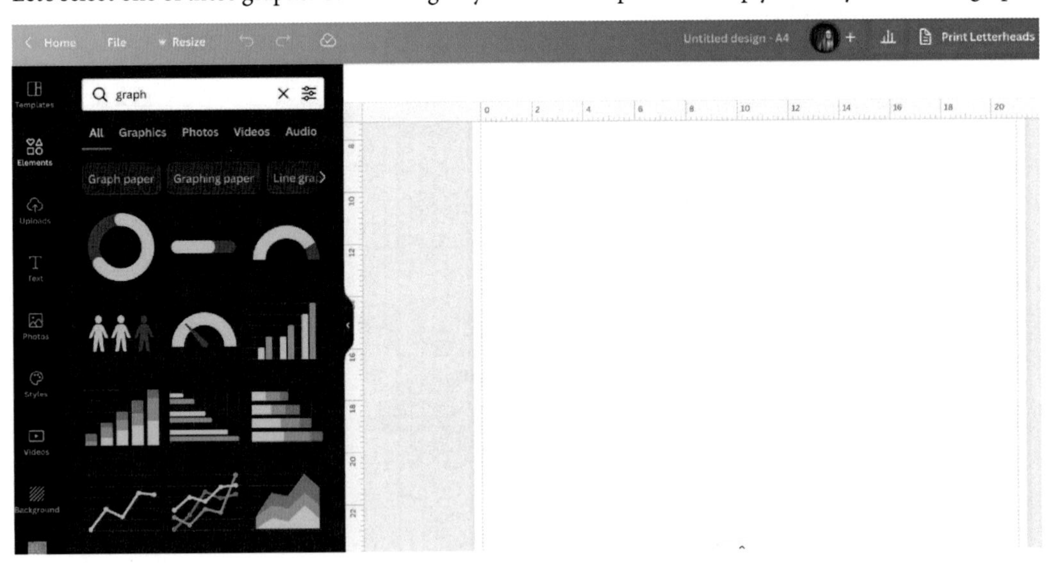

Figure 6.26 – Finding graphs in Canva

The simplest graph is the **Progress ring** graph. On the left, you have two slide bars: **Percentage**, which moves the blue ring around, and **Line weight**, which changes the thickness of the ring. You also have the option to add the percentage number to the middle of the graph and change the roundness of the endpoints:

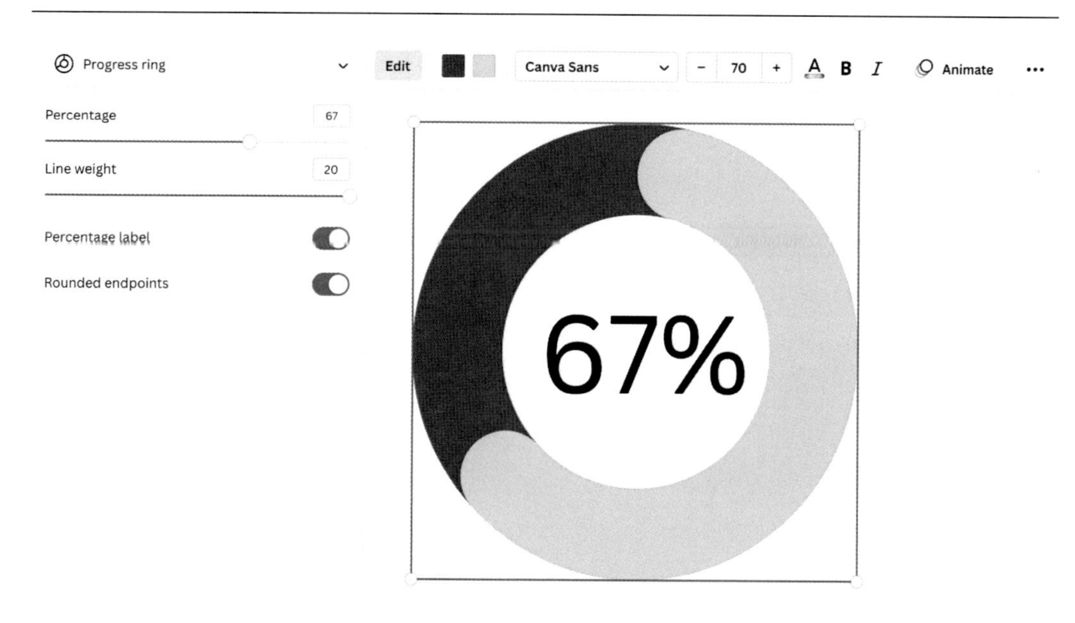

Figure 6.27 – Editing a basic graph

If you're looking for a graph with a lot more detail and different options that you can add yourself, select the **Stacked bar chart** option or a similar graph. This gives you the option to upload your own CSV file of information or you can manually type it into the boxes on the left. As you do so, the graph on your design will start to change:

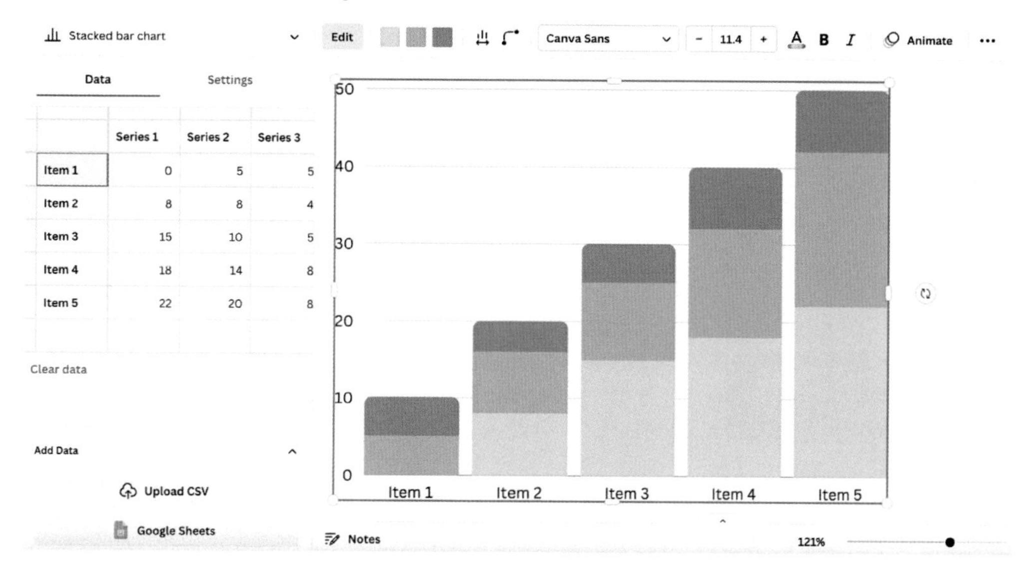

Figure 6.28 – Adding and editing a stacked bar chart

Click on the **Settings** tab, and you have a few more options to customize your graph:

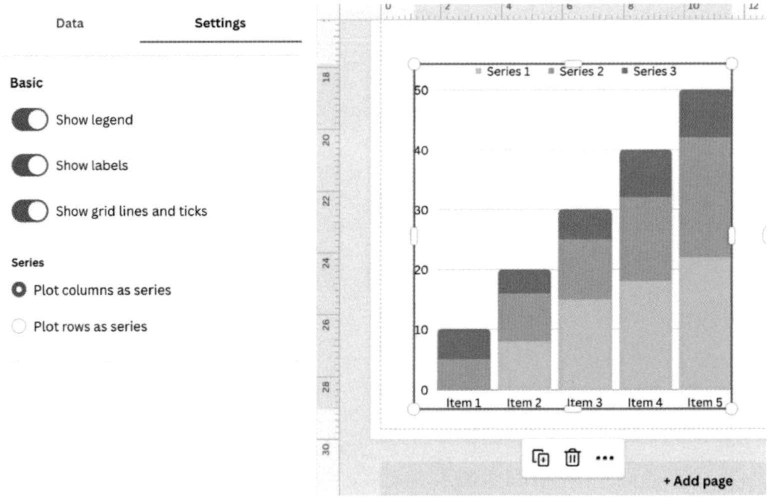

Figure 6.29 – Stacked bar chart settings

There are several types of graphs you can add to your design: progress rings, bar charts, pie charts, and line graphs, to name a few. All of these have the option to add information and customize the graph for your own uses:

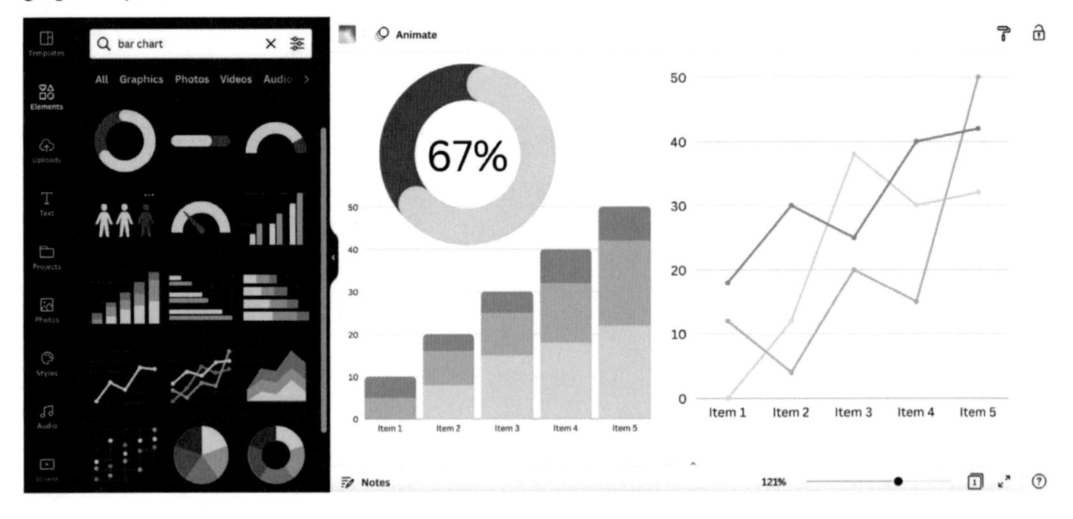

Figure 6.30 – Selection of graphs

Graphs are perfect for visually getting across information, helping to keep a hold of someone's attention, rather than just offering plain text. In the next part of this section, we will be looking at tables.

Tables

Tables are ideal for creating designs such as planners, calendars, leaflets, and brochures, as you can create squares for your information with the click of a button.

There are several styles of tables available, some with colored lines, others with blocks of color, and some with more prominent headers. Let's look at a couple of examples:

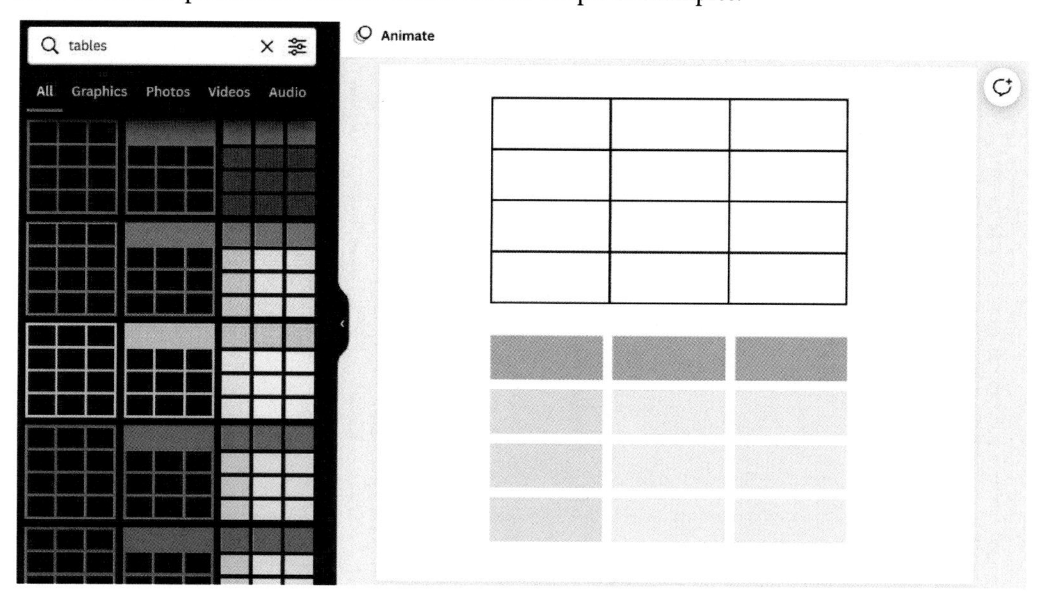

Figure 6.31 – Finding tables in Canva

Each table gives you a selection of options to help you to edit it. You can add or remove columns and rows by selecting your table and then pressing the three-dot icon that appears, either on the left for rows or at the top of the table for columns. This will present you with a list of additional options, including moving your rows and columns up and down and sizing them equally:

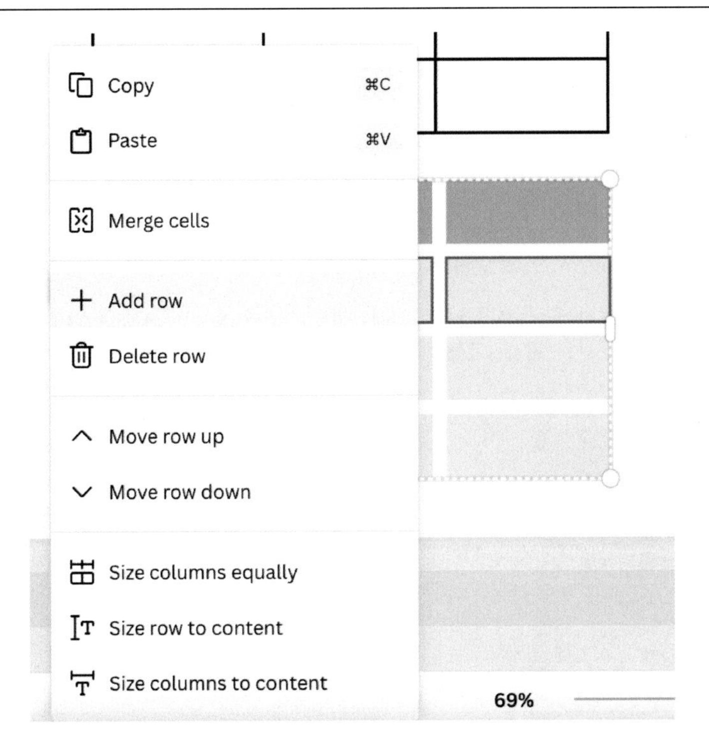

Figure 6.32 – Options for tables

Once you have the correct number of rows and columns, you will want to add information to your table. To do this, click on the square you wish to edit and start typing. You can also change the color of the individual squares, by selecting your chosen square and then clicking the color block at the top:

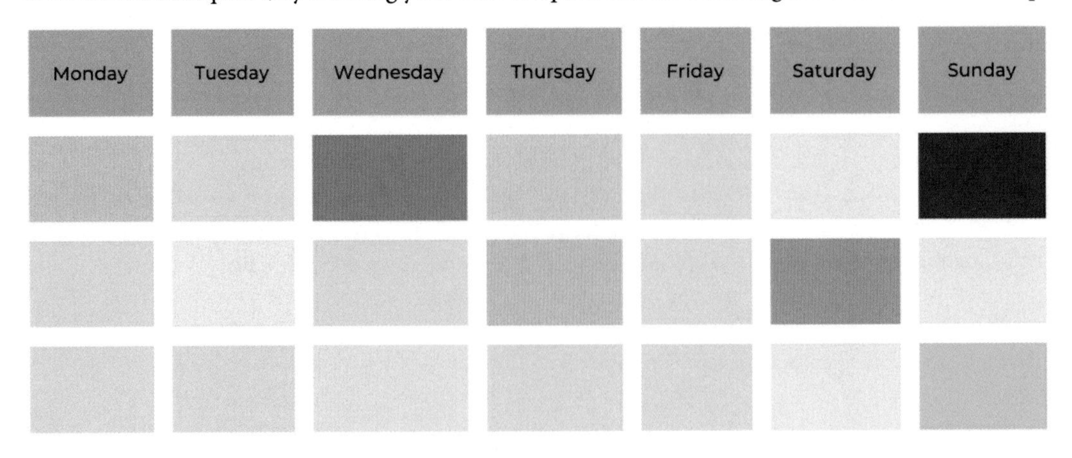

Figure 6.33 – Block table with text and color

Along the top bar, you have a couple of additional options to edit the space between your column and row cells, and to edit the space in the cell:

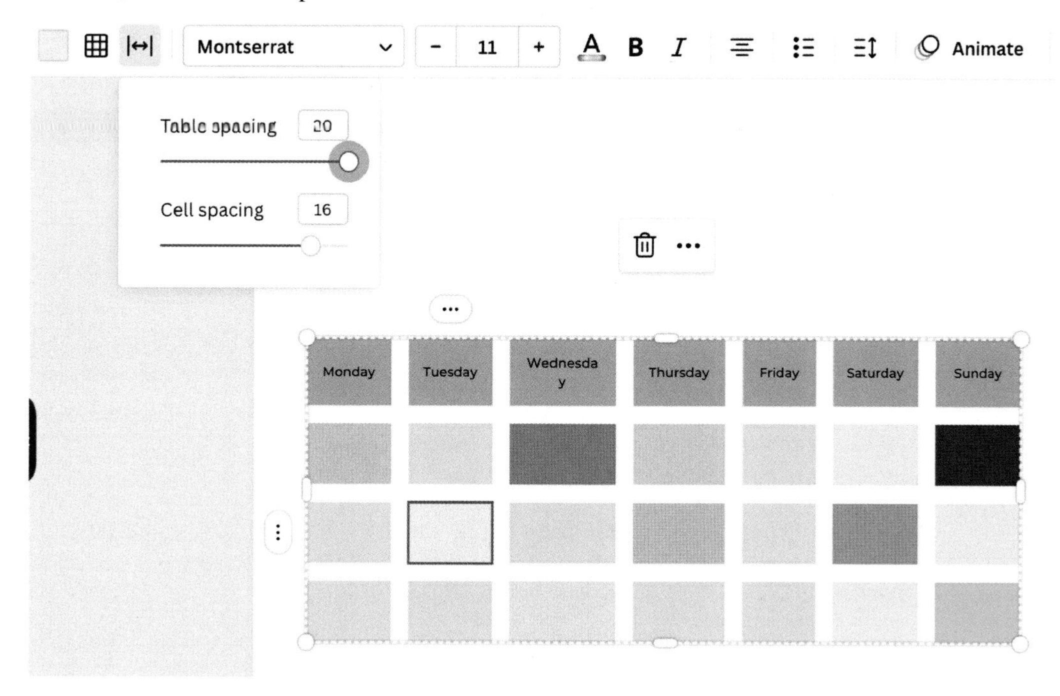

Figure 6.34 – Table spacing and Cell spacing options

Lastly, there is also the option to change the color, thickness, and style of the lines:

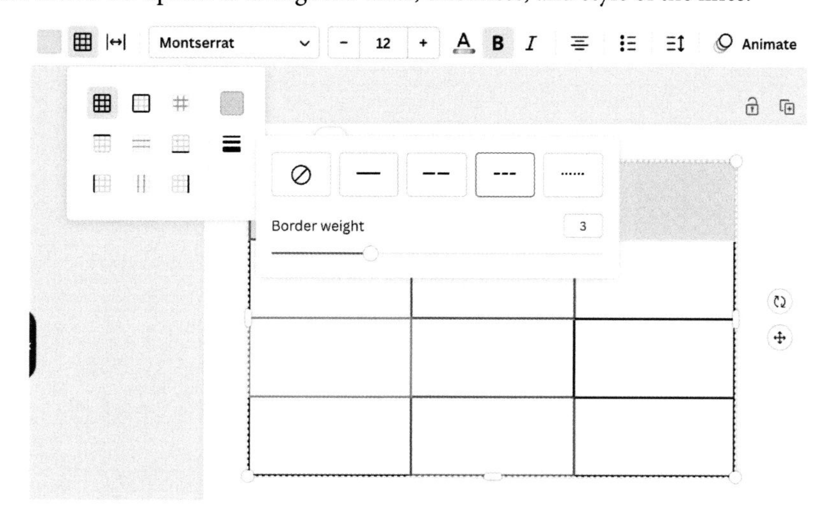

Figure 6.35 – Changing the color, thickness, and style of table lines

Tables and graphs are great features to have a play with, especially if you have a lot of information to present. I love that you can change so much about tables. They're not plain and boring; they are vibrant and fun, making our designs so much better.

We've now come to the end, so let's take a look at what we've learned in this chapter packed full of useful features to help you quickly create great graphics.

Summary

In this chapter, you've looked at a lot of different features – ones that can save you time but also help generate great graphics. The introductions to these features were more like tutorials, as each one you could follow along with. Looking back at this chapter, you have learned how to create and add a gradient as a background to your design, bringing out the information. You've also discovered and learned how to use the **Quick Create** feature, generating multiple graphics for different platforms at the same time. You can now add in grids and frames, and also add color, images, or video. You've even learned how to add and create a graph for your information-based social media posts. That's an amazing amount of information so far!

However, none of this is going to produce fantastic graphics without you being able to understand the basic design principles and knowing how a design works, so in the next chapter, this is exactly what we are going to look at.

7

Five Graphic Design Principles You Need to Know

Design principles are guidelines that designers use and apply to their work. They are hugely important in the design world and are the difference between good and bad design. Using these principles will help you to gain a good understanding of what a well-balanced and fully finished design should look like. And it will also help you spot the difference between well-thought-out designs and ones that just look unfinished.

In this chapter, we are going to cover the following main design principles that will help you with your Canva designs:

- Contrast
- Balance
- Hierarchy
- Alignment
- Repetition

By the end of this chapter, you will understand what each of these principles is and how to use them together to create amazing designs for your business.

The first one is my favorite – we're looking at contrast.

Contrast

I've always loved contrast. As a keen amateur photographer, I look for opportunities to take photos of really contrasting objects or places.

Contrast is the difference between two points in your design; for example, it could be the background and the main focal point, one being light and the other dark. Contrast helps draw the viewer's eyes to the exact point you want them at. It is light and dark, bold and thin, big and small, and soft and hard. Don't overdo the contrast, though; the subtle contrasting points need to fit in with the rest of your design and flow so that it all works together.

Color

Color is the most common contrasting point of a design. For example, this one is a basic black-and-white magazine cover. The contrast of just using two colors is big, but it works well with the overall design:

Figure 7.1 – Black and white magazine cover

If you want to use different colors, keep your color palette simple or on brand. Try to avoid colors that clash as the contrast will be too great and look out of sorts. The following design has a lovely leaf background, and the main focal point, which is the text, has been placed centrally. It also uses the same color palette, keeping the design on brand, flowing well, and the contrast balanced throughout:

Figure 7.2 – Leaf patterned design with text as the main focal point

When using colors, make sure that the background is very different from the main focal point of your design so that it stands out accordingly and draws the eyes of the viewer. Note that we can also do that with the size of our elements.

Size

Size is another contrasting factor; you can have big and small elements within your design working well together. Adding a large logo or image next to a block of text will naturally draw the eye first and toward the smaller textboxes second. This way, you are leading your viewer through your design in the way you want.

Size also helps with perspective; it gives you an idea of the size of things in relation to other elements in your design. For example, we know that a dog is smaller than a house in the real world, so if you were to add these into your design, you would make the dog a lot smaller so that our perception of the design is correct:

Figure 7.3 – Large dog and small house; looking at perspective

Size and color are two contrasting factors to think about when creating a design, but another is our font. When it comes to fonts, we don't often think about them in terms of contrast but style, size, and color play an important part when putting our design together from a contrast point of view.

Typography (or font)

Your typography or fonts also have a part to play with contrast. As most fonts these days can have color, thickness shape, and sizes applied, you can do a lot with your font. Choosing two contrasting colors, which means two colors from opposite sides of the color wheel (we looked at the color wheel in *Chapter 5, Exploring the Awesome Creative Tools for Branding*), will help to bring out your information and make it more visible for your viewer.

Here, we have a font with one color for the outline and one for the inside of the text. Contrasting colors are usually light and dark:

Figure 7.4 – Contrasting colors in fonts

Try to stick to two or three fonts within any design, though, and make use of the different typefaces for them, as they often come in thin, medium, and bold. You're using the same font, but the different typefaces will give it a contrasting look.

For example, the **Agrandir** font has multiple different typefaces:

Agrandir

Agrandir Black

Agrandir Grand

Agrandir Medium

Agrandir Narrow

Agrandir Thin

Agrandir Tight

Agrandir Wide

Figure 7.5 – The Agrandir font typefaces

Don't use more than three fonts as more makes it look cluttered and unbalanced, which is what we are going to be looking at next.

Balance

Balance is the placement of elements within your design so that it has equal weight on either side – this will give your design a pleasing look. Each and every element that you add to a design has a weight, which is how much space it takes up on the design. You can liken it to decorating your office – you wouldn't put all of the furniture in one corner or all of your pictures on one wall, rather you would spread them out in a way that makes the room look equal and cozy.

Without balance, your design can look messy and might not catch a viewer's eye.

Symmetrical designs are the most popular and create an equally weighted design. For example, this design has a symmetrical look and feel because it has its elements spaced equally throughout the top and bottom:

Figure 7.6 – Balanced floral design

Alternatively, you could go the opposite way and have a larger weighted element on one side and a cluster of smaller elements on the other side. These smaller elements equal the larger one, resulting in balancing out the design:

Figure 7.7 – Showing larger elements on one side with a cluster of small ones on the other

When adding balance to your designs in the beginning, just try and make it look symmetrical. Don't overthink it, and have a go at moving the elements around to different places. Think to yourself, does that give my design symmetry? If not, try moving it somewhere else.

Next, we're going to learn how to add hierarchies to your design.

Hierarchy

Visual hierarchy is something that you've probably come across and maybe not realized that it's incorporated into every design, especially marketing or advertising graphics. It is used to highlight the part of the design that you want people to see first, so you can control where and how someone views the design. You're drawing attention to one part of the design over other parts.

Take the following poster as an example. When you first look at it, it's the title that stands out, big and bold, across the design. This is the simplest way to add hierarchy to a design – by using size. Take one part of your design and make it bigger than everything else. You've grabbed the viewers' attention first by announcing the store is open. This then draws the eyes down the poster, in order of size, and finally reaching the store's opening hours:

Figure 7.8 – An example of hierarchy use on a clothing store poster

This can also be done by using a bright or bold color to help parts of your design stand out. The following example uses a colored background to make the white text the focal point:

Figure 7.9 – Romantic author graphic showing the use of color

Additionally, you can create hierarchy within your design by making use of white space, or negative space. This is the blank area around your elements, that is, the gap between the textboxes and borders. Don't be afraid to use this space, as it gives your text room to breathe and forms a border around it, drawing the eye to the text or focal point. Take a look at the space around the following example design. You can see how keeping it clean and clear helps you to navigate it more easily:

Figure 7.10 – Negative space example on a cream graphic

So, now you understand a bit more about using contrast, hierarchy, and balance within your designs. Next, let's look at alignment and how to create organization.

Alignment

Alignment helps to keep your design organized and mess-free. It keeps everything clean and clear and easy to understand, helping your viewer to stick around and check out what you have to say.

It can be used by adjusting the spacing between elements or adding a block of color. Alternatively, it can be used by adding a line element – we looked at lines in *Chapter 2, Discovering and Editing Templates*.

Now, try adding a block of color under your text to create alignment:

Figure 7.11 – Simple graphic using a color block

Use lines to separate information, as adding a line gives a more organized look; it can be a small subtle line – it doesn't have to be a big bold line if your design doesn't need it.

Have a look at this example – a small line can make a lot of difference. Two have been used here – one to divide the text from the image and one to divide the two textboxes:

Figure 7.12 – Yellow graphic showing the use of lines for alignment

In addition to this, dividing your design by adding all of your text down one side and an image or element on the other, as we have done in the preceding screenshot, also aligns your information and balances it. We read a graphic the same way we read a book, from left to right, so experiment when adding information to a design. Try adding it to either side and see how it works. You will often find text works better when placed on the left-hand side.

Canva has a brilliant alignment feature, which can be found under the **Positions** tab. We also looked at this in *Chapter 4, Designing Eye-Catching Graphics Through Useful Features*:

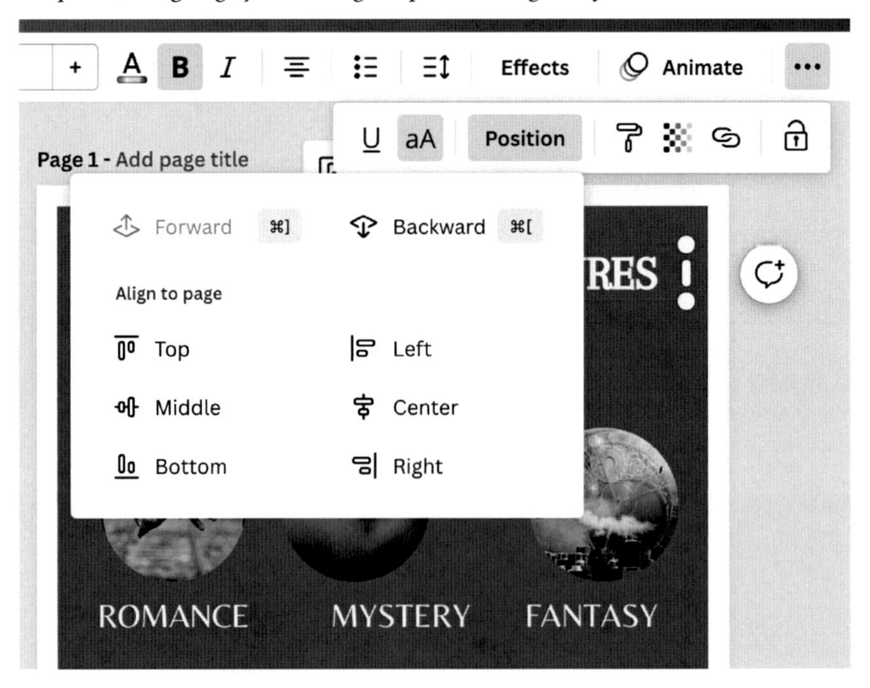

Figure 7.13 – The Position tab for aligning elements

Alignment really does help to keep your designs organized and clutter-free. Something else that helps with keeping designs organized is repetition, which we will look at next.

Repetition

Using repetition in your designs does not mean you have to create boring repeated creations. It's more to do with staying consistent. It will help someone to navigate and understand your design a lot easier if things all look similar and fit well together. For example, use elements that have the same feel to them. Don't use a soft pastel floral element and then use a neon comic element within the same design. And if you're creating a collection of templates for a project or your business, keep everything within them the same style – that is, the elements, fonts, color palette, and imagery – across the board.

The following example of a template pack is using repetition. The same color palette, fonts, and imagery have been used in all of them, creating consistency, yet each one can also be used on its own:

Figure 7.14 – Podcasting template pack using the same branding throughout

Also, repetition is used in spacing – this is the space between your elements. Keeping spaces between elements consistent helps to organize your design and stops the eye from being drawn to uneven spacing; for example, the following design is okay, but it could benefit from having its spaces equaled:

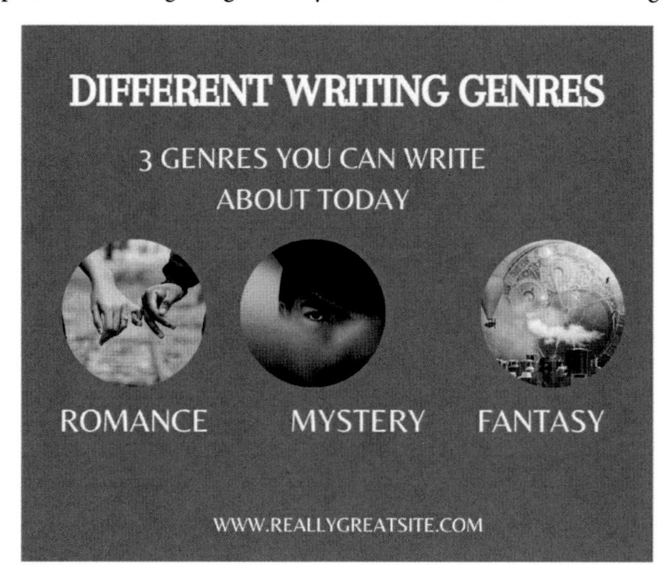

Figure 7.15 – Unevenly spaced gray design

Do you notice the unevenness of it? Is your eye drawn away from the elements and to the edges? By making a few tweaks to keep everything aligned, our design will look a lot better:

Figure 7.16 – Gray graphic with the spaces evened out

Design principles are important for our design work. Even if we're just creating graphics for our social media channels, having a basic understanding of them will help you to create better graphics.

We've now come to the end, so let's look at what we have learned.

Summary

In this chapter, you learned about five different design principles. We looked at contrast, and you now understand how to apply colors, size, and typography to your designs so that they complement each other. Additionally, you learned about balance and how to move elements around so that you can achieve a pleasing look and not add too much weight to any particular side of the design. You also understand the importance of hierarchy and how to draw a viewer's eyes to the parts of the design you want them to look at. Alignment also plays an important part, as you now know how to align elements in Canva and how this tool tidies and organizes your design. Finally, you can now create repetition throughout the template packs, and you have learned that using the same or similar elements throughout brings consistency to your designs.

In the next chapter, we're going to look at creating logos, using templates, and the basic guidelines you need to know for your business logo.

Part 3: Let's Get Creating

The last part of this book is all about creating, that is, building your graphics, and getting used to using Canva as a daily tool for your business. Here, we will look at how to create your own logo, the use of icons and shapes, as well as the guidelines behind trademarking with Canva. This is important to learn about. We'll also look more at creating specific graphics you need for your business and how to animate them, as well as using and editing video. Social media platforms love video, so this is a good aspect to learn about with regard to visibility on social platforms. Another important factor for many businesses is being able to share graphics and connect with their audience in as many ways as possible. So, we will look at sharing, creating clickable links, and downloading your designs as well, covering every part of this wonderful platform.

This part includes the following chapters:

- *Chapter 8, Creating Your Perfect Logo*
- *Chapter 9, Making Social Media Graphics with Canva*
- *Chapter 10, Leveraging Video and Animation within Your Business Marketing*
- *Chapter 11, Downloading and Sharing Your Designs*
- *Chapter 12, Tips and Tricks for Printing*

8

Creating Your Perfect Logo

Creating a logo for many business owners is crucial as it helps define the brand, can be added to everything we do. and becomes recognizable for our community and customers.

We can create logos in Canva, and there are lots of amazing templates available; but, as with many platforms, there are terms and conditions that determine what can be done with the content and best practices when it comes to using templates in Canva.

In this chapter, we will cover the following main topics:

- Creating a logo in Canva and using templates
- Brand guidelines for logos
- Using icons, text, and basic shapes in logos
- Creating different logo versions

By the end of this chapter, you will have a good understanding of how you can use a logo created in Canva and know where templates are and how to edit them to suit your brand, how to add icons and shapes, and how to create different versions of your logo for a variety of uses.

Creating a logo in Canva and using templates

Canva has an amazing array of templates for logos, templates that Canva or freelance designers create, so you know you're getting a good logo template.

To find the templates, use the search term `logo` in the **Create a design** tab; this will open up a 500 px x 500 px blank design for you.

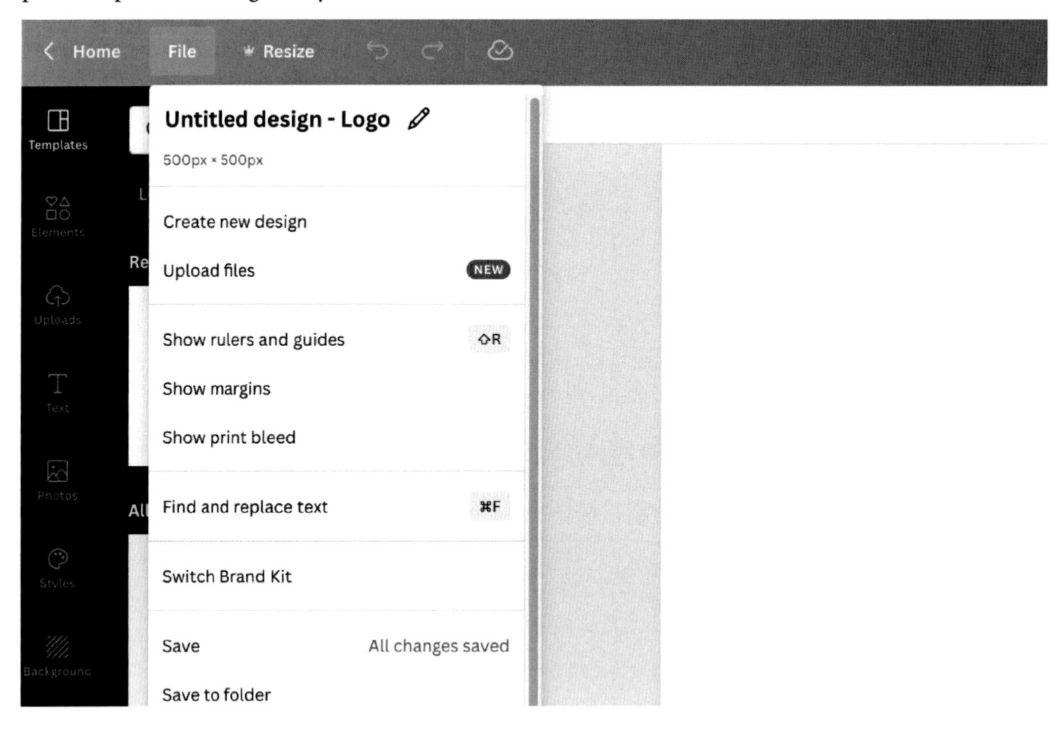

Figure 8.1 – Drop-down menu showing template size

> **Tip**
>
> Once you've finished your design, resize it to 5,000 px x 5,000 px, as this gives it a sharper look when used. The 500 px x 500 px size is OK but can look blurry when used on large items such as printed banners.

Have a scroll through the logo templates; there are thousands here, so it can be a bit tricky to find one that will suit your business and brand. At the top is a search bar, so you can add a keyword here to bring up suitable logos, or you can use the suggested tabs under the search bar; this will help in narrowing down your search results.

For example, I have typed in `bakery` as my keyword; let's assume I run a small bakery and require a new logo. These are the results that are shown to me, keeping in mind the ones at the top are the most used, so if you want one that is less likely to be like other bakery shops' logos, scroll down:

Figure 8.2 – Selection of bakery-related logo templates

Your logo should represent you and your business, and it should be simple and easy on the eye. Complicated logos with lots of small elements and text are very difficult to understand when small and are more likely to be ignored than a logo with a simple, clear design.

We like to be able to recognize and understand shapes as quickly as possible; otherwise, we move on. Social media is a great example of this. It's a very busy place to be and we need to catch our viewer's eye quickly.

Have a look around you at a few big-brand logos; they are usually just a simple icon and are easily recognizable.

Once you have found a template that you like the look of and could possibly work with your business, it's time to edit it.

We edit templates because they are available to over 100 million people worldwide and we want our logo to be as unique as possible. By editing the template in a few ways, we are achieving this goal.

The main ways we can edit our logo template are by changing the following:

- Colors
- Fonts
- Text
- Icons

For this example, I'm going to use this template to show you the different changes I will make:

Figure 8.3 – Pink cake boutique logo

First of all, I've decided I like the style of this template and the arch of the text at the top, but I run an (imaginary) gardening business, for example, so the baking theme doesn't work.

I will need to change a few things, but I will start with the text. First, it needs to display the business name, so to do this, click on the textbox and start typing. In this template, the textbox already has a curve, but if you would like to add one, take a look at *Chapter 2, Discovering and Editing Templates*, where you can see how it is achieved:

Figure 8.4 – Pink cake boutique logo being edited

Once you have your information in place, change the font style. I've changed it from **Dream Avenue** to **Noto Serif Display Light**, but this should be your brand font.

The next things I will change are the icons, as the cupcake one doesn't suit the business type at all. Delete the icons you don't want and replace them with new ones from the **Elements** section.

I need something that works with the brand, and leaves are a nice, simple pattern. It is easy to work out what they are, and they can be recognized when small, so they seem a suitable option for this logo.

In the **Elements** section, type in the `leaves` keyword, and lots of options will appear for you. I have chosen these watercolor-style leaves, which are free to use:

Figure 8.5 – Green gardener logo with pink background

I've also changed the two smaller icons to leaves, completing my logo. The last thing I would like to do with this is to change the background color to white, giving it a nice, clean-and-clear look that suits my branding:

Figure 8.6 – Finished gardener logo

My new business logo is complete. It also looks quite different from the original.

Have a go at editing your own logo. Search for one within the templates and change the colors, text, font, and icons, and see what you can achieve yourself.

If you have an idea of how you want your logo to look, create a custom template sized at 5,000 px x 5,000 px and create a logo from scratch using the elements, lines, and fonts available.

Creating a logo from a template in Canva is great if you are just starting out in business or you would like to update an existing one. However, there are a few guidelines when it comes to content in Canva, and logos, more specifically. Let's take a look at this further in the next section.

Brand guidelines for logos

Logos in Canva come with a few guidelines that you need to be aware of when creating one for your business.

You can use a template to create a logo, or you can create one from scratch using elements, fonts, shapes, and lines. This is not a problem; there are no main restrictions on the actual creation of a logo in Canva.

When you are creating your logo and would like to have a look at the licensing related to a particular element, click on the three dots next to it and then click on the **i** symbol:

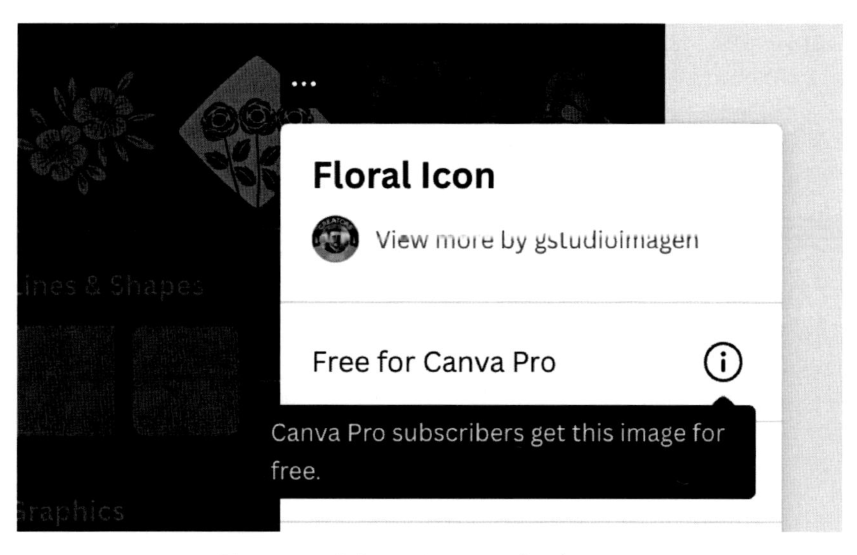

Figure 8.7 – Information point for elements

This then brings up a page where you can see the top level of the license agreement:

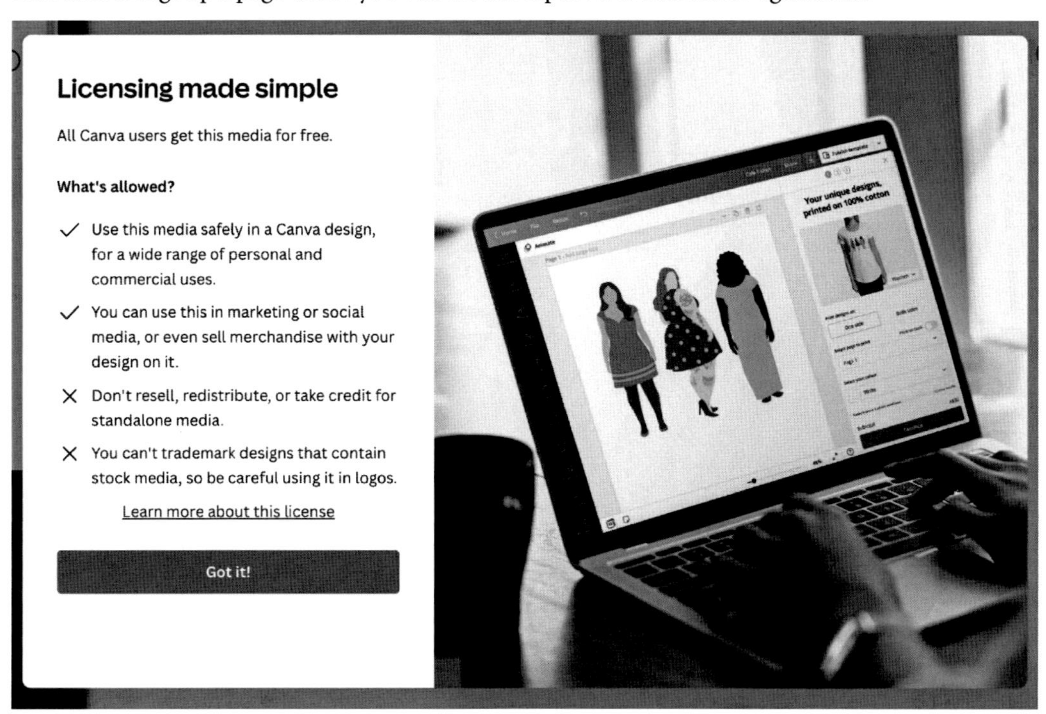

Figure 8.8 – Licensing overview for free-to-use elements

Where the restrictions come into play is at the point you want to trademark a logo. This is a common practice, and a lot of businesses want to make sure their logo is different from everyone else's and cannot be copied by another business; this is why we trademark a logo. The problem is that all of the templates in Canva for logos are currently made available to 100 million users worldwide, and so are all of the elements, images, and content. You cannot create a unique logo in Canva; the chances are there are a lot of other people who are using the same template or elements as you. Plus, the content in Canva has been created by a designer or Canva itself, so it does not belong to you. Hence you are unable to trademark your logo.

If you are happy with a logo that may look similar to someone else's, or you've used a template and changed it to suit your brand, and you're not worried about trademarking, then that's absolutely fine. I've created my logo in Canva, and I'm happy with it. However, I know if I wish to trademark it in the future, it will need to be redone, so it is unique.

If you would like to read through the Canva guidelines, you can find them all here: `https://www.canva.com/policies/license-agreements/`.

Creating a logo using basic lines, shapes, and free fonts is the best way to go if you would like your logo to be different from others, as using elements or images makes them very recognizable to others, so next, we'll look at using basic lines, shapes, and free fonts in your logo.

Using icons, text, and basic shapes in logos

If you want to use a logo that has a unique look to it, then have a look at creating a simple logo using free fonts and lines in Canva. This may sound slightly boring, but they can look very effective, and as we've mentioned, keeping your logo simple will help it to be more recognizable when small.

Here's a selection of logos that have used lines, basic shapes, and free fonts:

Figure 8.9 – Selection of simple logos using free fonts and shapes

Each one of these logos uses a free font and a basic shape to help create the look of the logo, so a simple logo can be created in Canva that looks professional.

To create your own, you need to decide on the style of the logo first. Is it a round logo, letters only, square, or oblong?

Round tends to work well, especially with social media profile images, email signatures, and social media graphics, but you don't have to stick to a round logo if it doesn't suit your business. Create round submark logos instead; we will be looking at these later in this chapter.

To get started with creating a blank design, as mentioned previously, create a custom design that is 5,000 px x 5,000 px, so you get a sharp logo.

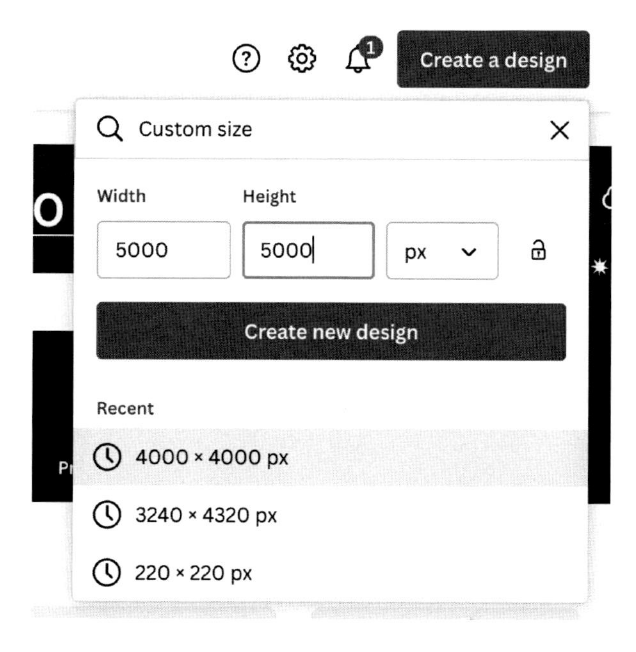

Figure 8.10 – Creating a custom size for a logo template

Once you have your blank design and have decided on the style of the logo (for this example, I'll go for an oblong-style logo), add a textbox that has your business name in it, then add a rectangle around the textbox using the `shapes` keyword in the **Elements** section:

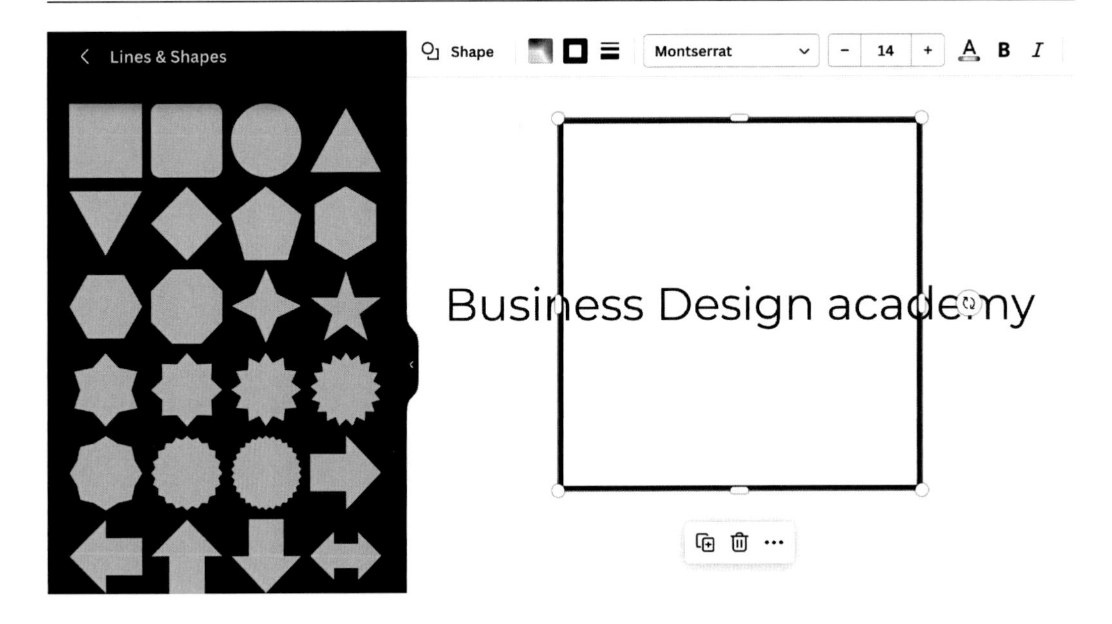

Figure 8.11 – Adding a shape to a logo template

Adjust the size of the rectangle shape by dragging the white corners. This will also change the thickness of the box. Once it's at the required thickness, place it over your textbox, dragging out the side lines to fit:

Business Design Academy

Figure 8.12 – The beginnings of a basic oblong logo

The business name in this example is quite long, so I'm going to take the word **Academy** and move it below, changing the font as well, so it's in line with the brand. Keeping in mind we're using simple and free fonts, I've changed it to Montserrat, a very common free font that is widely available:

Figure 8.13 – The building of a new oblong logo

The logo is beginning to come together, but it is still missing something and looks unfinished. In this instance, you could add in a white block square using the **Shapes** option and place it on the bottom line, effectively adding a break in the oblong, then place the word **Academy** over the top. This gives it a more unique and different look. I've also changed the main text to uppercase, so it stands out better:

Figure 8.14 – The finished logo

Now I have, a nice, simple, professional-looking logo I can use for my business that I have created myself. I've not used any recognizable elements or images that will relate to another business; this logo is unique.

But this logo may not work on all formats; it would look good on a white background, but what about a dark background or a patterned one? Or what if it's too long? How would I overcome this problem?

This is where submark logos come into play. None of the logos we've looked at so far use any content that you can't trademark, so let's look at some examples of elements that you can add to your log and submark that you cannot trademark.

Content you cannot trademark

To give you an idea of the type of content that you can use for your logo but cannot trademark, let's type the words `Floral icon` into the **Elements** section. Here you will find a large selection of hand-drawn, watercolor, or digital icons that have been created by someone else:

Figure 8.15 – A selection of icons that can be used for logos but not trademarked

Any one of these would work well as a business logo icon, but they have been created by and belong to another designer. If you hover over an element and click the three dots that appear, you can see who created it, and you can click the name to see their other elements available in Canva:

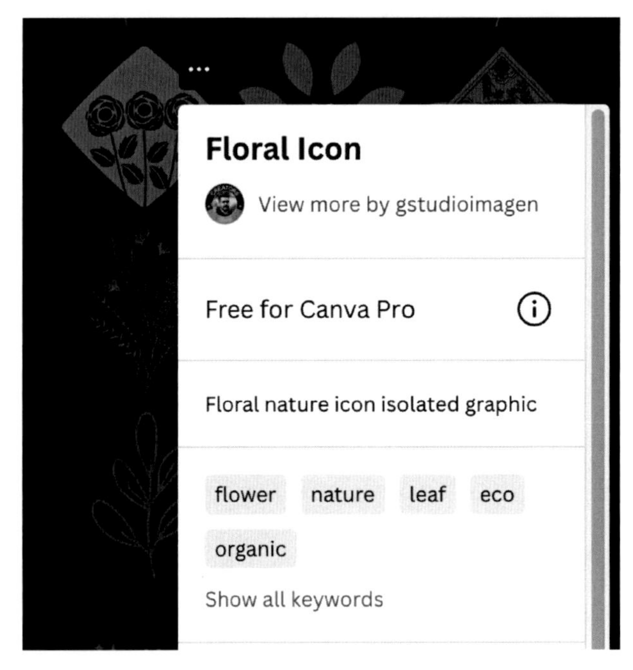

Figure 8.16 – Dropdown to find the creator of an element

It also states that this element is free for Pro users, so anyone on a Free account will be required to purchase a license to use the element, usually a couple of dollars. This means you have access to the use of the element within a design of your creation on both Free (with a purchased license) and Pro plans, but you cannot trademark the element or any design that uses that element.

We briefly mentioned other types of logos you can create, called submark logos, so this is what we will be looking at next.

Creating different logo versions

Creating different-style logos for a variety of uses means you will always have a version of your logo that will work on every platform, online and offline.

Keep your original logo to hand, as you will need to use this as a basis for your submark logos. They will all have a similar look and feel to them as they belong to the same brand and need to be relatable to each other.

Start with creating a logo that would work on a dark background; we currently have one for a white or light background.

Simply swap the colors around. Here, I've changed the background to black and changed the text and oblong to white:

Figure 8.17 – A dark version of the finished logo

I now have my first submark logo.

Next, create a submark logo that would work as an icon or button by simplifying it even further. You could use just the first letters of your business name; these are often reduced in size when used, so need to be simple:

Figure 8.18 – Submark logo using business initials

Don't forget to create different versions so that they will work on both light and dark backgrounds. Sometimes you may want to remove the background, and other times adding a circle can help to make it stand out more. Trial different types and keep all of them in a file for when you may need them:

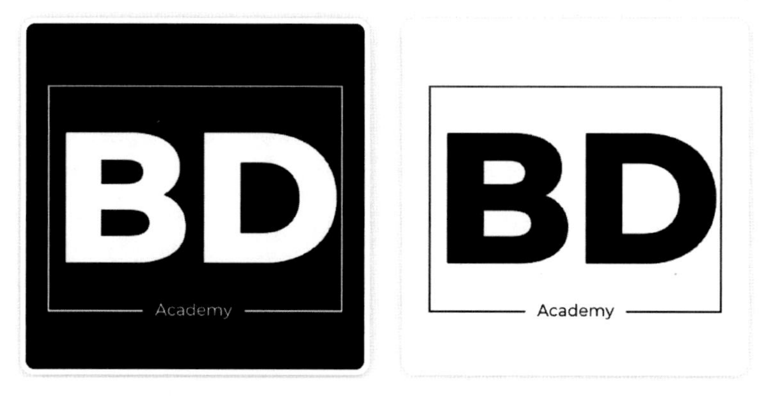

Figure 8.19 – Submark logos showing light and dark versions

As we've created an oblong logo and square submark logos, it's a good idea to add circle logos to the group. These work well as round icons, buttons, and social media profiles and look good in the corners of social graphics:

Figure 8.20 – Round submark logos showing light and dark versions

To do this, add a circle from the **Shapes** section in Canva. All of the shapes in this section are free to use and have been added and created by Canva, so you are safe to use these within your logo. Then change the colors over so you have a light and dark version of your submark logo.

We now have our finished collection:

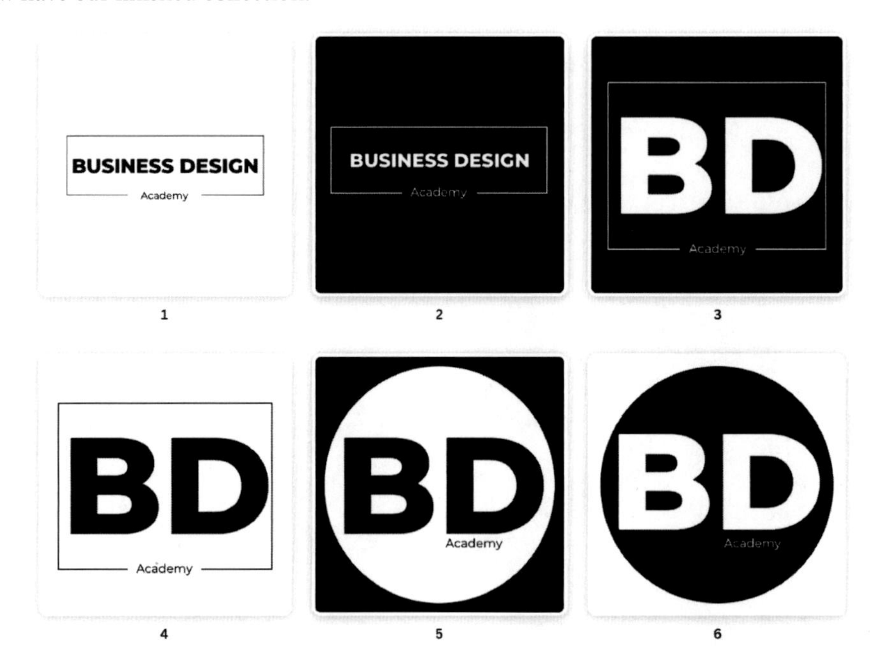

Figure 8.21 – The complete collection of logos and submark logos

You will soon find that you have built up a great collection of submark logos in your Canva account. These are all useful in different situations, so make sure to keep them safe.

You don't have to stick with this design or color palette. Your logo will and should grow with you as your business grows, your style changes, and your business evolves, so make sure you review your logo on a regular basis to make sure it still represents what you do.

I've changed my logo quite drastically over the years to make sure it still fits with my business and branding.

So, that's the end of this chapter. I hope you've found it useful and that it helps you to create a logo you love in Canva.

Summary

In this chapter, you've learned how to find logo templates in Canva and edit them using color, text, fonts, and shapes. You've also learned how to create a custom-sized template to start a new logo from scratch. You have also discovered more about Canva licenses and why you are not able to trademark a logo created in Canva. Lastly, you have learned the reason why submark logos are needed and how to create a collection of your own submark logos for your business. This chapter has been all about logo creation, so let's move on to something more fun and look at how to create different graphics in Canva that we need for our businesses and social media profiles.

9

Making Social Media Graphics with Canva

This is a fun chapter, as we're going to create some social media graphics. These are all useful designs that will get you using many features in Canva, whether for social media, physical printed products, such as business cards, or advertisements, so have a good read-through of this chapter first, and then open up Canva on your computer and follow along.

In this chapter, we are going to create the following graphics:

- A profile frame
- A Facebook banner
- An animated Instagram story
- A business card
- A magazine or leaflet advert

By the end of this chapter, you will be able to use all of the features needed to create social media graphics and will have a range of designs you can start using for your business.

Creating a profile frame

A profile frame is a graphic you can add to your social media accounts; it's often the first thing someone will see when looking at your business or profile page, so it's a good idea to use it to showcase you and your business.

There is a Facebook profile size template you can use in Canva; this should also be suitable for other platforms where you can add a profile image. It is 1500 x 1500 pixels in size.

To find this size, click on the **Create a design** tab at the top of your Canva account and type in or search for `Profile Frame`; it will appear in the dropdown. Once you have found it, you may notice a lot of templates suitable for frames appear on the left-hand side. This is because you have chosen to view a specific style and Canva will bring up the templates for that style:

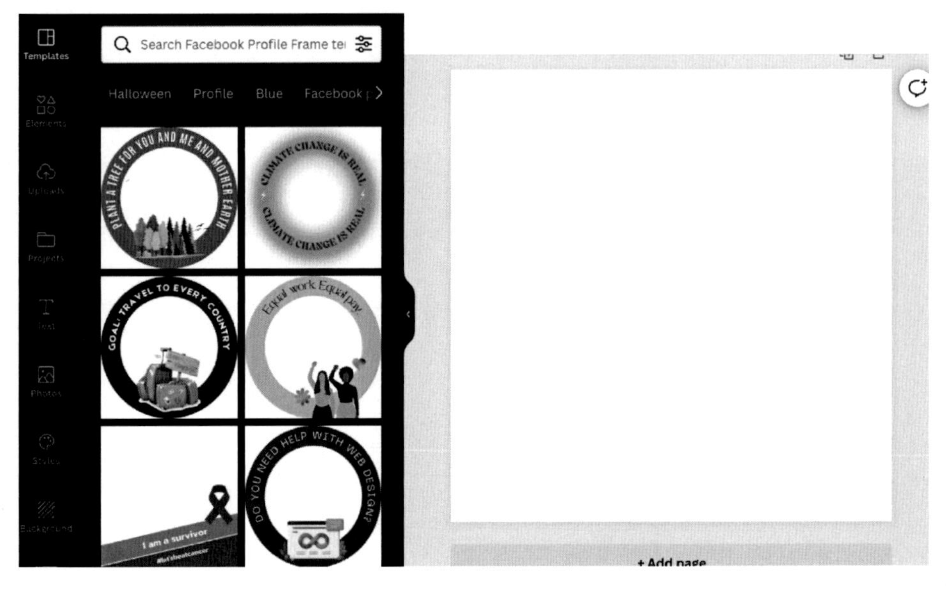

Figure 9.1 – Profile image frame templates

A profile frame is designed to have an image in the background. For social media, a natural-looking photo of yourself is the most appropriate one. As people buy from people, they like to see who is behind the business, so you don't have to use your logo here. Once you have a nice image of yourself, you are ready to create your frame.

Profile frames suit a circular design, so we are going to create one from scratch using a colored circle. Search in the **Elements** tab for `Circles` and a large selection of different styles will appear. For this tutorial, we are going to use a basic chunky circle such as this one:

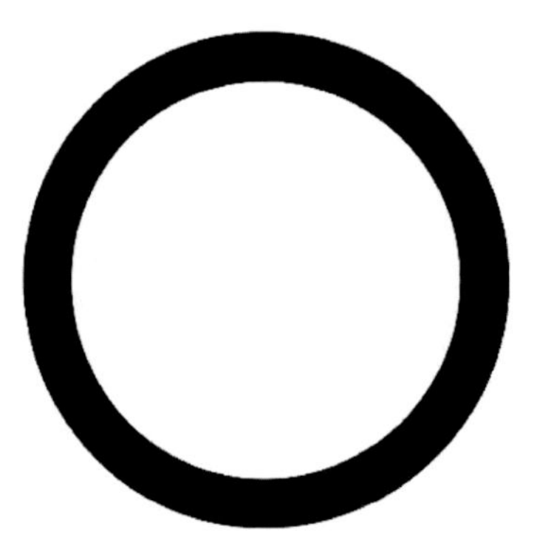

Figure 9.2 – Circle element

The first thing to do is to change the color of the circle to suit your branding. After you have done this, add a textbox and populate it with your business name:

Figure 9.3 – Circle element and text box

Now, we get to use the curved text feature. This is a great feature and perfect for profile frames. Select your text box and then click on the **Effects** tab at the top. At the bottom of the text styles that have now appeared on the left, select **Curve**. This will curve your text for you, place the curved text over the top of the colored circle, and stretch it out to fit. You can use the **Curve** slide bar to adjust the ratio of the curve:

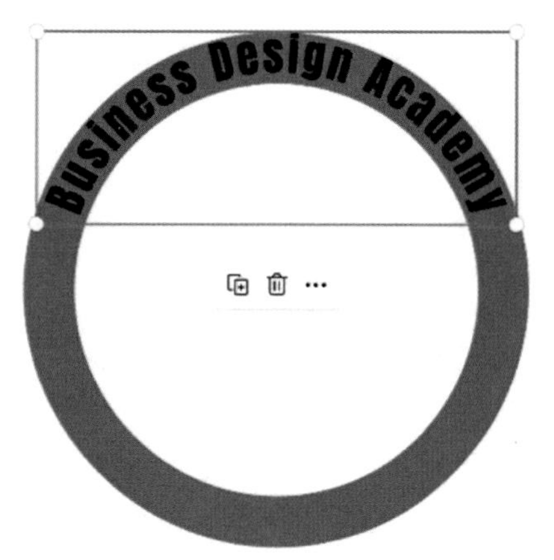

Figure 9.4 – Circle element and Curve text feature

Change the color of the text to white if you've used a darker color for the circle so it stands out, and then search for `frame` and add a circle frame from the **Elements** section. You will drag and drop your photo into this:

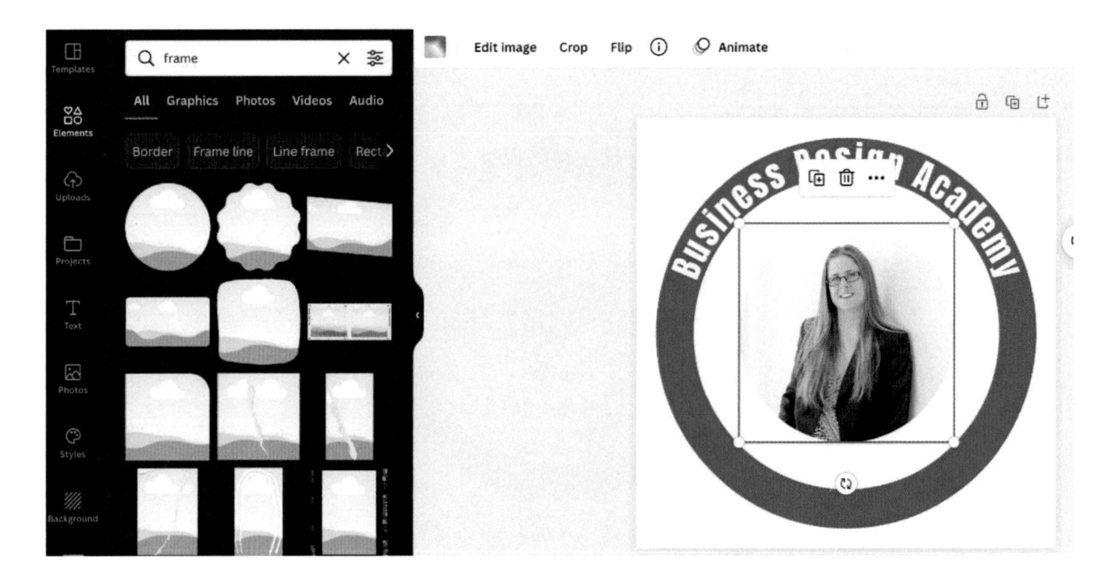

Figure 9.5 – Adding an image to a frame design

You can see that it's beginning to come together. Increase the size of the photo by dragging out the corners to cover the colored circle and then use the **Positions** tab to send it to the back – it will now fit your new frame.

You can add elements or your logo to the frame as well, but please be aware that many profile spaces for these images are round and will cut off the corners of the template, so don't add anything to the four corners.

You can now download your finished design to use:

Figure 9.6 – Finished profile frame

I've added a colored element to the preceding example, which uses my brand colors. Along with a profile frame, you will probably need a banner image. This can be created to match your profile frame and will give it a professional look and feel, so let's have a look at creating one next.

Creating a Facebook banner

Facebook banners are a great way to advertise your business; it's the space at the top of your group, page, or personal profile and it is free to populate with an image. However, there are often sizing issues with banners. I get asked a lot about them and how to size them correctly.

If you use the sizing in Canva for Facebook banners, then when uploaded, it will look slightly blurry. This is because Facebook compresses all images, even though you've used the correctly sized template according to Canva and Facebook.

How do you overcome this?

You will need to create a custom-sized template for your page or group banner. We will look at this in a moment, but first, I'd like to mention profile banners, as these are slightly different:

Figure 9.7 – Current mobile profile frame with a circular profile image on the left

One thing to be aware of when creating your personal profile banner for Facebook is that they often tend to move your circular profile image from the left to center and then back again, sometimes covering the information on your banner with your profile image. This is especially prominent on mobile devices, as the profile image covers more of the banner than on a desktop. You may find it best to have two banners at the ready, one with your information in the center and one with the information on the right, so you can swap them over if the profile image moves.

Groups and page banners

First of all, it's good to get the correct size from Facebook, so have a look on Google for the most recent sizes.

At the time of writing, the following applies:

- 820 x 312 pixels on computers
- 640 x 360 pixels on smartphones

As you can see, both desktop and mobile are different, so this needs to be taken into account as well.

Once you have your sizes, take the widest width and tallest height, giving you 820 x 360 pixels, and triple these numbers.

So, you have 2,460 x 1,080 pixels – these are the numbers to use to create your custom template. This will help cover both mobile and desktop and by tripling them, it will help to make a sharper image after Facebook compresses it upon uploading.

This image gives you an overview of the sizes:

Mobile version size 1920px x 1080px Desktop version size 2460px x 936px

SAFE SPACE TO USE

1. Google the current sizes for mobile and desktop Facebook banner sizes
2. They are currently:
   - 820px x 312px desktop
   - 640px x 360px mobile
3. Triple these sizes to stop quality loss in the banner after you have uploaded it to Facebook
4. Create a custom sized template in Canva using your new sizes
5. Create 2 oblongs the same dimensions as the original tripled sizes, lay them on top of each other, adjust the gradiant of one, so you can see both, then use the safe oblong space you have now created in the middle of them to design your banner.

Figure 9.8 – Facebook banner size guide

Click on **Create a design** and add these numbers to create your custom template.

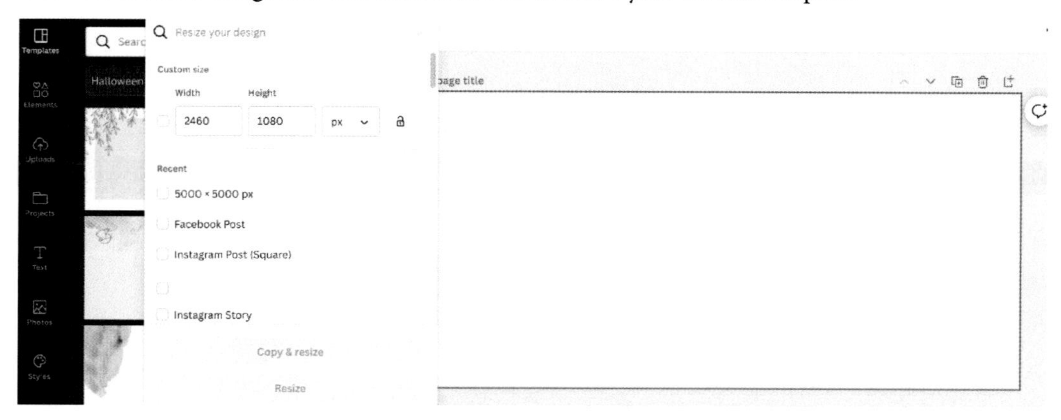

Figure 9.9 – Creating a custom template for Facebook banners

Before you start creating, you need to determine where the safe space is so that you can add all of your important information here, knowing it will be visible on both desktop and mobile screens.

To do this, you need to add two squares. Take the two numbers you have above for desktop and mobile and triple them so they will now work on your new template:

- 2,460 x 936 pixels on computers
- 1,920 x 1,080 pixels on smartphones

Add a square from the **Shapes** section and drag out the corners to the first dimensions. As you drag out the corners, you can see the numbers in the black box:

Figure 9.10 – Adding a square to a Facebook banner

Add another square shape and do the same with the second dimensions – overlay them both in the center of your template. At this point, adjust the **Transparency** settings of one so you can see the other underneath:

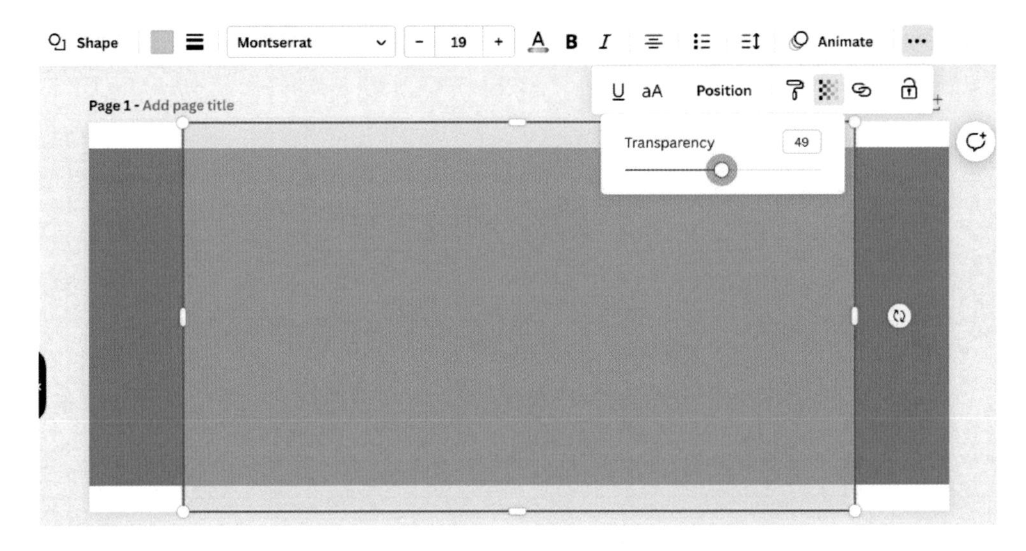

Figure 9.11 – Changing the transparency of a square

You can now see a square has appeared in the middle between your two larger squares; this is the safe area to design your banner. Add a light-colored square over this area and lock it in place so that it will not move until you have finished designing your banner:

Figure 9.12 – Locking a square shape on a Facebook banner

At this point, you can delete the two squares you added at the beginning; you don't need these anymore. You can now start to add in your information, images, and elements, making sure the important things are kept within the light-colored square:

Figure 9.13 – Facebook banner design

Here, I have added two textboxes, both kept within the light-colored square, and an image.

Next, add an element or color block at the top and bottom. This goes outside of the central box because the outer edges are still visible on either mobile or desktop:

Figure 9.14 – Simple Facebook banner design in progress

Alternatively, add in a background image that can stretch the entire span of the template:

Figure 9.15 – Patterned background Facebook banner in progress

Once you've finished, it's time to unlock the light-colored square, delete it, and see what your design looks like:

Here, we have two finished designs, one simple and clean:

Figure 9.16 – Finished simple Facebook banner

The other is more creative and fun, but both show the important information on all devices:

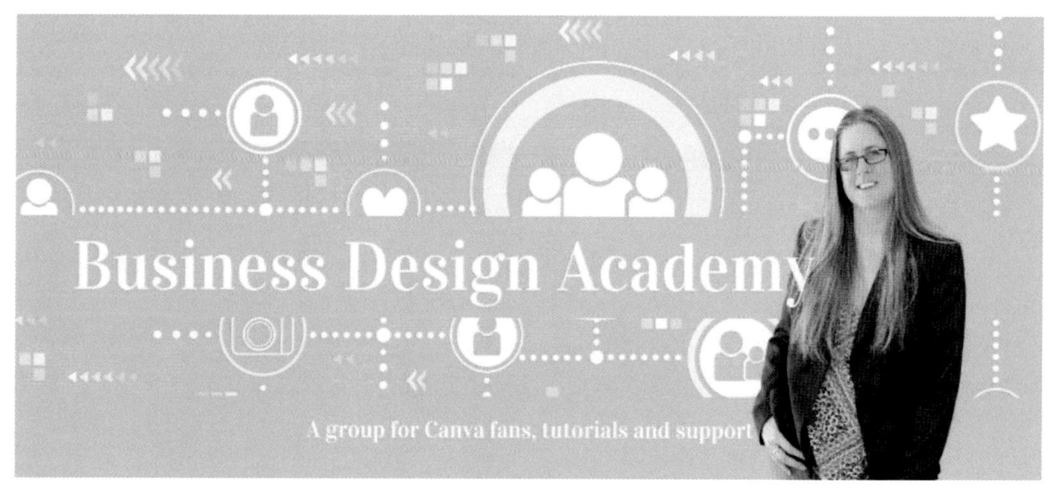

Figure 9.17 – Finished Facebook banner design with a patterned background

Use your branding when creating your Facebook banner, and make sure any images work with your business. Adding an image of yourself works well and followers can relate to you if they can see you. Make sure you keep your information in the middle.

So, that's our Facebook account sorted. Let's look at creating a story for Instagram using animation.

Creating an animated Instagram story

Instagram stories are extremely popular and gain a lot of engagement; these are a good type of design to create and promote your business. You can also animate your story with elements, animation features, or video. Stories on both Instagram and Facebook work better when they have an aspect of movement to them.

You can use an Instagram story template on Facebook as well.

Let's look at the different types.

Adding animation using the Canva features option

Search for the `Instagram story` template size using the **Create a design** option. By now, you probably know that there are lots of templates for this size to the left of the design. You can either use a template or create your own from scratch using the elements, textboxes, and images.

If you are creating from scratch, remember to make use of your branding. Use your color palettes, fonts, and branded imagery to stay consistent throughout your design.

Follow along to create this Instagram story in Canva:

Figure 9.18 – Finished Instagram story design

1. Search for and add a grid from the **Elements** section to your template. Make sure it is the one with four image spaces – this will automatically resize to fit the template:

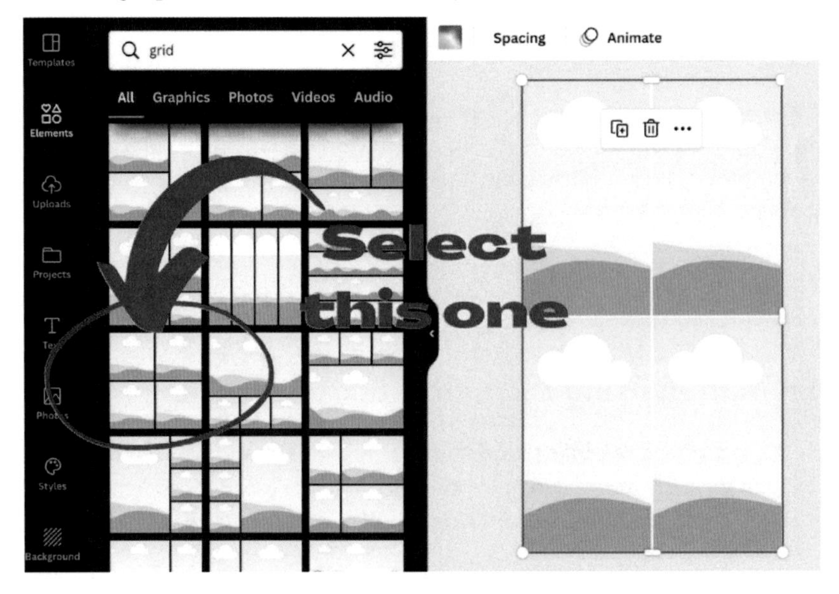

Figure 9.19 – Selecting the four-grid element in Canva

2. Then, select the upper-right frame and change the color to white. After this, either upload your own images or search for images in the Canva **Photos** library. If you are a product business, use images of your own products. For service-based businesses, search for `Flatley` in the **Photos** library. Many are suitable for services:

Figure 9.20 – Adding images to the grid

3. In the white, top-right corner, add a textbox. In this box, add either your business name, product, or service, use the **all-capitals feature**, and then add another textbox beneath it and add some information. You can then add a third textbox with how to contact you, using your website or social media handle. The text sizes should decrease in size order.

You now have a finished design to add your animation to:

Figure 9.21 – The finished design

To add animation, click on the **Animate** tab at the top. You can now add animation to the whole design – hover over each option and it will show you how it will look on your template. Choose the one you like, and you can use this on your socials to promote your business.

If you prefer to have a more subtle animation, you can select a part of your design, a textbox, for example, and then click **Animate** to just animate that part, leaving the rest of the design static. Otherwise, you can add an animated element, which we are now going to look at.

Adding animated elements

We can use the same design as we have in the previous section, but rather than clicking on the **Animate** tab, we're going over to the **Elements** section and searching for `animated lines`. I like these – they work well around text and help parts of the design stand out.

Scroll down until you find this element – it is free to use – and add it to your design:

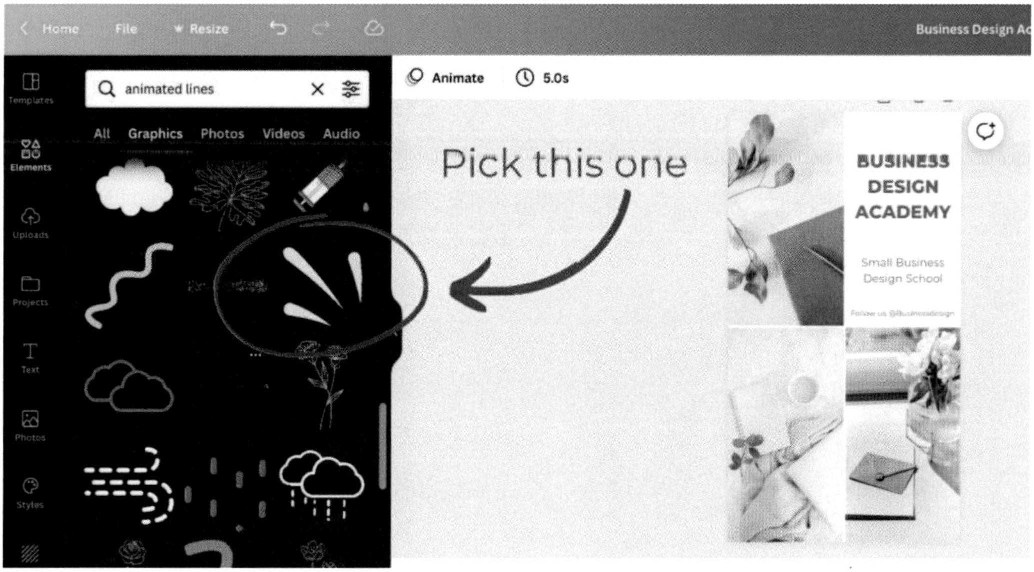

Figure 9.22 – Selecting an animated element

Reduce the size using the circles in the corners and move it to the side of one of your textboxes, whichever one you want to stand out the most, and then duplicate it, flip it, and move it to the other side of the textbox:

Figure 9.23 – Adding animated elements

Tip

As these are animated, you cannot change the color of these in Canva, so you need to find an animated element that has a color relevant to your branding or template color palette.

You can now see how long your template will play for in the top-left corner and can watch it before downloading by clicking the play icon on the upper right:

Figure 9.24 – Showing the play icon and animation length

These are both great ways to add a touch of animation to your story template, but you can also add a video. We will be looking at videos in greater detail in *Chapter 10, Leveraging Video and Animation within Your Business Marketing*, so let's look at creating the next design in this chapter: a business card.

Creating a business card

Business cards are still being used, even in the modern world of technology and everything else being moved online. If you go to networking events, for example, or have a face-to-face meeting, being able to give someone a business card will help keep you and your business top of mind.

It doesn't have to be complex or include absolutely everything. As long as you make it clear who you are and what you do, and give them a way to contact you easily, that will be just fine.

Start by using the **Business Card** size template from the **Create a design** tab. It will give you multiple options to create different shaped designs but stick to the classic size, which is the first option in the dropdown.

As this design is to be printed, make sure you select **Show print bleed** so that it will be there ready when needed, either printed by a third-party printer or through Canva itself, which we will be looking at in *Chapter 12, Tips and Tricks for Printing*:

Figure 9.25 – Blank business card template

Start by adding the information you would like on your business card. Add the following into individual textboxes so that you can change the font and text size of each section, in this order:

- Your name
- Your business name
- A short description of what you do
- Your contact email address
- Web address or social media handle

Align them to the left. Once added, increase the size of your name, and decrease the size of your contact details, making your name and business name the focal points of the business card:

Laura Goodsell
Business Design Acdemy

Canva templates and traingings for small businesses

laura@businessdesignacademy.co.uk
www.businessdesignacademy.co.uk

Figure 9.26 – Business card details

It's looking a little plain on this side, so add an element in the corner, and you can even add a splash of your brand color to the side by using a shape and changing the color. I've also added a line element to the side where the textboxes align:

Figure 9.27 – Business card design

Once you have the main information side done, it's time to add another page to this design and create the front of your business card. Select the plus symbol next to the main page at the bottom and it will produce another page:

Figure 9.28 – Adding another page to a business card design

This will be the front, so it should either have a textbox with your business name or you can use your logo.

For a simple but effective front, use the same color as you have used on the back, and then add a square shape from the **Elements** section stretching across the design. Leave this white, and then add a textbox with your business name along this shape:

Figure 9.29 – Front page of a business card design

To finish, search for a pattern in the **Elements** section – for example, search for `leaf pattern`, add one to your design, stretch it to cover the entire page, and turn it white. Lastly, select the **Position** tab and send it to the back:

Figure 9.30 – Front and back of the finished business card design

When you're ready to print your business card, on the download option, select **PDF print**. This will then give you the option to select the following:

- **Crop marks and bleed** – These show the printer where to trim the paper
- **Flatten PDF** – Merges all individual elements into one
- Select the **CMYK** option (the color option for all printers) in the **Color Profile** dropdown

All are often required by printers, so Canva has added these options for you. However the **CMYK** option is a Pro only feature.

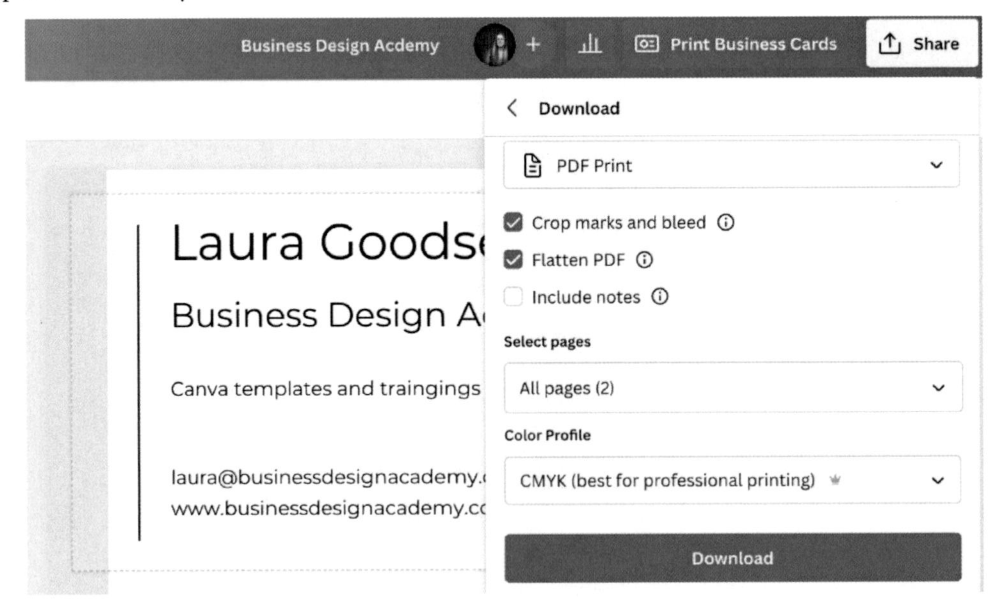

Figure 9.31 – Crop, Flatten, and CMYK drop-down options

So far, you have created designs for your social media channels and gotten a business card ready, but what about advertising your business? Adverts in magazines, leaflets, and local fliers are a great way to promote your business, so let's have a look at this style of design next.

Creating a magazine or leaflet advert

Magazine or leaflet adverts can really help with promotion, giving you another platform to showcase what you do.

As with business cards, when you create your advert, keep in mind that it may be printed for a physical magazine, so turn on your print bleed and select the **Crop marks and bleed**, **Flatten PDF**, and **CMYK** options when downloading it.

Now, the sizing of this one is more down to the publisher that you will be sending it to; they may have certain sizes that they require your article or advertisement to be in. This is where you would need to create a custom design. There is a possibility they will request it in inches or millimeters, so you can use the dropdown to change the measurement:

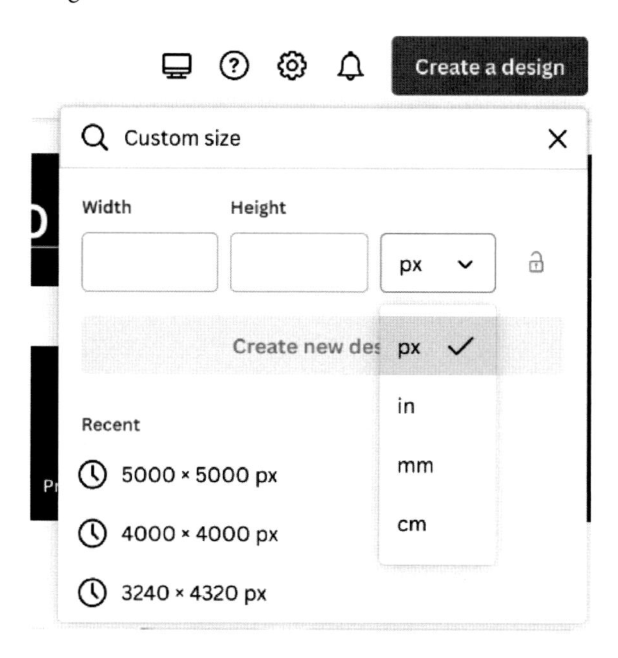

Figure 9.32 – Different custom design sizes

Once you have your blank design template, it's time to start creating your advert. Keep it simple and clear, staying consistent with your branding throughout. This is a place where you are promoting your business, so every aspect needs to be on brand.

Let's create something similar to this:

Figure 9.33 – Basic advert design

If you don't know the size that's needed, search for `advert` in the **Create a design** section. It will bring up a poster size; you can use this as a basis and then resize it once you have the correct measurements.

Search for `gradient` in the **Elements** section and select one to add as a background, preferably one that you can change the colors of to your own branding, and then add a single grid to the bottom half of the template, which is where you will add your main image, making sure it overlaps with the edge of the template:

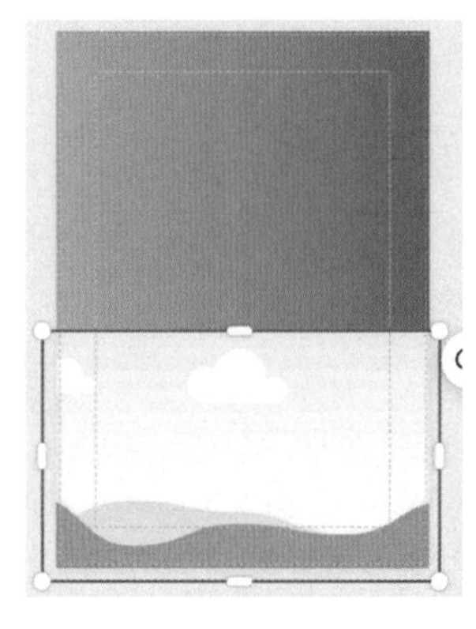

Figure 9.34 – Advert gradient background and image placement

To find the ribbon element across the middle, search in the **Elements** section for `corporate ribbon`. Lots of different types will appear. These particular elements are Pro, but there are a lot of different free elements available as well. Use the element to cover the line between the grid square and gradient color here, stretching it across the width of the design:

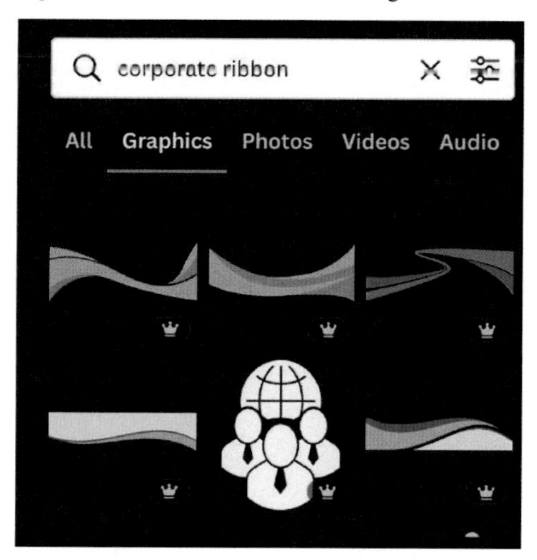

Figure 9.35 – Selecting a corporate ribbon element

These elements are also color-changing, so you can add your brand colors to them. Once you have the background of the design in place, you need to add textboxes – one at the top with your business name, for which you should increase the size and use the **all-capitals feature**, and one beneath for your short business description:

Figure 9.36 – Adding textboxes

Next, it's time to add the images. Search for `Circle frame` in the **Elements** section and add two of these to your design. These are free to use. Drag and drop in your images, either from the **Photos** library or your own that you have uploaded:

Figure 9.37 – Adding a main image and two smaller images

Lastly, you need to add contact details. To do this, find the square shape with rounded corners in the **Elements** section, and then use the white lines at the top to reduce the height to form a button shape:

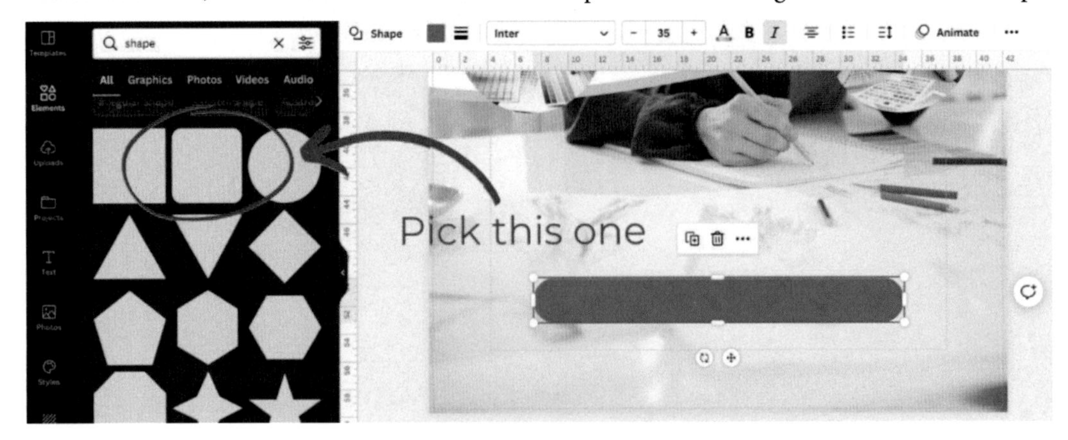

Figure 9.38 – Selecting a shape to create a button background

Change the color of this shape to match your brand and then add a textbox with your contact information – this could be your phone number, web address, email address, or social media handle, whichever is the best for someone to contact you via:

Figure 9.39 – The finished design

You can add more information to this as and when it's needed, without having to always start from scratch, but this gives you the basis to start with.

> **Tip**
>
> If you want to make your contact details stand out more, add icons – for example, add a phone icon to go next to your phone number.

I hope you've enjoyed this chapter and have created some amazing graphics that you can now use for your business.

Summary

Wow, this has been a packed chapter! By now, you should have several graphics created that you can use for your business, including a profile frame, a Facebook banner, an animated Instagram story, a business card, and a magazine or leaflet advert. While you've been creating these, you have also learned how to correctly size a Facebook banner and that the platform compresses images. You've also learned how to create a profile frame using a circle element. You've seen two different ways to add animation to a design and how to create a business card ready for print by knowing how to add bleed marks and crop marks and how to flatten a PDF. We've also looked at creating an advert-style poster, which involves looking for different types of elements to use.

Earlier on in this chapter, I mentioned you could add videos to your design as part of the **Animation** section, so that's exactly what we are going to be looking at in the next chapter.

10
Leveraging Video and Animation within Your Business Marketing

Making the most of video and audio in your marketing materials and social media channels will help boost your profile and visibility. Platforms such as Facebook often prefer videos or posts that have an aspect of movement in them as they tend to get better visibility and, as human beings, we capture movement better than a static images. So, if you can create moving graphics, that will have a beneficial impact on your business.

In this chapter, we are going to cover the following main topics:

- Creating presentations
- How to add and edit audio
- How to add and edit video
- How to add animation
- Recording directly into Canva

By the end of this chapter, you will have a good understanding of the impact of video and how to add and edit video and audio files to your Canva designs, as well as how to create a basic presentation, record directly, and add animation.

Creating presentations

Canva is just getting better and better when it comes to presentations by adding new features all the time so that you can create amazing-looking interactive presentations for business and personal use. These are brilliant for those who create courses, run training or zoom calls, or would just like to present something in a fun way.

There are several presentation options in Canva, but we're going to stick with the first one in the list: **Presentations (16:9)**. If you click on this option, it will open up a blank presentation template:

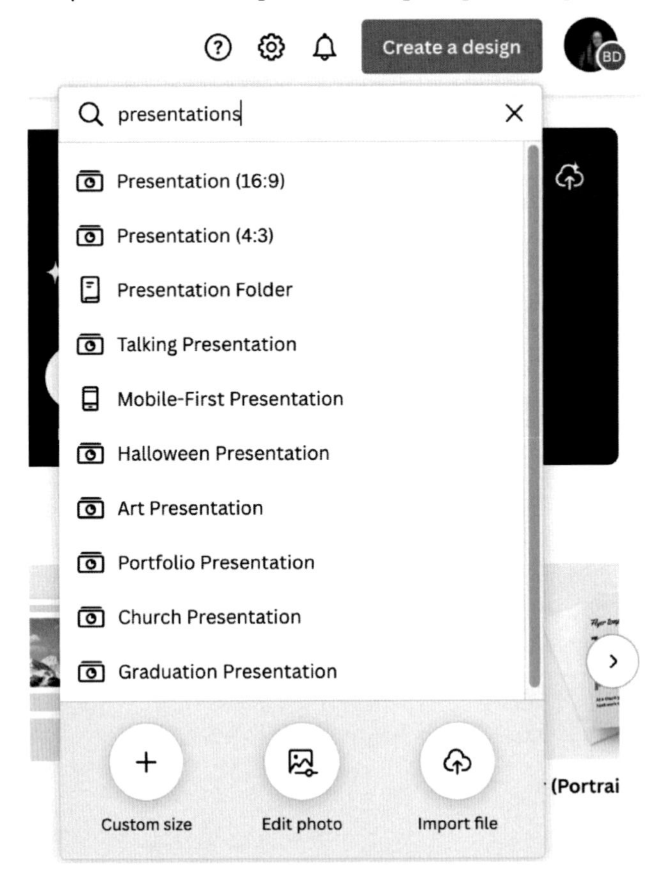

Figure 10.1 – Finding presentation-sized templates in the Create a design tab

With presentations, you may notice that the pages run along the bottom of the screen rather than underneath each other. This way, you can see how the pages will work together:

Figure 10.2 – A blank presentation page

You can create a presentation using elements, images, and shapes but you also have access to hundreds of templates on the left that you can use and edit to suit your needs.

Use the search bar at the top to find one that will suit your niche. When you click on a template, you will find that many of them have multiple pages. You can either pick and choose which ones you would like to add or click the **Apply all x pages** option to add them all. They can be individually deleted if they're not needed at a later date:

Figure 10.3 – Adding a template to your presentation pages

For this example, I've chosen to add all pages to the presentation. They are now lined up along the bottom and I can edit each page as I would a normal Canva template, changing text, images, and colors to suit my branding. Click **styles** on the left, then choose your branding colors (if you have them set up in the PRO version) and click the **apply to all pages** button. This will populate your branding across the entire presentation:

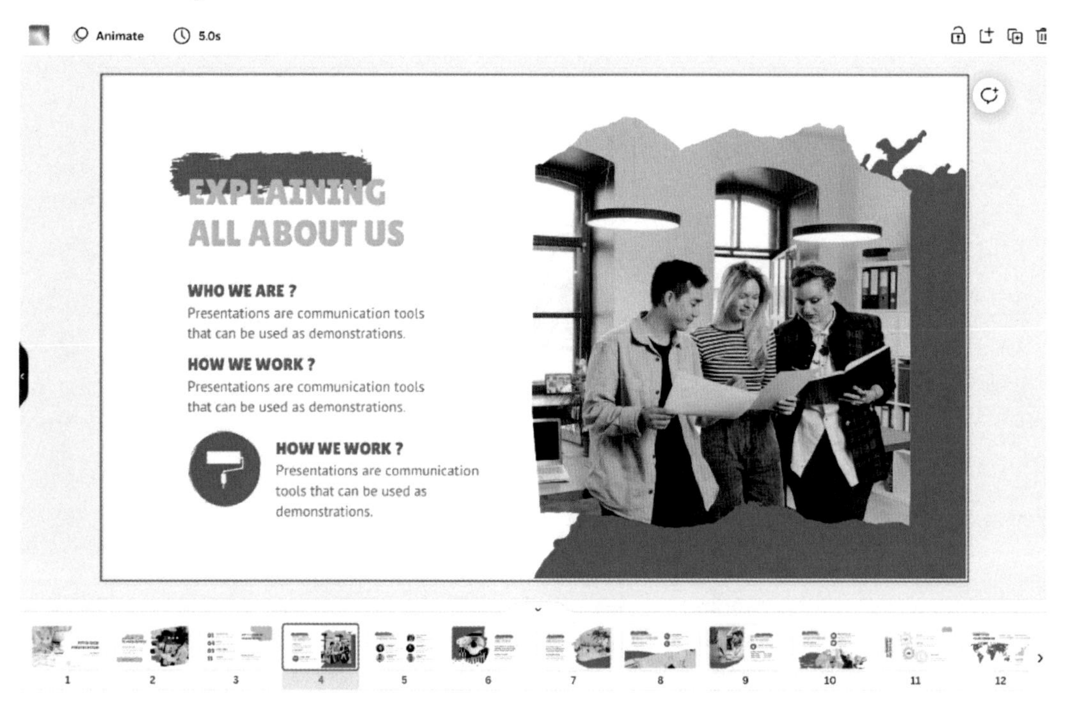

Figure 10.4 – Changing the color of your branding

This is already starting to look very different.

Once you have added your information, changed your images, and removed any pages you don't need, it's time to choose how to present your presentation.

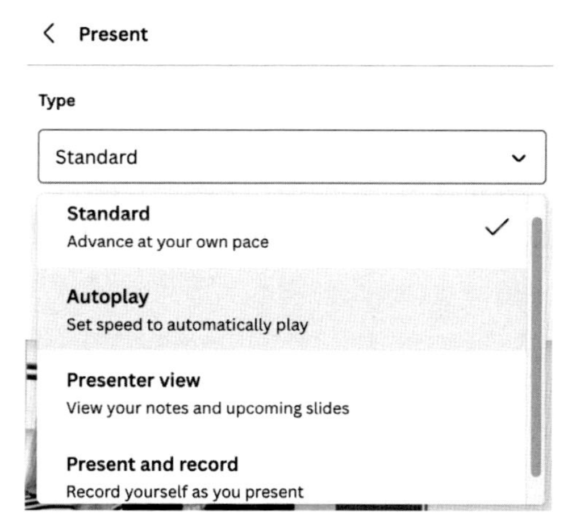

Figure 10.5 – Different presenting options

On the **Present** tab, there are four options:

- **Standard**: Allows you to go through the presentation in your own time, moving on to the next page when you're ready, and is in fullscreen mode:

Figure 10.6 – Standard presenting mode

- **Autoplay**: You can select how long you would like each page to play for. Then, it will go through your presentation automatically for you. This is also in fullscreen mode:

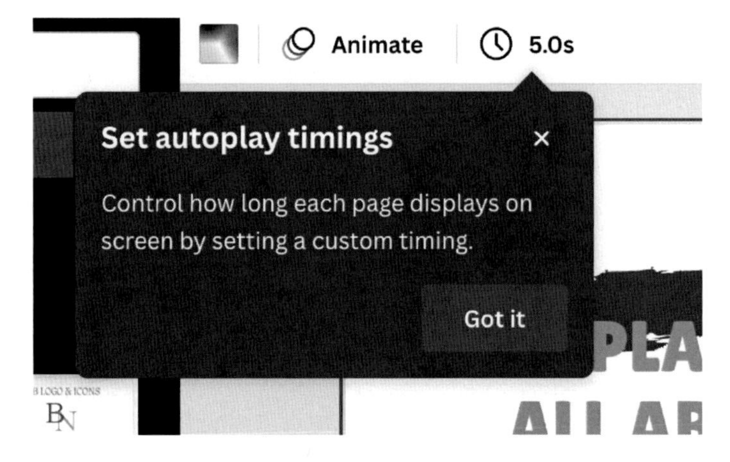

Figure 10.7 – Setting autoplay on presentations

- **Presenter view**: You get two windows with this one. You can place the first window on the screen you will be looking at:

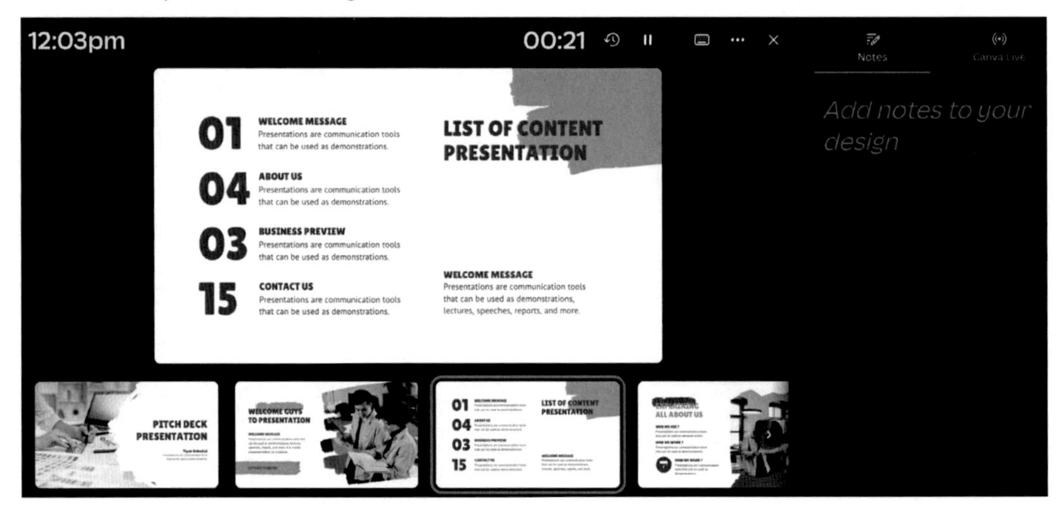

Figure 10.8 – Presenter mode with notes and pages

The second one allows you to display information to your audience. This way, you get to see your presentation pages and notes to guide you through:

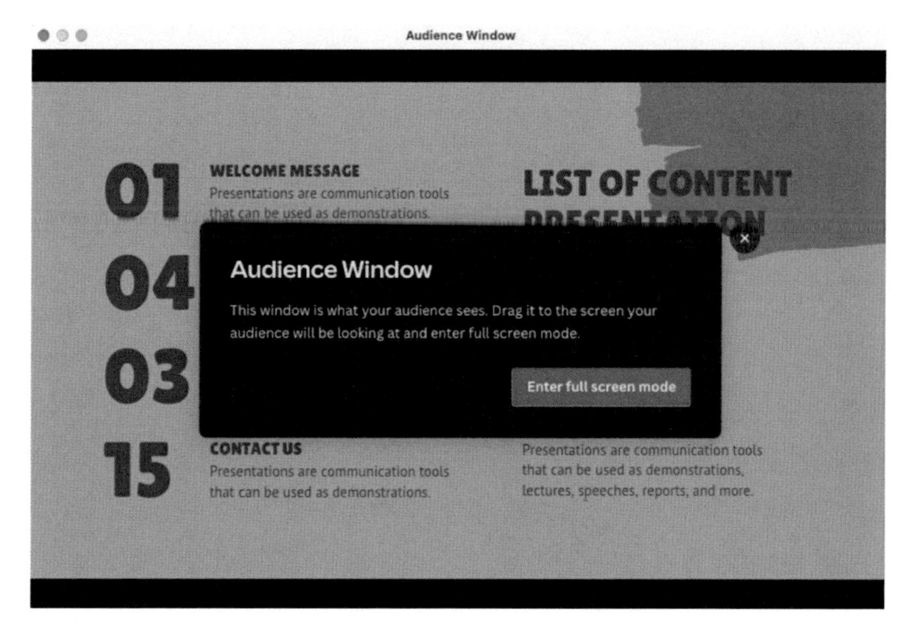

Figure 10.9 – Presenter mode for your audience

- **Present and record**: My favorite one, this option lets you present your presentation while recording it. It shows a small recording of yourself in the corner, which is perfect for prerecorded courses. Once selected, it will take you to the recording studio:

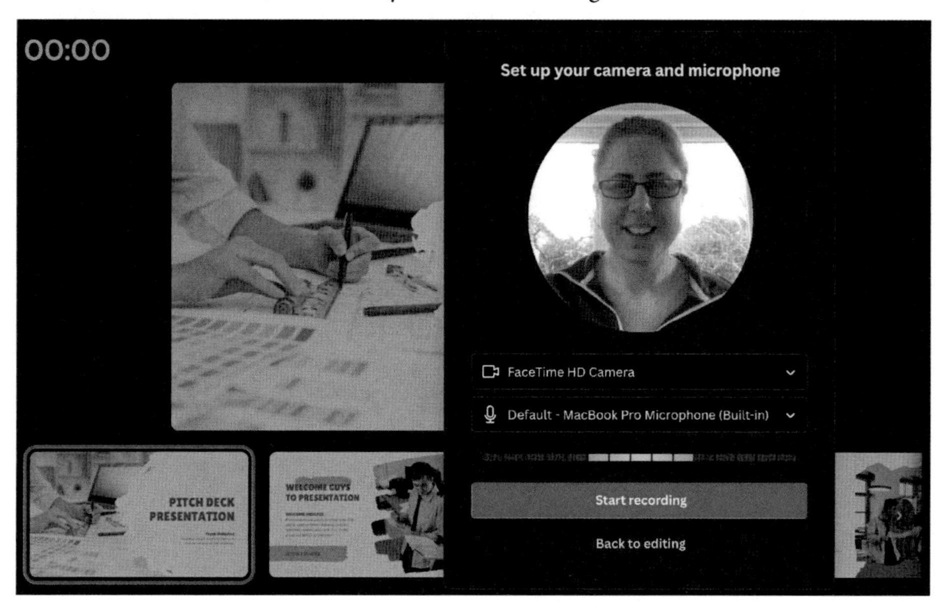

Figure 10.10 – Setting up to present and record at the same time

This is where you can check the camera and microphone settings before recording. This option also gives you the notes on the right and pages along the bottom, but the result will show the full screen and your small video in the corner only:

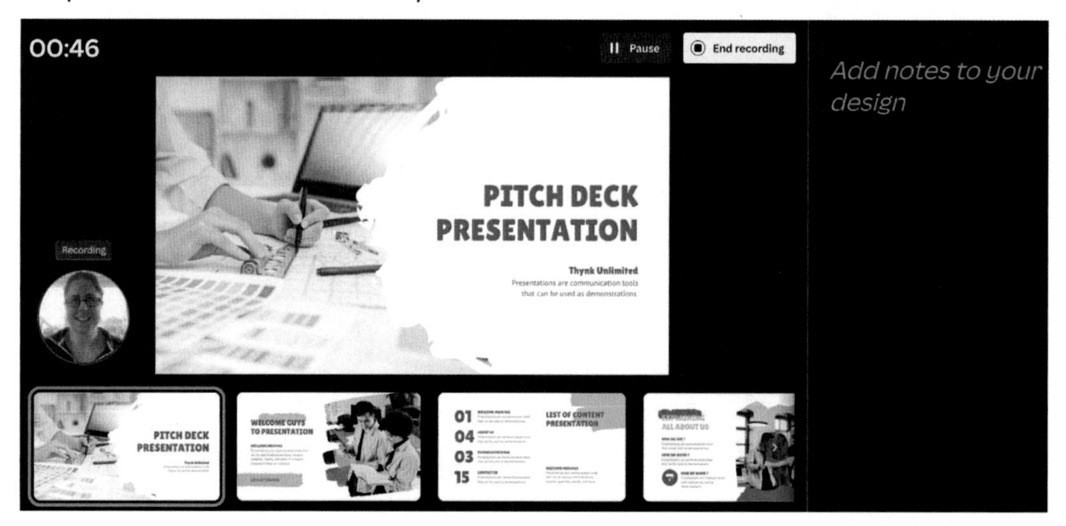

Figure 10.11 – Presenter mode with a small video of yourself during the presentation

Once you have finished recording, you will be given the option to either share a link to the presentation or download it to your computer for later use.

One more thing I love about presentations is the keyboard shortcuts. Canva has added various keyboard shortcuts that bring up small animations throughout. While you are presenting, press one of these keys and watch what happens:

- *C*: Confetti
- *D*: Drum roll
- *Q*: Quiet emoji
- *U*: Curtains fall
- *O*: Bubbles
- *B*: Blur
- *M*: Mic drop

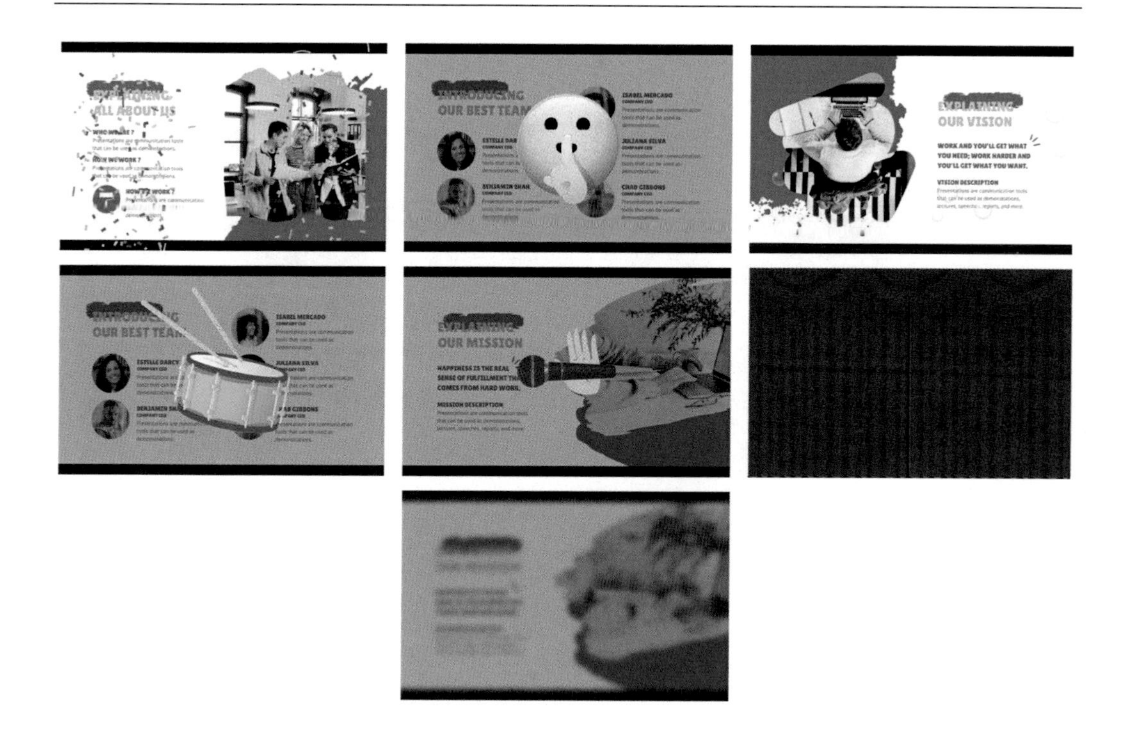

Figure 10.12 – The different animations you can add to a presentation

Presentations are great fun, especially with the added animations. Now, let's look at how to edit and add audio and video to your social graphics, hopefully helping you with more visibility.

How to add and edit audio

Adding audio to your design is often used on platforms such as YouTube, Instagram, or TikTok, as well as others platforms that like video, but often, you may not want the original sounds of the video being heard. Alternatively, perhaps you've created a video with no sound. Being able to add audio to it can help finish it off, making it more appealing to your audience.

Both the **Audio** and **Video** options in Canva can be found on the left menu once you have your design open. Scroll down to the bottom; in the very far left corner is the **Apps** tab:

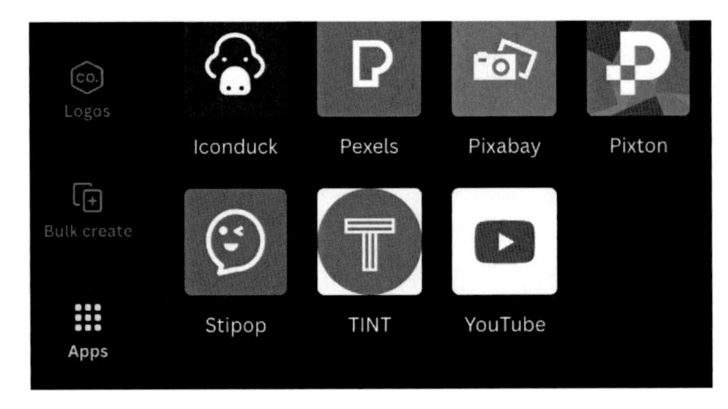

Figure 10.13 – The Apps tab's options

Let's go through how audio works, how you can find different audio files, and how you can add them to your Canva design:

1. Click the **Apps** option; both **Video** and **Audio** will appear at the top. Clicking on them individually will place them in your menu:

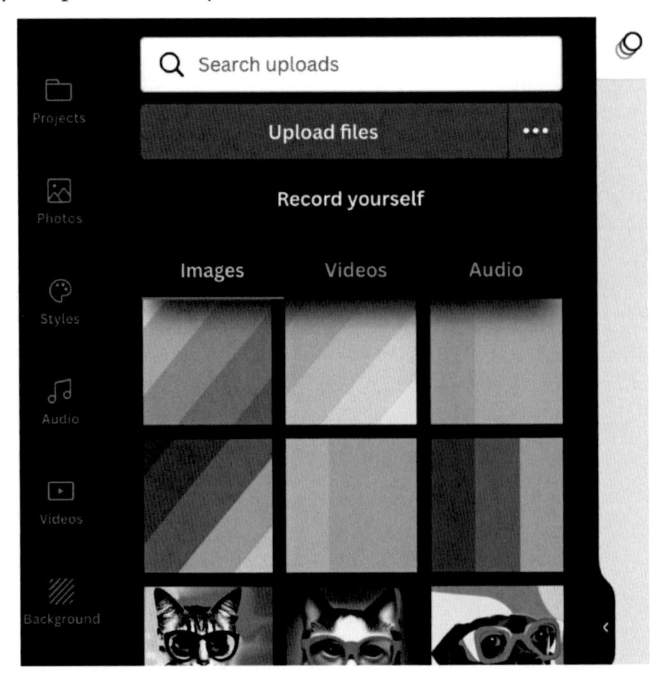

Figure 10.14 – The video and audio apps in the sidebar

2. For this section, we're looking at adding audio to your design, so click on the **Audio** option to open up the search results.

   From here, you can search for different types of audio you would like to use; the option buttons beneath the search bar are useful for this. Alternatively, you can scroll down to look at recently used or different popular audio files:

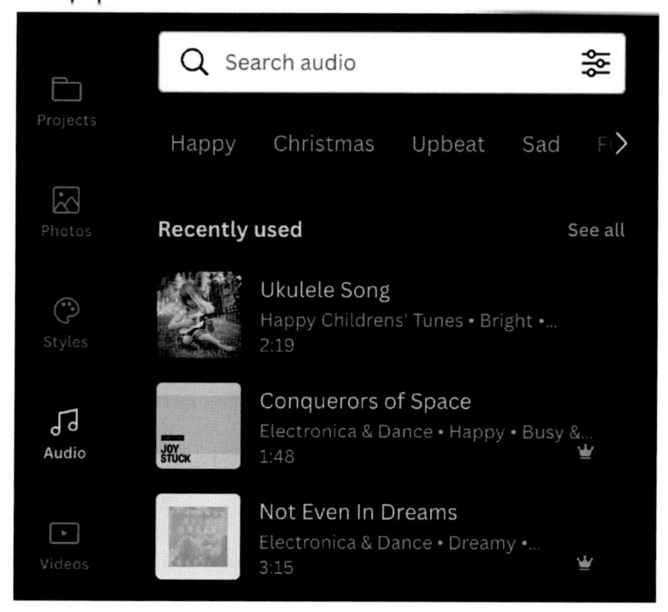

Figure 10.15 – Audio search tab and different audio files available

3. Next, to play an audio file, hover over the image icon; a play button will appear. Click this to listen to the audio before adding it to your design:

Figure 10.16 – The chosen audio file

4. Once you've found a piece of audio you like, you can add it to the design. It will appear along the top, giving you a section of the audio that will be played. To change this, drag the blue bar section along the audio:

Figure 10.17 – Audio playing along the top of a design

5. In this example, the section of audio that will play is only 5 seconds long. To increase or decrease this, you need to adjust the time frame of the design rather than the audio file. The audio will always play to the same length as the design. So, to increase the length of the design, first, you need to remove the audio by clicking the delete icon in the top-right corner:

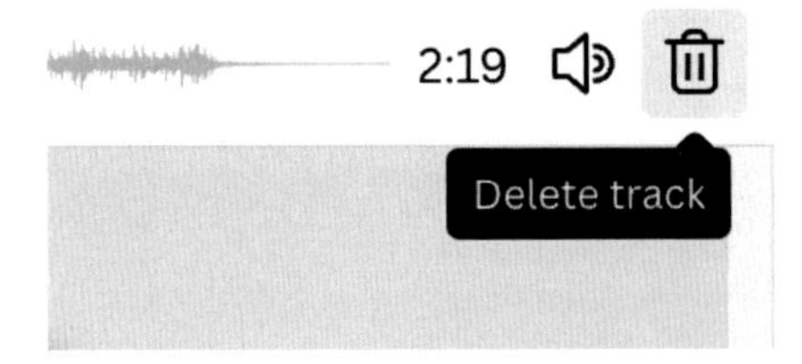

Figure 10.18 – Delete option for removing audio

6. The normal top bar will appear again. Here, you can adjust the length of the design (the preset time is always 5 seconds), change the time in the box, and hit *Enter*:

Figure 10.19 – Changing the length of a template

7. Now, you can add your audio back in and it will adjust itself to fit:

Figure 10.20 – Adjusting the length of an audio file

You can only add one piece of audio at a time. If you wish to add another, drop it in; it will replace the old one. The other option you have regarding audio is to adjust its volume by using the speaker icon in the top-right corner.

Let's take this a step further now and look at how to add and edit a video.

How to add and edit video

Canva has a fantastic video library. Usually, you can find something to suit your needs, but you can also upload and edit a video as well as remove the backgrounds of a video. However, this is a PRO feature, though it's worth mentioning here.

To upload a video into Canva, head on over to a blank or existing template and click on the **upload** tab on the left. This will allow you to upload images and videos directly from your computer. Once you have a video in the **upload** section, click on it; it will be placed into your template. From here, you can edit it using the options from the top bar:

Figure 10.21 – Adding a video and the different video editing options

Clicking on the **Edit video** tab will bring up the **Background Remover** app on the left of the screen, along with options to adjust aspects of your video on the right, including warmth, tint, brightness, and contrast:

Figure 10.22 – The Effects and Adjust tabs for videos

But let's look at the background remover app and have a look at this video before and after clicking **Background Remover**.

This is the video before with full background:

Figure 10.23 – Video before background removal

This is what it looks like after with the background removed:

Figure 10.24 – Video after background removal

I can now add this to a design using any color background, grid, or frame to make my video and design stand out more. In the same way, I can add an image to grids and frames, and I've also reduced any clutter.

The next thing I can do with a video is cut or trim it. If I have a part at the end that makes it look unfinished – for example, when reaching over to click **end**, after recording, it's often a good idea to trim this part out – you can do this by dragging in the purple lines at either end of the video in the top bar and click **Done**. This will trim your video and will show you the reduced video length time in the box on the left, which currently says 9.1 seconds:

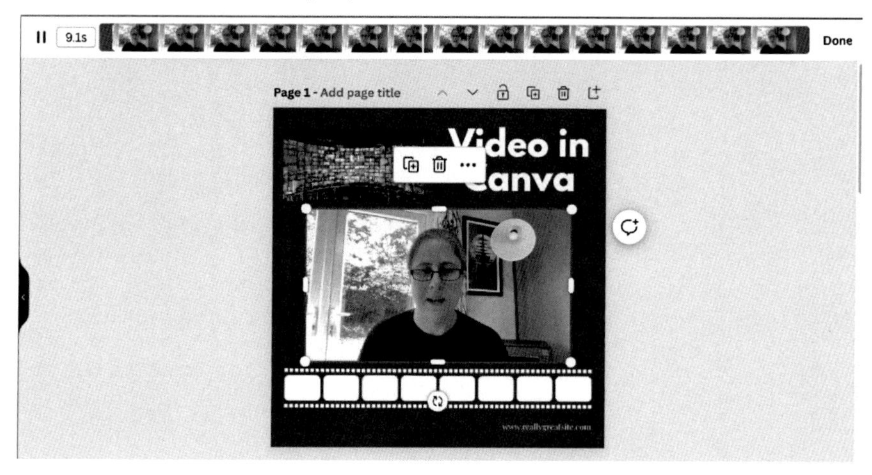

Figure 10.25 – Adjusting the length of a video

There are also two **Playback** options where you can loop the video forever so that it will play over and over until it has been manually stopped. You also have the option to autoplay the video, rather than you having to press play when presenting your video:

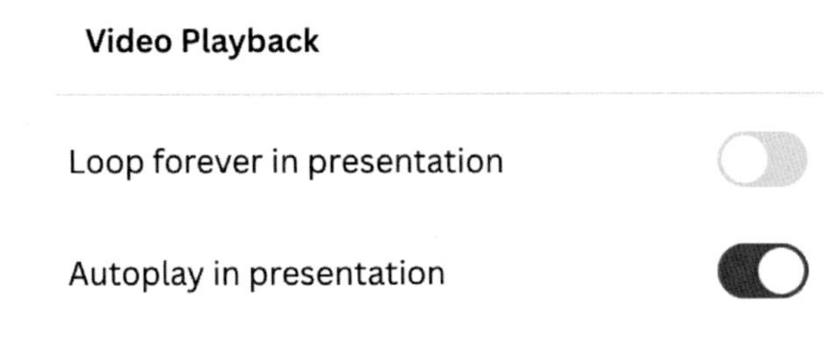

Figure 10.26 – The different playback options for video

Also, on this top bar, you have the option to crop the size of the video by dragging in the white corners. This allows you to remove objects or people in the background you would not like to be there:

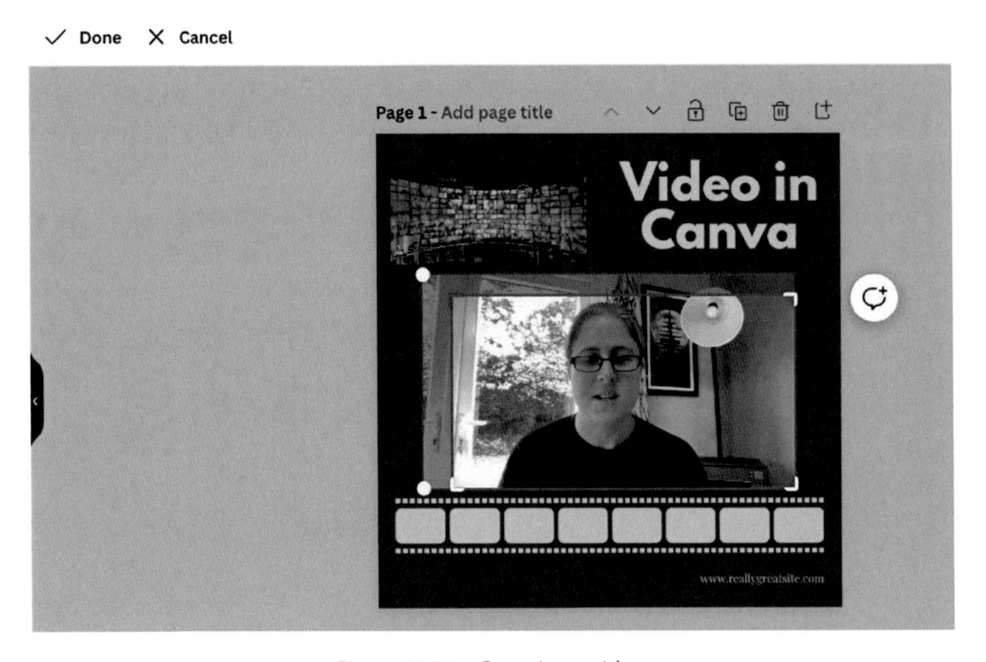

Figure 10.27 – Cropping a video

Finally, you have the option to flip or rotate the video and animate it as you would any other template or element, which is exactly what we are going to look at next. Let's look at animation in a bit more detail.

How to add animation

Animation is a great alternative to adding video. If you don't want to go through the hassle of recording a video or can't find one on Canva that could work for you, you can add animation to turn your design into an MP4 file, and you will still have your movement and video for your social media channels.

There are a few ways to add animation and animate different aspects of your design.

You can animate the following:

- The entire design as one
- Individual text boxes
- Individual elements
- Individual images and videos

Depending on which aspect of your design you select, different options will appear on the left. Whenever you select an element, text box, or image, click **Animate**. A new animations box on the left will appear with two columns – one for the item you have selected and one for the entire page, giving you the option of both:

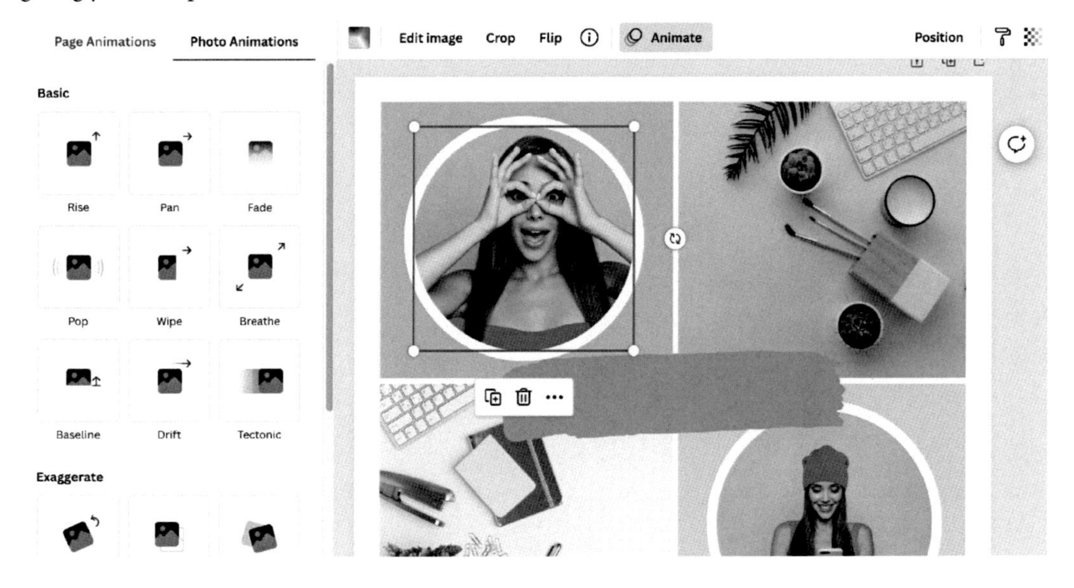

Figure 10.28 – Photo animations

Hover over any of the animation boxes and you will see it applied to your design, giving you a view of how it will look. Click on the **Page Animations** option and hover over them; it will do the same, except that the animation has been applied to the entire design.

Animations for elements and images (and videos) are very similar, apart from three additional image/video options. If you scroll to the bottom, you also get these, which are image/video-specific:

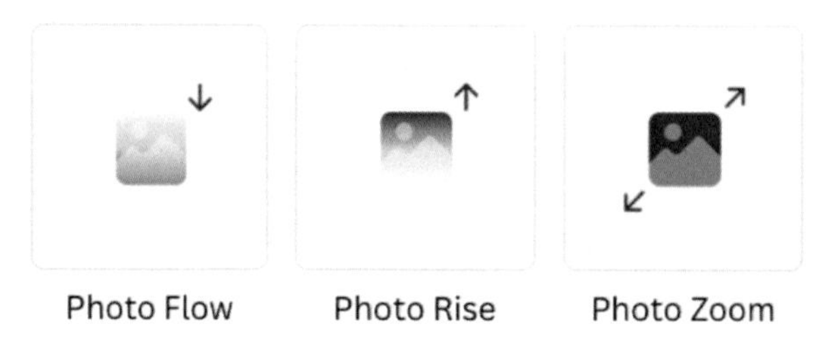

Figure 10.29 – Three additional photo/video animations

The text boxes are slightly different but you get a few new options, such as the **Typewriter** effect. These are text-specific and can make your writing stand out:

Figure 10.30 – Text box animations

As we mentioned in *Chapter 9*, *Making Social Media Graphics with Canva*, you can also add animated elements and stickers to your design, giving you the element of movement. These can all be found in the **element** section. You can also search for video and audio here as well.

Now that we know how to add video and audio, let's look at how to use Canva to record directly into it.

Recording direct into Canva

This is a great feature that can save you a lot of time when you want to record something and add it to a Canva template. Usually, you would need to use a third-party platform or dig out your camera, then upload it to your computer before adding it. The record direct feature has cut all of this out and it's so super simple to use.

To find the feature, you need to be on the design where you would like to add the recording. I've created the following mock-up:

Figure 10.31 – Template ready to record direct into

I would like to add a short video below the text **Video in Canva**

To do this, go over to the menu on the left and select the **Uploads** option. Here, you will find the **Upload files** button and, below that, one that says **Record yourself**. Select it:

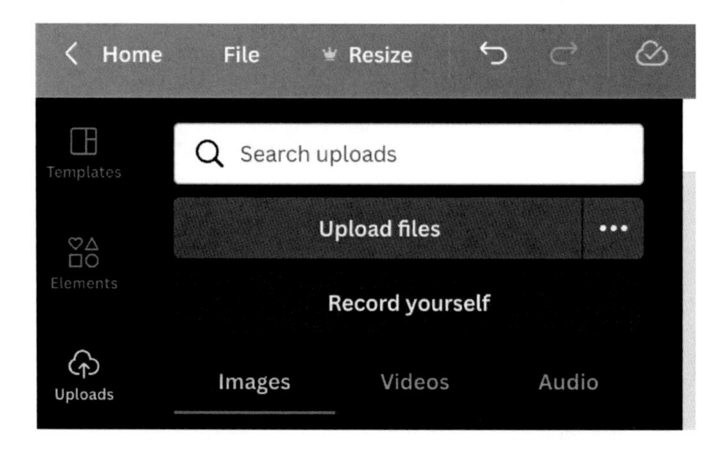

Figure 10.32 – Upload and record options

A new window will open with your template in the background and a small version of yourself in the bottom-left corner:

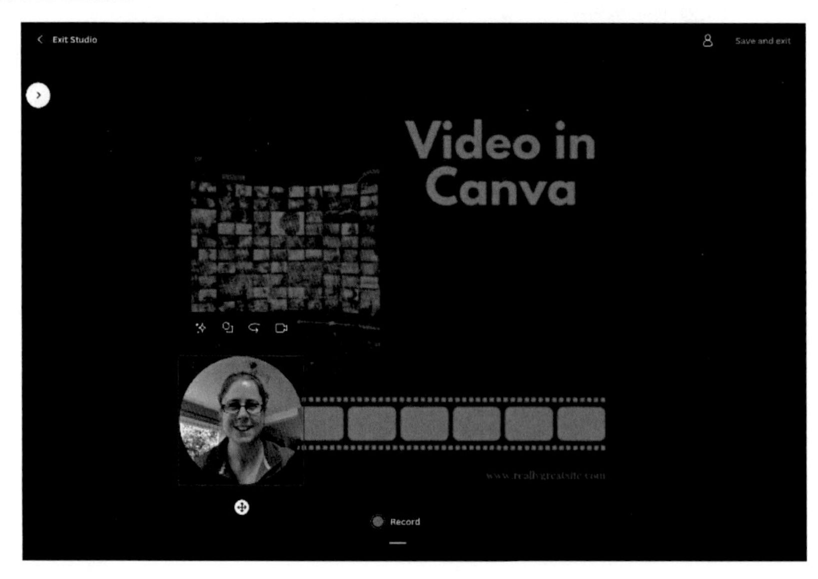

Figure 10.33 – Recording directly into your template

Above this window you will find four options, as follows:

- **Filters & effects**

  Here, you can add different filters to your video. Currently, there is just one effect, which is skin smoothing:

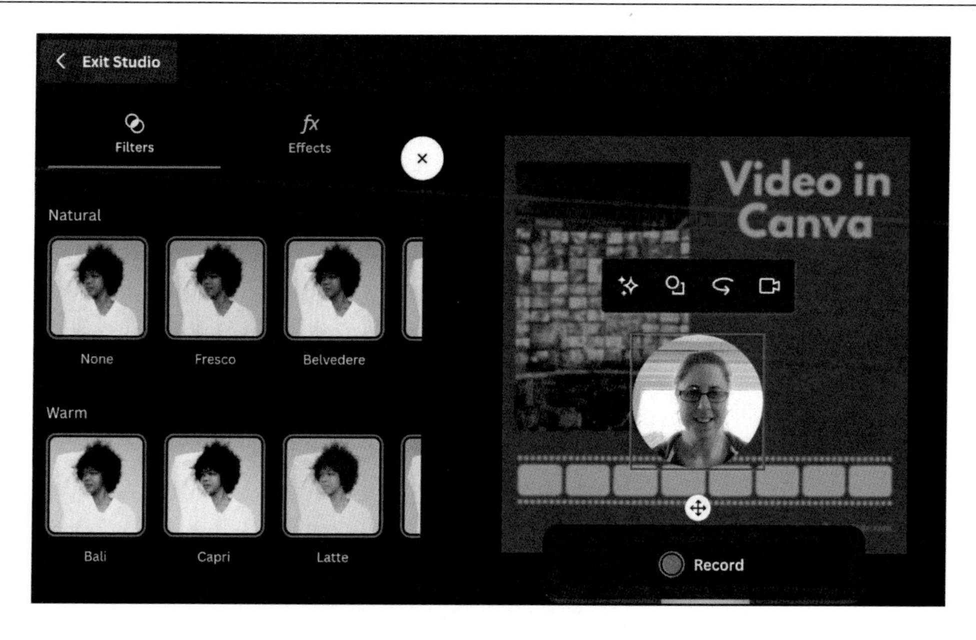

Figure 10.34 – Adding filters to your video

- **Change shape**

  This gives you the option to have either a circle- or square-shaped video:

Figure 10.35 – Changing the shape of your video

- **Mirror Camera**

  This option flips or mirrors the camera for you so that any writing or text is the right way around:

Figure 10.36 – Flipping or mirroring your video

- **Turn camera off**

  This option turns the camera off so that you can record audio only:

Figure 10.37 – Recording with no video

For this example, leave all of these settings as they are and click the record button at the bottom. You will see a 3, 2, 1 countdown; then, it will start recording automatically. After that, a red circle will appear with the word **RECORDING** underneath so that you know you are live:

Figure 10.38 – Recording for your template

Once finished, press **Done**. It will process the video for you. Then, click the **Save and exit** tab in the top-right corner. The video will be added to your design. All you need to do now is drag and drop it to wherever you would like it to be, and then save and download your finished design ready for use:

Figure 10.39 – Finished recording and complete template ready to use

Being able to record directly into Canva is a huge time-saving feature. You can also add your own pre-recorded videos and use any of Canva's video library, as we saw in this chapter.

With that, we've come to the end of an action-packed chapter. I hope you've enjoyed it and will put the video information you have learned here into practice.

Summary

In this chapter, we covered a lot about video, audio, and animation. Now, you can search for and add videos and audio files, as well as record directly in Canva and edit a video's length, crop it, and flip it. You also learned how to add various animations to the full design or just aspects of it. After this, we covered presentations. You can now create a presentation, present and record it, and also add fun animations while presenting. One thing we haven't covered yet is how to download and share these great designs you are creating, which is exactly what we will look at in the next chapter.

11
Downloading and Sharing Your Designs

We're now at a stage where you have a great understanding of how to use Canva and create some amazing designs for your business, so in this chapter, we're covering the downloading and sharing part – how you can share your designs with others and link them to social media.

In this chapter, we're going to cover the following topics:

- How to download a design
- How to share your design
- Linking to social media
- Creating clickable links
- Apps you can connect to Canva
- How to create a QR code

By the end of this chapter, you will know how to create your own QR codes, link to your social platforms, and download any design and share it directly with other people. Let's jump straight in and look at downloading.

How to download a design

Downloading a design in Canva is, like many other features, very straightforward. Once you've finished creating your design, all you need to do is click on the **Share** button at the top: this gives you a lot of options, but we're focusing on the **Download** button. A dropdown will appear where you can select a variety of download options – the main one for the majority of designs would be **PNG**. This is an image file, and we covered these in *Chapter 3, Tools and Features for Using Elements and Images*, and we're going to be looking at the PDF options in *Chapter 12, Tips and Tricks for Printing*. So, let's select the **PNG** option for this exercise:

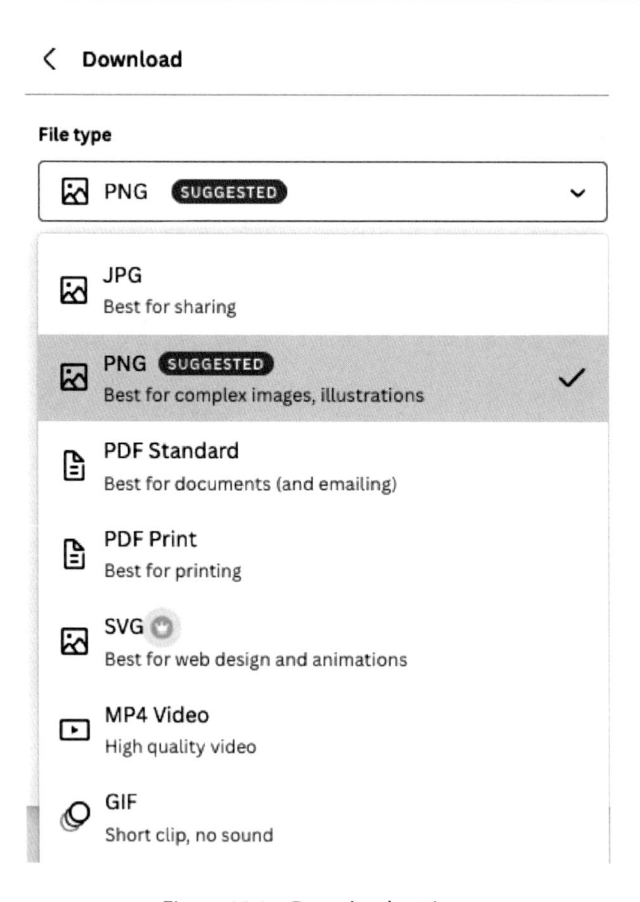

Figure 11.1 – Download options

After selecting **PNG**, it takes you to a page of further options. If you have Pro, you can choose to download your file with a transparent background and compress the file size. There is also an option to save the download settings so that when you create another design, it automatically chooses these settings for you:

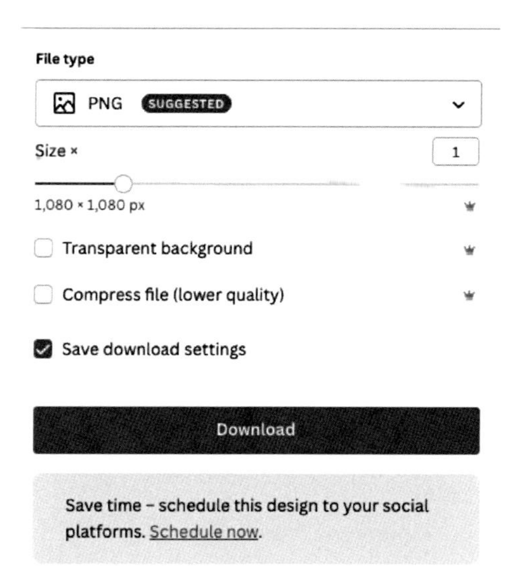

Figure 11.2 – Additional download options

Then, all you need to do is select **Download** and it will send the design to your computer or phone, depending on which device you are using to download your design.

This celebration box often appears with a link you can copy and use to send the design to someone or post on social media:

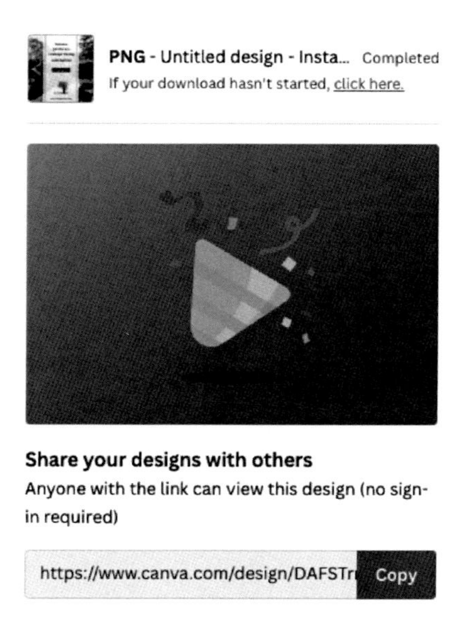

Figure 11.3 – Share your designs with others popup

And that's about it for downloading your design – nice and simple – so let's look at sharing your design directly from Canva.

How to share your design

Sharing Canva designs can be really useful – for example, if you use a virtual assistant and need to share ideas, or you want to share something with family members or on social media. You can even send graphics directly to Mailchimp for use later in your emails.

All the downloading and sharing options are in the same place – click on the **Share** button, and then for sharing options, click on **More**:

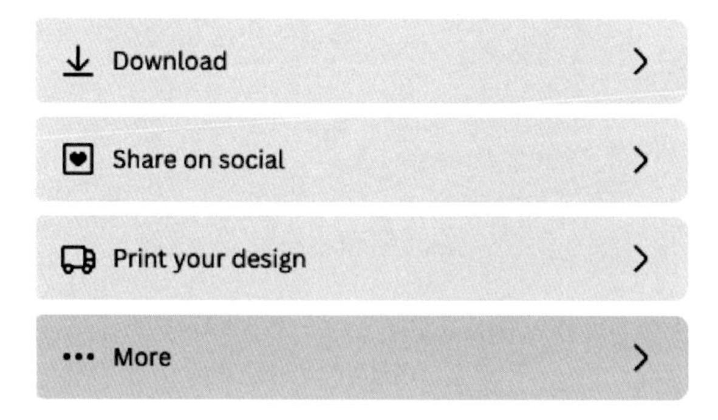

Figure 11.4 – The More option

From here, you can see every option has been put into its own group. There are the following:

- **Share**
- **Social**
- **Save**
- **Messaging**
- **Design**
- **More options**

The main **Share** section will be the most used. From here, you can click **Template link** and a link you can copy and paste will appear. However, this will add the design to someone else's Canva account, allowing them to edit and use it without you knowing what they are doing with it:

Figure 11.5 – Template link

There is also the option to present your design and record it – we looked at that in further detail in *Chapter 10, Leveraging Video and Animation within Your Business Marketing*

You can copy it to a clipboard, save the link to a folder on your computer, or select the **View-only link** option to send someone a link where they can view but not edit your design:

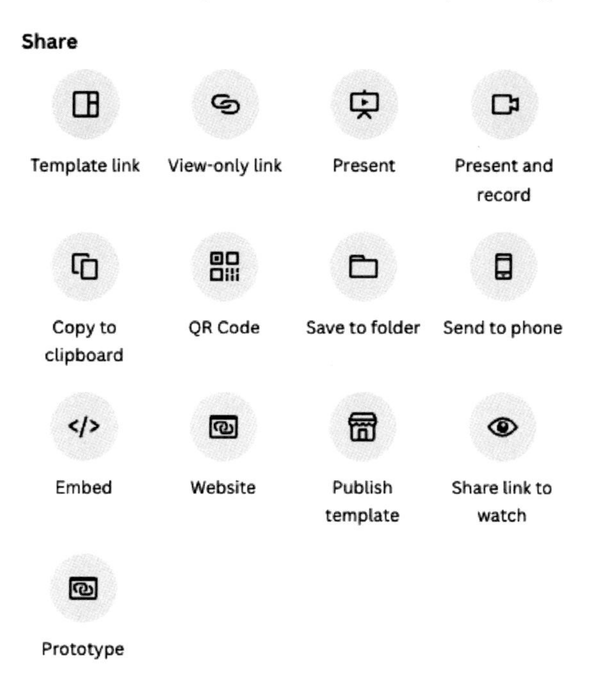

Figure 11.6 – Share options

Next is the **Social** section, where you can connect and send your designs directly to your social accounts. Have a look at the next part for more information on this section.

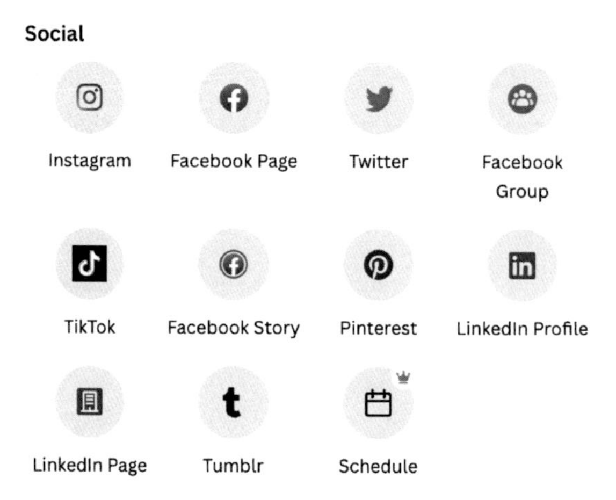

Figure 11.7 – Social linking options

Keep scrolling down and you will get to the **Save** and **Messaging** sections; here, you can save your design to a variety of places, including Google Drive and Dropbox, so that you can then go on to share your designs with others from these platforms.

Messaging allows you to open the design in a messaging platform, ready to share, including email, Facebook Messenger, and Mailchimp:

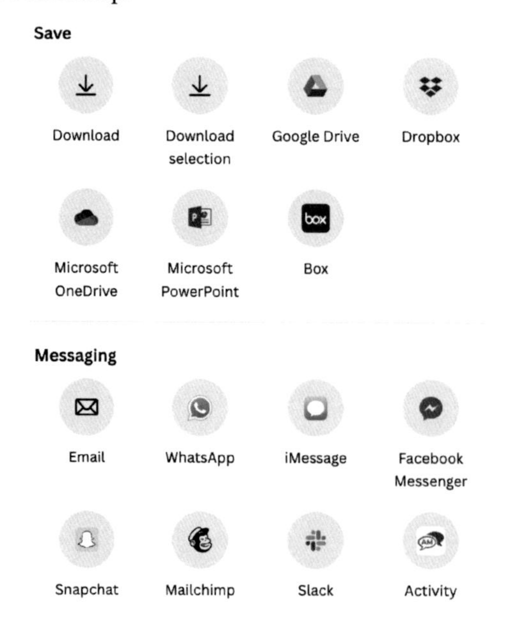

Figure 11.8 – Save and Messaging options

Click on the **Mailchimp** option and a simple box appears to save your design into the image section of your account.

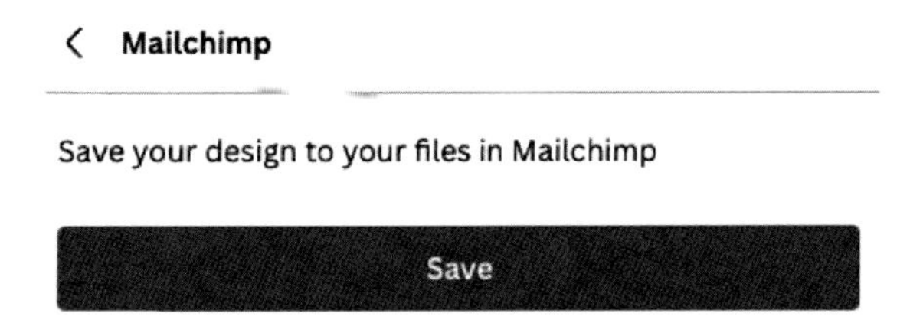

Figure 11.9 – Saving designs directly to Mailchimp

So, sharing your design is really quite straightforward. Canva is adding more and more places and apps all the time to which you can connect and share content. However, before you can share anything, you need to connect your social accounts to your Canva account and give them permission to share your designs directly, so let's have a look at that next, and then you can connect and share away.

Linking to social media

The majority of social channels that you can connect to your Canva account are straightforward – they all just require your login details. I believe it's only Facebook that asks for an extra step to be completed. Let's look at the simple way first and then we can look at Facebook.

So, once you have your design finished and ready to share, just click on the **Share** button in the top-right corner, and then click **More** and choose your platform. Canva will bring up a box asking you to connect:

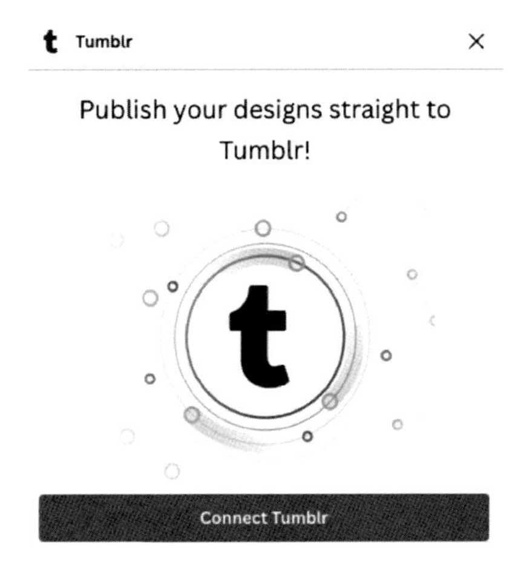

Figure 11.10 – Connecting to a social media platform

Once you click on the applicable **Connect** button, a box from the social platform pops up asking you to log in securely. Once done, you're all set up and ready to post directly:

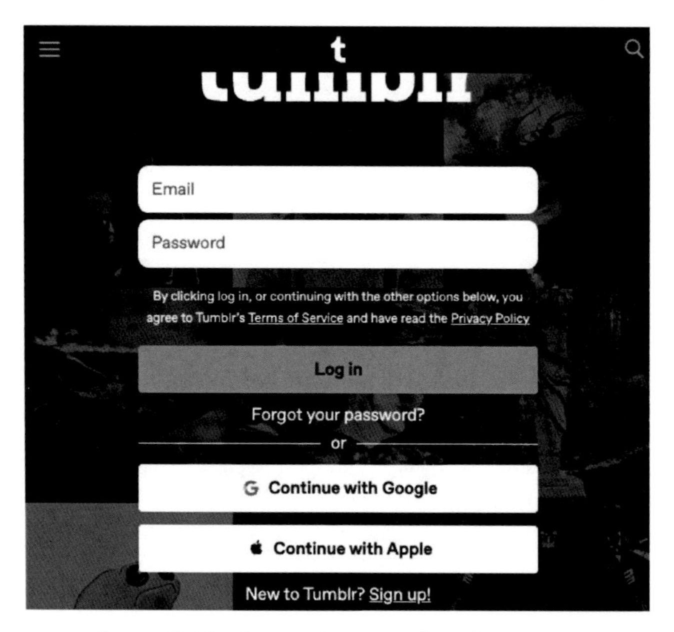

Figure 11.11 – Connecting a social media account

Now, I don't use Tumblr, but I do have Twitter – every time you want to post to your social platforms, it will bring up the necessary boxes for you to create your post, along with a character count restriction so you don't add in too many characters:

Figure 11.12 – Creating a post directly in Canva to send to a social media platform

With Facebook, they ask you to give Canva permission to connect from within your Facebook account. Upon trying to connect, this message will appear, giving you instructions on how to connect the two platforms:

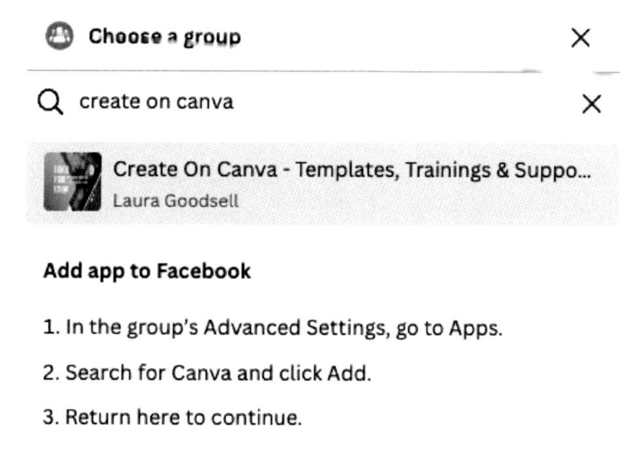

Figure 11.13 – Steps to connect a Facebook account to Canva

You will need to log in to your Facebook account and follow the step-by-step instructions to connect, but once you have done so, you can now post directly to Facebook as you would any other social account you have connected. You can share to a Facebook group as well as a page, but not your personal profile yet:

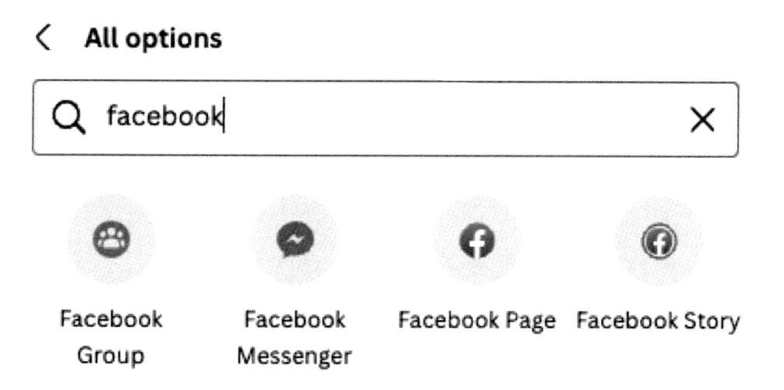

Figure 11.14 – Different Facebook sharing options

As well as automatically sharing to social media platforms, you can schedule this with the content calendar by clicking on the calendar icon in the bottom-left corner of the post. If you would like a refresher on this feature, have a look at *Chapter 1, Setting Up Canva on Desktop and Mobile*, where we covered this in more detail:

Figure 11.15 – Scheduling a social media post

Lastly in this section, you can find all of the apps and social channels you are connected to by going back to the home page, clicking on the icon in the top-right corner, and then clicking **Account settings**:

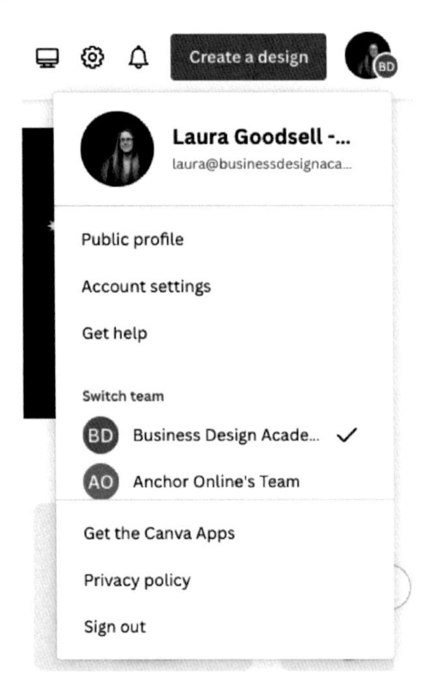

Figure 11.16 – Account settings tab

Scroll down and there will be a list of all linked accounts – it also gives you the option to disconnect each one:

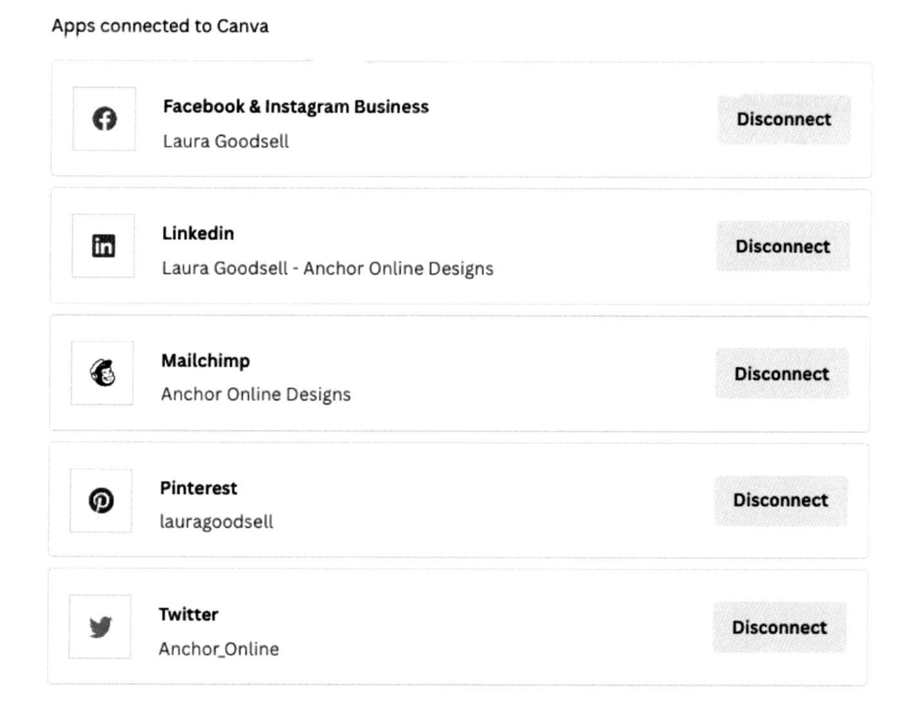

Figure 11.17 – Apps and social media channels connected to your account

Connecting your accounts to Canva helps save you time and reach your audience faster, as you don't need to download your images and then upload them to the various platforms.

Another way to connect to your audience is by adding links to your designs, giving the option to direct readers to where you want them to go – your website or social media channels, for example – so we're going to look at how to create clickable links.

Creating clickable links

I love to create clickable links in my documents; you can add your website to your e-book, your social channels to infographics, and your email address to a lead magnet. Plus, it couldn't be simpler – Canva has made it a nice, easy process for us to attract more people to our business with clickable links.

To add a link to your design, you need to create a button, or even a simple line of text will work. I've chosen to use this media kit page as an example:

Figure 11.18 – Media kit page

On this page, I've added some social media handles. These are normal textboxes at the moment, but I want to turn these into clickable links so that when I email this out, the end user has access to all of my social media feeds:

Figure 11.19 – Textboxes to be turned into clickable links

Select just one of your textboxes on your design, and then click on the two-linked-circles icon at the top:

Figure 11.20 – Two linked circles icon for creating links

This brings up a search bar. Just enter your web address or social media address and it will link it for you:

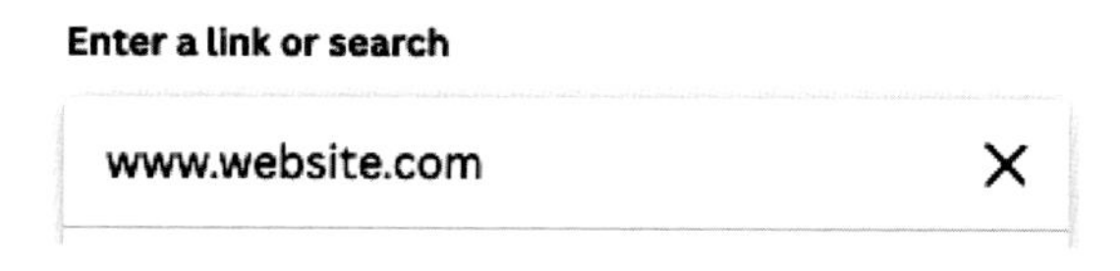

Figure 11.21 – Entering a URL to create a link

> **Top tip**
> When adding social media channels, make sure you enter the full address. Don't just add `@socialchannel` – you need to input `www.facebook.com/page/socialchannel` for it to work.

You can tell when it has worked, as a line will appear underneath your text that now has a link attached:

Figure 11.22 – Creating a clickable link

I mentioned adding a button earlier on in this section. There isn't a specific button you can add, but you can make what looks like a button by searching for and adding an element shaped like a button:

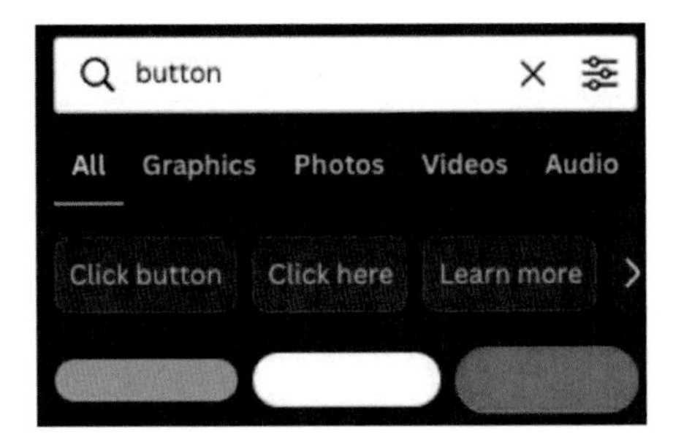

Figure 11.23 – Searching for buttons in the Elements section

Then, you can add your textbox over the top with the attached link, giving it the look of a button rather than plain text:

Figure 11.24 – Creating buttons for links

Top tip

Anything you want to download and use as a PDF document can have clickable links built into it, but unfortunately, PNGs, JPGs, and videos cannot have clickable links in them. It's not currently possible to add them to images or videos.

Now that you know how to connect your social media accounts and connect your audience to your PDFs, did you know there are lots of apps you can connect to your account as well? This gives you access to some amazing content and features.

Apps you can connect to Canva

Connecting apps to your Canva account feels like a huge bonus because Canva is a great platform as is. They are now giving us access to so much more through this route, so I wanted to show you some of my favorite apps that you can connect and use. All the apps can be found in the **Discover apps** section on the left-hand side of the home page; I encourage you to have a good look around there.

The first one I'd like to share is the **Text to Image** app, which allows you to input text, and Canva will generate an image based on your description:

Text to Image

Type what you'd like to see, and watch it come to life.

Figure 11.25 – Text to Image icon in Canva

Open up the app and click **Use in a new design**, and then select any template size. It doesn't really matter, as all images created in this app are square. On the left, you can now see a box to input your description and some inspiration points, and then the option to choose a style:

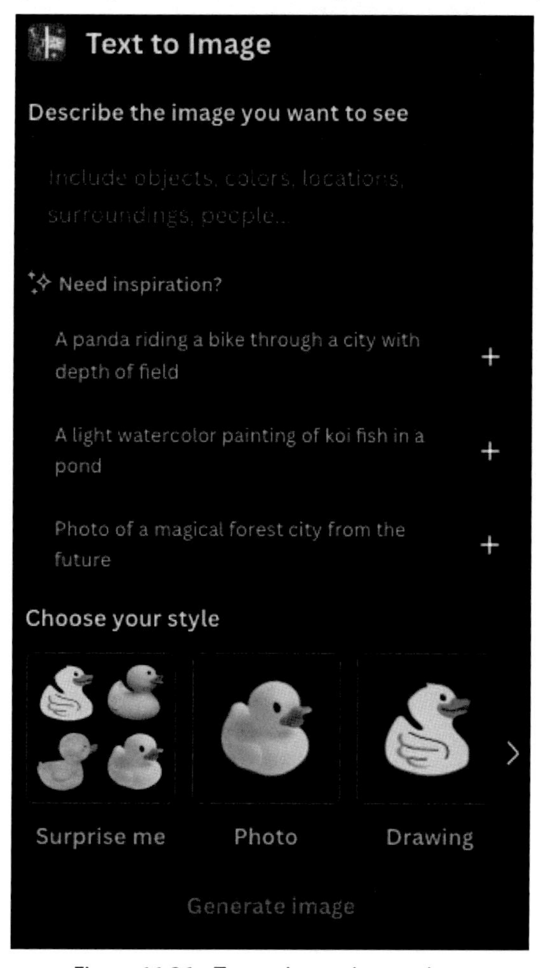

Figure 11.26 – Text to Image instructions

I've added `Dog wearing sunglasses in the rain` as my description, and then clicked on **Surprise me** for the style. These are the images Canva has created for me:

Figure 11.27 – AI-created images in Canva

These are four very quirky images that I can now use in any of my Canva designs.

Have a go and see what you can create – this is such a fun app!

Next, I'd like to show you the **Draw** app – this is a lovely, basic app that lets you create a drawing yourself:

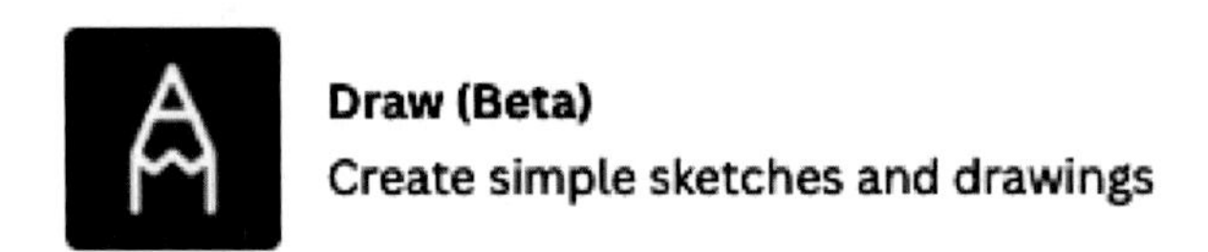

Figure 11.28 – Draw icon in Canva

Once you have clicked on the app, select **Use in a new design**, and the left-hand menu will show you the pens and settings you can use. There are currently four pens to pick from, a pen nib size sliding bar, a transparency bar, and color options. Upon selecting a pen to use, the **Eraser** option appears:

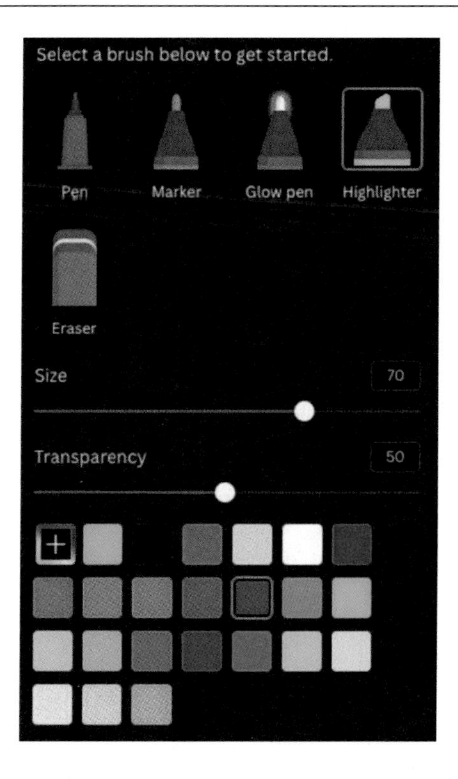

Figure 11.29 – Draw app pen selection and options

Select your pen and color, and then use your mouse on a desktop, your mouse pad on a laptop, or your fingertip on a tablet to draw. Once finished, click **Done** at the top or **Cancel** if it's not right and you want to start again. Once done, it will turn into an image for use in your design.

Here's an example of how the different pen options look – my favorite is **Glow Pen**:

Figure 11.30 – Examples of the different pen types

Next, I'd like to show you the **Shadows** app – this app allows you to add a shadow to an image. You will need to have the background removed from the image for this app, as the shadow fits around the object:

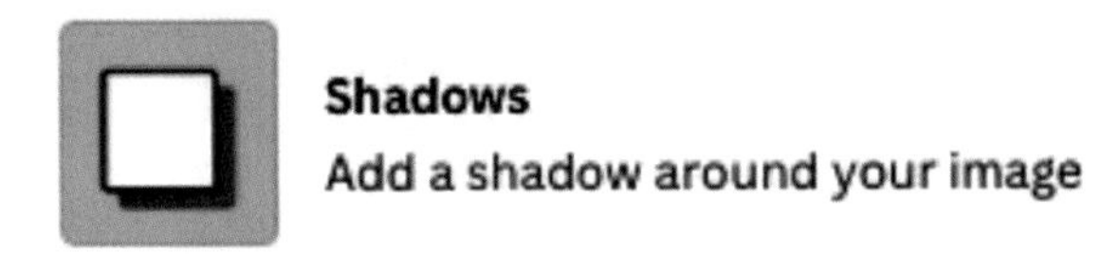

Figure 11.31 – Shadows app icon

When you would like to use this app, click on the **Use in new design** button and a new template will open up for you. A sample image of a girl in a red hat will appear on the template, but you can delete this and add your own image by going to your **Uploads** section or finding one in the **Photos** tab:

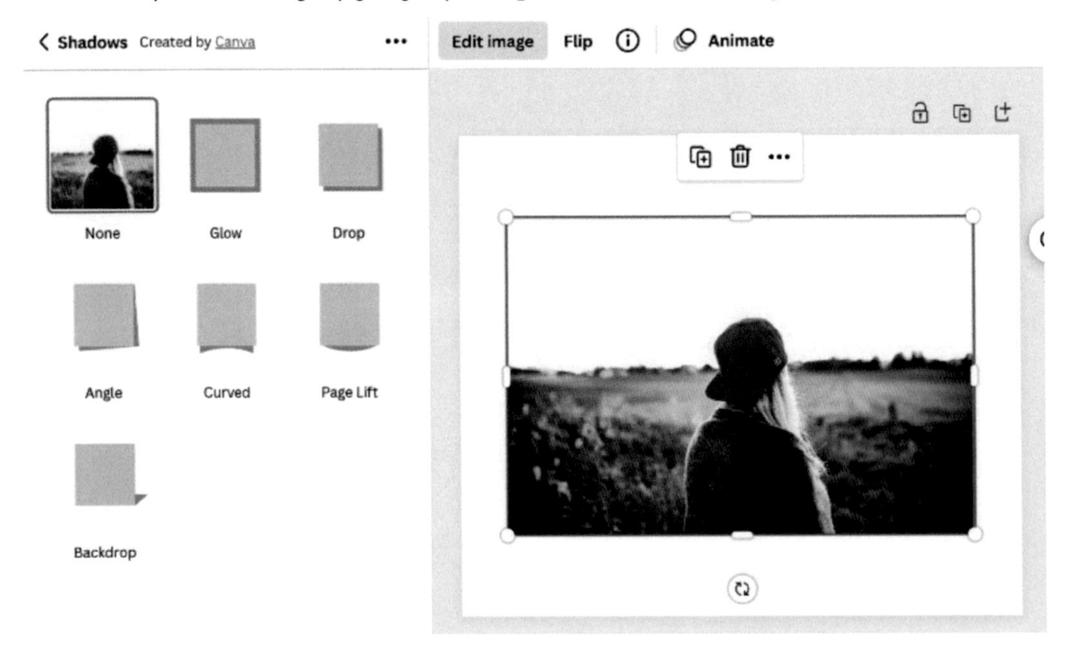

Figure 11.32 – Sample image of a girl in a red hat on the Shadows app

Once you have your image ready, click on **Edit image** at the top, search for **Shadows**, select **Drop** (this is one of the shadow options), and then click it again to open up the settings:

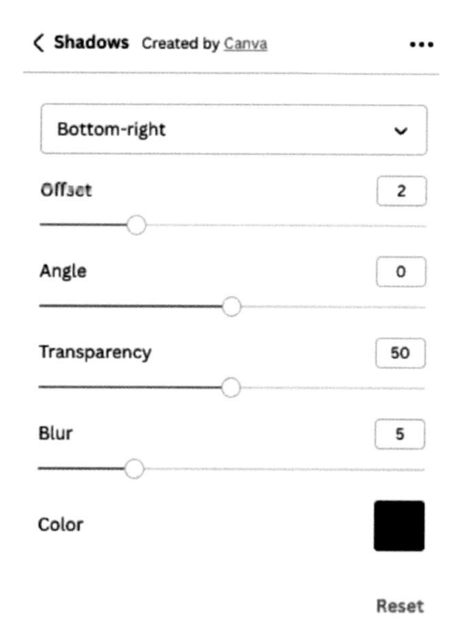

Figure 11.33 – Shadow apps options

From here, you can adjust the intensity and direction of your shadow, extend the blur, and even change the color, resulting in a 3D effect.

Here's a before and after of the same image:

Figure 11.34 – Before and after image using the Shadows app

Adding a shadow gives your images depth.

Lastly, I'd love to show you the **Character Builder** app. This is relatively new, and I can see it only getting better. It helps you to create your own character and give them clothes, features, and different colorings. You can also use these characters in any of your designs:

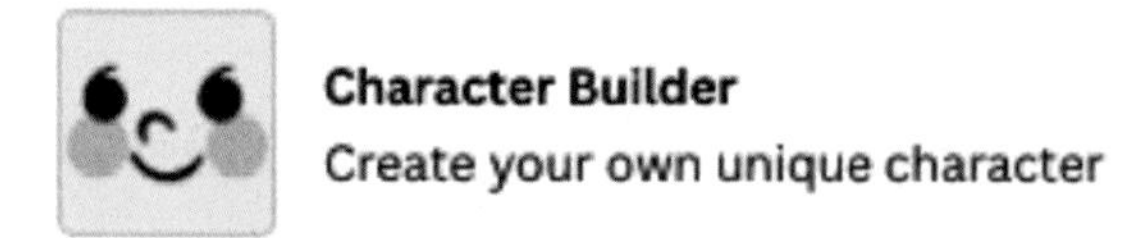

Figure 11.35 – Character Builder icon in Canva

Click on the app, then on **Use in new design**, and, as with the other apps, the menu on the left-hand side will change. Here, you now have all of the parts you can use to create your character. You have the **Head** shape and **Face** features, **Body**, **Skin tone**, and **Hair color**:

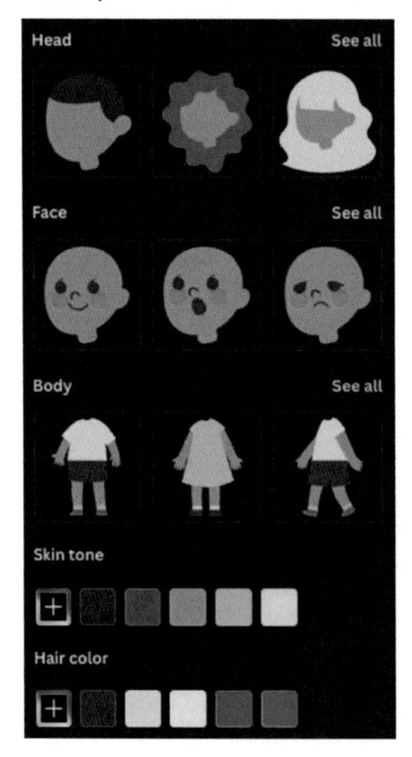

Figure 11.36 – Different sections of Character Builder

To see more of each part, click on the **See all** tab. There are lots of different shapes and styles for you to choose from and build your character. Select each option and it will appear on the blank design. This is my character created in just five clicks:

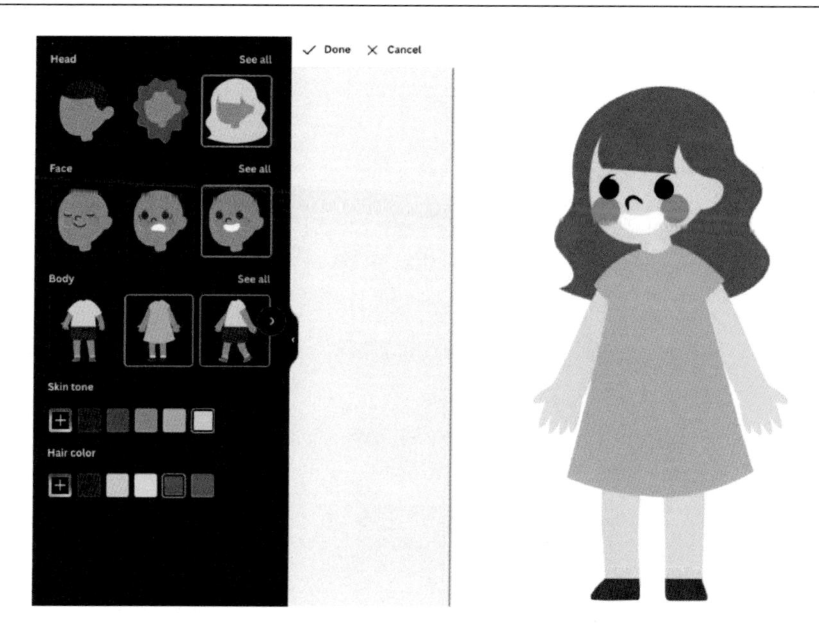

Figure 11.37 – Character Builder

I like these characters because you can make them your own, unique to you, and use them within your business – they could be your mascot or icon.

You can also import your media, edit your photos, and share and publish to different platforms all through the apps you can connect to your Canva account:

Import media

Google Drive
Add your Google Drive photos to your designs.

Google Photos
Add images from Google Photos to your designs.

Embed
Add video, music and online media to your designs.

Discover content

Text to Image
Type what you'd like to see, and watch it come to life.

QR code
Add QR codes to your designs.

Emoji
Add your favorite emojis to your designs.

Photo editing

Background Remover
Remove the background of your image in one click.

Auto Enhance
Automatically enhance your photo

Shadows
Add a shadow around your image

Share and publish

Heyzine Flipbooks
Page turn effects and slideshows for your design

Smartmockups
Publish to Smartmockups to create stunning mockups

Publuu Flipbooks
Save designs to flipbooks with page turn effects.

Figure 11.38 – Selection of apps available through Canva

One last app I'd like to share with you is the **QR code** app; this is a great feature you can add to your designs and is perfect for business use, so it has its own section.

How to create a QR code

A QR code is like a bar code. Someone can use the camera on their phone to scan the QR code and it will open up whatever link has been attached to the QR code in the design. Often websites, social media links, and email addresses are added, but it can be anything with a URL.

Adding QR codes is done through an app. We discussed these in the previous section, so we're going to dive straight in.

Open up or create the design you would like to add the QR code into, then head over to the left-hand menu, scroll all the way to the bottom, select the **Apps** tab, and click on the **QR Code** option:

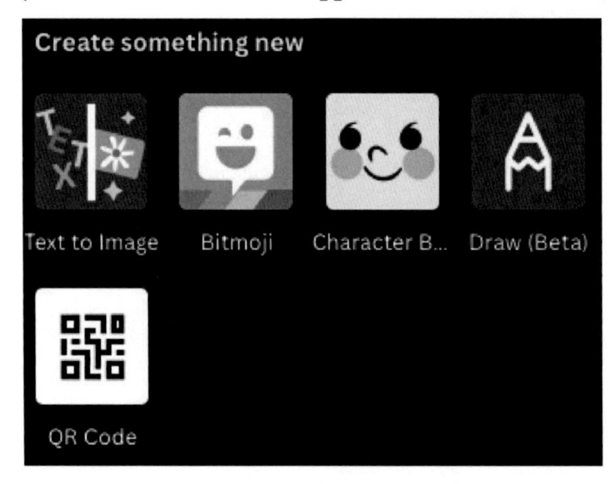

Figure 11.39 – App selection in the left-hand menu

It opens up a simple URL box. This is where you add the link you would like to attach to the QR code. You can leave it as a standard QR code or you can click on **Customize** and change the colors of the code to match your brand. **Margin** just changes the size of the border:

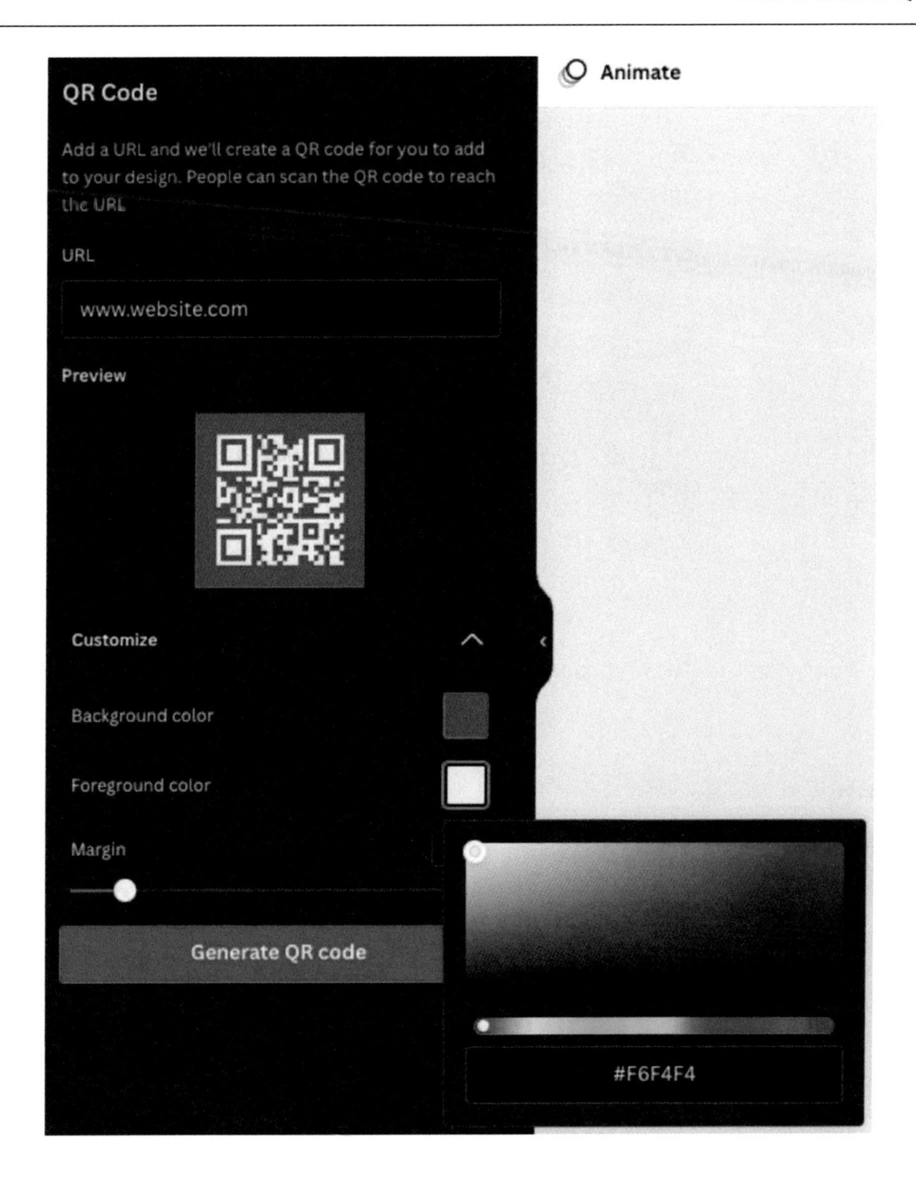

Figure 11.40 – QR Code customization

Once you're happy with how it looks, click **Generate QR code** and it will add it to your template. From here, you can adjust the size to fit anywhere within the design:

Figure 11.41 – QR code on a template design

You now have another way for your audience to connect with you and find your business or offers so much easier.

Summary

In this chapter, you've learned how to download a finished design. You can now share any design with anyone, and you've learned how to link your social media channels to your Canva account, as well as being able to create clickable links in your PDF documents. You have also discovered the vast range of apps that you can now connect to your Canva account, and you've learned how to create and add a QR code to your designs.

We've looked a lot at how to share your designs in this chapter, so we're going to take it a step further and look at getting your designs printed in the next and final chapter of the book.

12
Tips and Tricks for Printing

Being able to design great graphics in Canva is an essential process for the small business owner. So far, this book has shown you a lot of information, tutorials, and tips on creating and sharing your designs, but you can also print in Canva as well, not only through third-party printing companies but also directly through Canva. So in this chapter, the last in the book, we're going to look at printing and adding your designs to physical products.

In this chapter, we are going to cover the following main topics:

- Printing templates
- Designing multi-page documents for print
- PDF editing and printing
- Printing directly through Canva

By the end of this chapter, you will be able to set up a template ready for print, print any design through third-party printers or directly via Canva, upload and edit a PDF, and comfortably create multi-page documents ready for print.

Printing templates

Canva has a huge array of different-sized templates, ready for you to use a template or create a custom template for any aspect of your business. However, picking the correct one is important before you start designing, as many of them have additional settings on them:

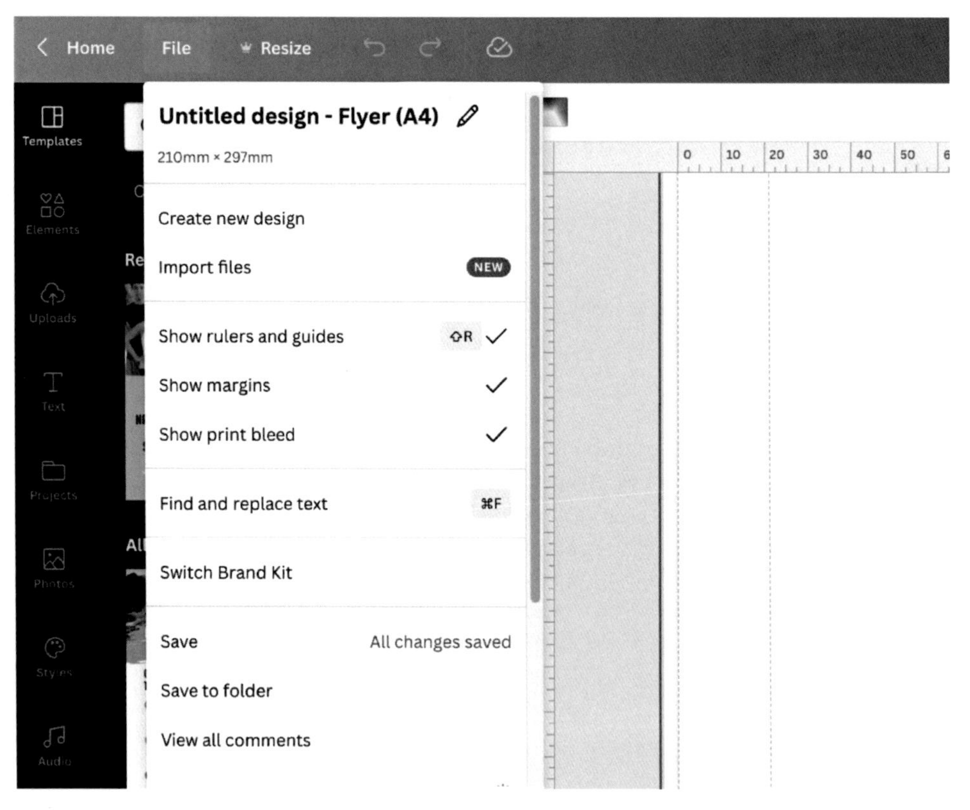

Figure 12.1 – Rulers, margins, and print bleed options

Here are a few examples of template sizes that you can look for and use for printing.

Mainly for business owners, creating marketing materials is an important part of our everyday task list, but you can also create printable designs at home, such as the following:

- **Flyers (portrait)**
- **Business cards**
- **Brochures**
- **Newsletters**
- **Infographics**
- **Invitations and cards**

All of these options have hundreds, if not thousands, of templates already set up for you to edit and use. They also have the margins and print bleed incorporated into the design for you, so let's look at what the print bleed and margins are in a bit more detail.

Margin

When the **Show margins** setting has been turned on, it shows a faint dotted line around your template, keeping all of your information inside of this dotted line. This ensures that nothing important gets cropped out during the printing stage:

Figure 12.2 – Dotted margin line

This would include any textboxes, images, or elements that you deem essential to the design – it gives the printer a margin of error to work with.

Print bleed

The print bleed is a second dotted line around your template – this is the original borderline. Canva extends the size of the template, usually by 3 mm, to ensure there are no white areas around the outside and that you avoid having white areas around your design, or extending your images, colors, or elements over the edges:

Figure 12.3 – Overlapping an image for print bleed

After you've created your design and made sure your information is within the margins and no images or elements overlap with the print bleed, you are ready to print. This is where you can select the **Share** button, and then the **Download** button will bring up your options. There are two PDF tabs – the best one for printing is the **PDF Print** tab. This ensures your print is of high quality, 300 DPI. The **PDF Standard** tab is only 96 DPI, and printing companies will always ask for the higher-quality 300 DPI document:

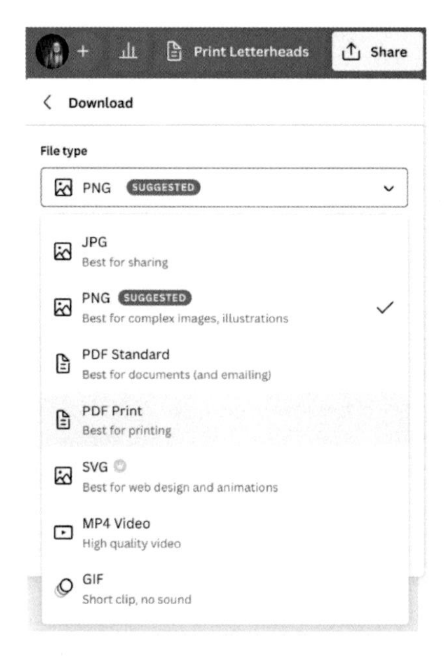

Figure 12.4 – PDF Print dropdown

Once you've selected **PDF Print**, it then gives you further options. From here, you can select the **Crop marks and bleed** and **Flatten PDF** options:

Download

File type

PDF Print

Crop marks and bleed

Flatten PDF

Include notes

Color Profile

RGB (best for digital use)

RGB (best for digital use)

CMYK (best for professional printing)

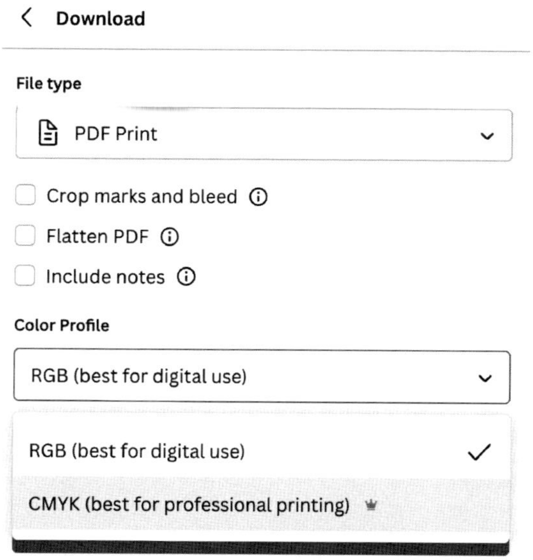

Figure 12.5 – Print options

We also mentioned both the **Crop marks and bleed** and **Flatten PDF** options in *Chapter 9, Making Social Media Graphics with Canva*, but here is a bit more information on what they both are.

Crop marks and bleed

Adding crop marks and bleed helps to show where your design will be cut by the printer. They show up as small lines at each corner and a very thin white border:

Figure 12.6 – Crop marks and bleed

These will not appear on your finished print; they are only for use by the printer.

Flatten PDF

To flatten a PDF means that every element within the design, such as images, color blocks, and textboxes, is merged into one – they are effectively grouped to form one element. When creating a Canva design, every element we add is separate so that we can move them around, change their sizes, animate them, and so forth, but for printing, they are best combined. This helps keep colors consistent during the printing stage.

Color Profile

The next part in the dropdown, under the **Crop marks and bleed** and **Flatten PDF** options, is the **Color Profile** settings. From here, you can now choose how you want to download your design, either **RGB** or **CMYK**. If you're planning on printing this document, select the **CMYK** option, which is used by printers and is the preferred option. If you print using **RGB**, the end result can look dull. The colors will not be as vibrant as using **CMYK**. However, if you only want to use this online or as a digital product, then the **RGB** option may be best suited to your needs:

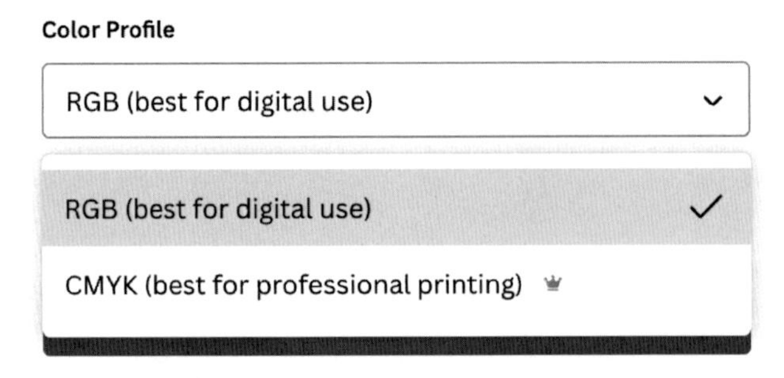

Figure 12.7 – RGB and CMYK print options

Once you have gone through and selected your options, you are now at the stage to click **Download**, and your design is ready to be printed.

However, there are a couple more points you need to know about if you plan on creating multi-page printable designs in Canva, so let's have a look at that next.

Designing multi-page documents for print

When creating a multi-page design in Canva, quite often, a lot of the pages are the same or similar, maybe with a variation in the title or images used; for example, a printed journal will have the majority of pages looking the same. When creating these types of designs, concentrate on creating the main page and then duplicate it as many times as needed so that you have the layout set, and then you can then go through and edit any titles, images, or information on each page.

Use the **Duplicate page** option in the top-right corner of the page you want to copy:

Figure 12.8 – Duplicate page option

This will save you a lot of time and keep your designs looking professional and consistent.

Canva also has a page limit for each design, which is currently set at 200. If you are creating a design that will be larger than this, then you will need to copy your design into a new template so that you have two of the same. By copying the first design, you're keeping your page layout, branding, and style the same. You then need to edit the second one so that it is in line with the first one – for example, if you've numbered your pages but can only get as far as 200 on the first document, then the second document will start at 201, and you would need to continue this way until you were at the end of your design.

However, at this point, you may hit another problem – you now have two documents that need to be combined into one, ready for printing or sending to a publisher if it's going to be a book. Unfortunately, this can't be achieved in Canva, so you would need to look into third-party platforms that can combine these.

Currently, both documents will have been downloaded using the **PDF Print** option and will include your **Print bleed**, **Crop marks and bleed**, and **Flatten PDF** options, so you can use a PDF merge website. There are a few about – some of the ones I would recommend are as follows:

- `https://www.pdf-merge.com/`
- `https://www.ilovepdf.com/merge_pdf`
- `https://www.sodapdf.com/pdf-merge/`

All of these have a free-to-use option for merging PDF documents into one file.

Being able to download as a PDF in Canva is very useful for anyone interested in creating lead magnets, or even bigger projects such as notebooks, journals, or books based on your niche, but you can also upload a PDF into Canva and edit it fully, so let's have a look at how that can be achieved.

PDF editing and printing

I think this is a brilliant feature and one that is often needed – being able to edit a PDF. I had a client who once had several posters made up for her and they were all PDFs. She loved the design but wanted to change the date and time so they could be used again. I uploaded them to Canva for her and changed them into editable Canva designs so that she could simply edit the information and then download it as a PDF to use as and when needed, and this is exactly what this feature is for.

To find the **upload** section for the PDF, click on the **Create a design** tab at the top. Then, at the very bottom of the dropdown, you will find three options:

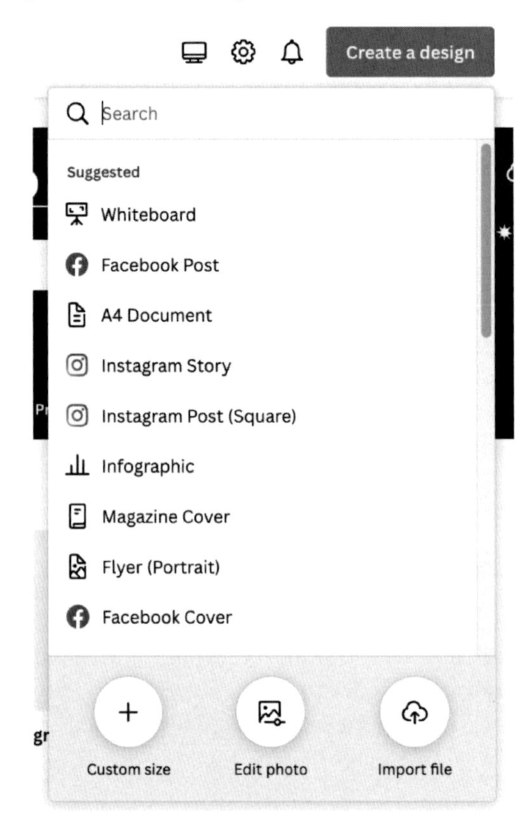

Figure 12.9 – Suggested design ideas and Import file option

For this example, we need the **Import file** option at the bottom right. When you click on this, it will open up your computer's documents file, so find and select your PDF. It will then import it into Canva and convert it into a normal Canva design.

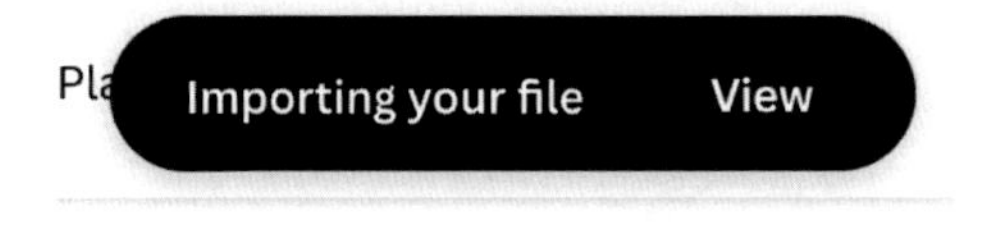

Figure 12.10 – Importing your file notice

It won't open for you; you will need to go to your **Recent designs** section, and it should be the first one:

Figure 12.11 – Uploaded PDF document

Click to open it, and you now have a fully editable PDF; all the textboxes can be changed, images can be removed and replaced, and any element can be changed. You can also add new content as and when you wish. Please be aware that at the time of writing, more complex PDFs may not convert correctly, and may look different from your original PDF. However, Canva is great at getting things updated, so I imagine this will be improved upon in the future.

Once you've finished editing your PDF, you also have all of the usual download options, so you can download it as a PNG, PDF, or video file.

We've now come to one of my favorite features of Canva – printing. I love that I can have products printed through Canva directly.

Printing directly through Canva

Canva has a fantastic array of printable products, where you can create a design and then have it printed onto a product and shipped to you all from within Canva itself.

This is set to get bigger and better as more features and printed products are added.

Let's have a look at some of the items you can have your designs printed onto. Have a look at the **Template** tab on the left-hand menu, and then scroll down to **Custom Prints**:

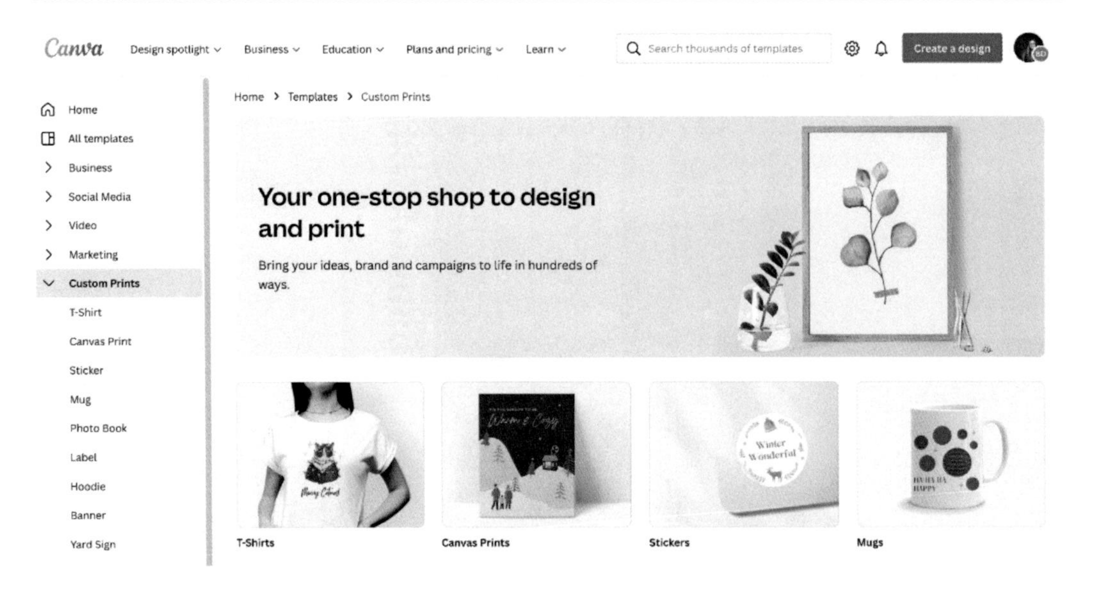

Figure 12.12 – Custom Prints product options

This opens up a new sub-menu of different product types. From here, you can choose what you would like to print, whether on T-shirts, mugs, labels, or jumpers, among other things:

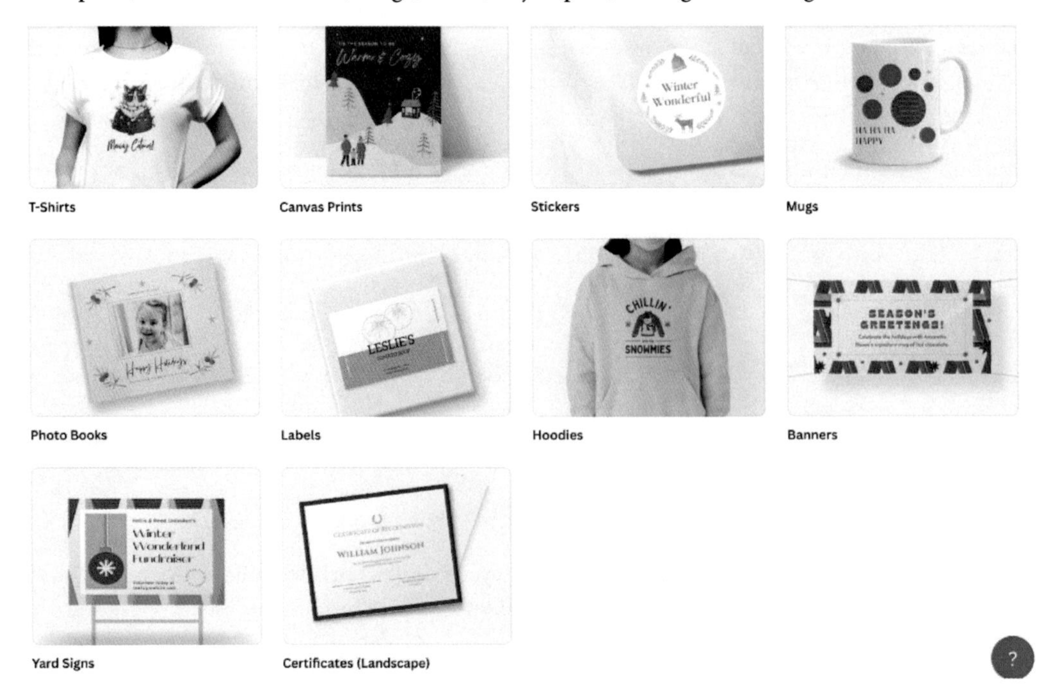

Figure 12.13 – Selection of different products available for print

Once selected, you are presented with a range of different template designs suited to the product, or you can select the first option on this page to create your own design from scratch:

Figure 12.14 – Templates for print options

Another way to create and print designs onto products through Canva is to start with creating your own design – you can then select the **Print your design** option in the dropdown:

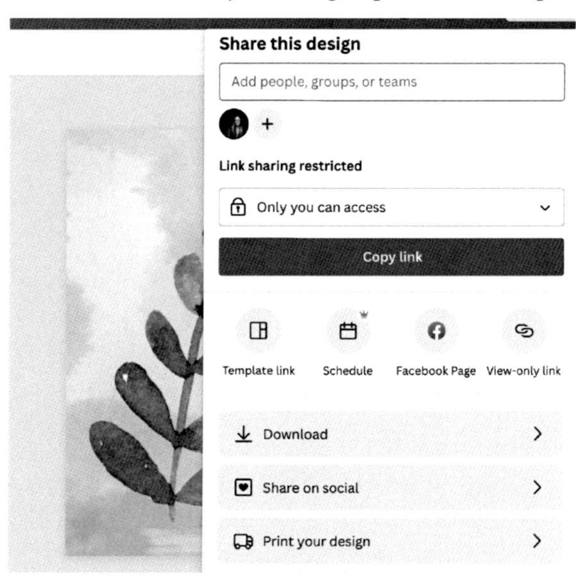

Figure 12.15 – Print your design button

Let's go through how to print a design by selecting the **Print your design** button.

First of all, you're shown a dropdown of different products. Here, there is a larger range of printable items. For example, you have coasters, stickers, notebooks, and tote bags, to name a few.

This results in a better option when wanting to print physical items:

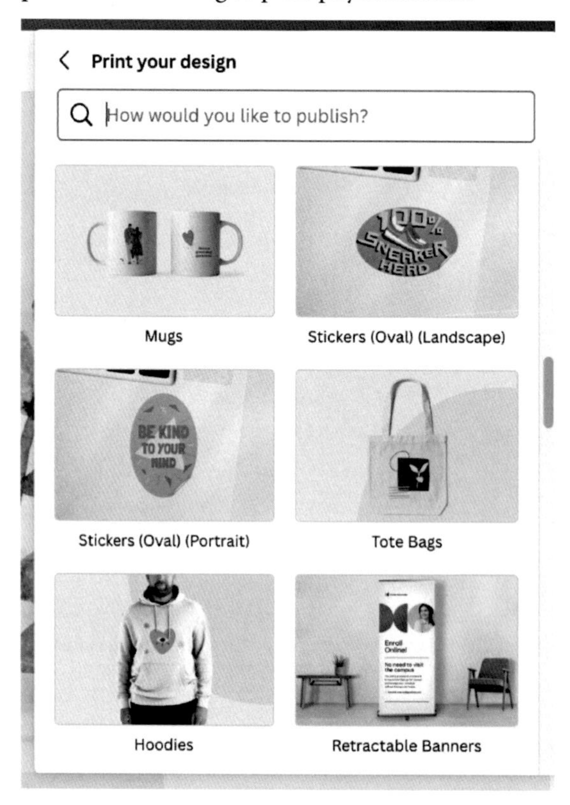

Figure 12.16 – Additional print products

Let's say we wanted to print our design onto a sweater: Canva will automatically resize your design to fit this, and then it will bring up options specific to the product – in this case, sizes and colors.

It also gives you the option to have a front and back design for clothing, with a view of how both sides will look:

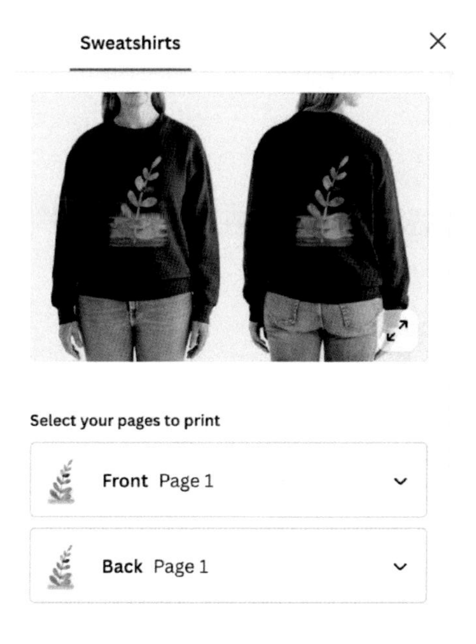

Figure 12.17 – Front and back options for printed sweaters

Top tip

If you would like to have a transparent background on your design so that there isn't a square shape around it, just make sure you leave the background white. If you add a color or image into the background, the shape of the template will appear:

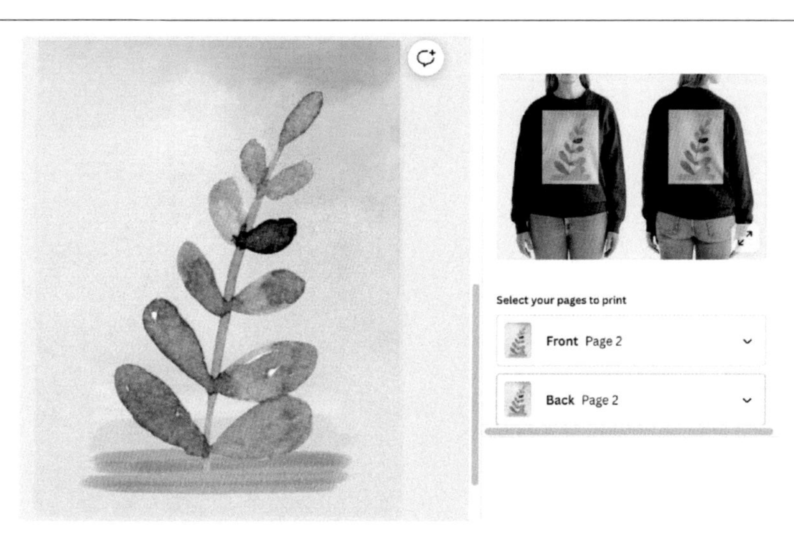

Figure 12.18 – Showing how adding a background to a design can look

Once you've selected the front and back designs, scroll down to the **Sizing** and **Color** options. With clothing, there are currently three color choices: **Black**, **Gray**, and **Navy**:

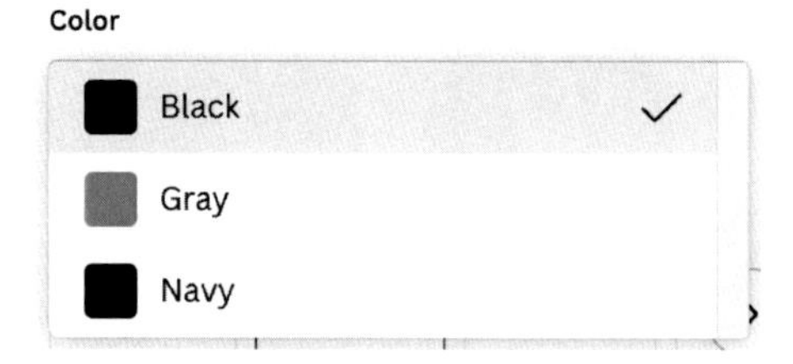

Figure 12.19 – Different color choices for printed clothes

Then, it's on to **Sizing** – it ranges from S to XXL, and with each option, it gives you the size in centimeters so you can measure to see whether it will fit:

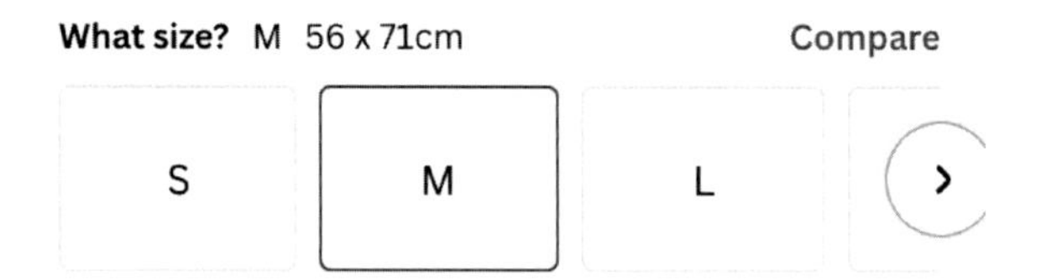

Figure 12.20 – Sizes for printed clothes

Lastly, the pricing – the more you purchase of the same item, the bigger the discount they give you. This example design is based on a double-sided sweater, which is £4 more expensive than the single-sided sweater:

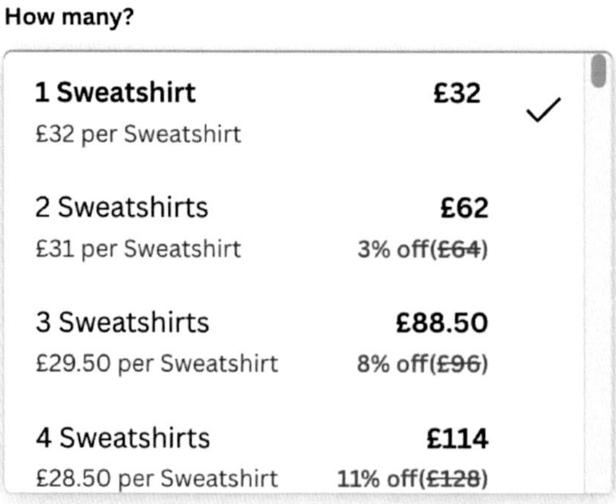

How many?

1 Sweatshirt **£32**
£32 per Sweatshirt

2 Sweatshirts **£62**
£31 per Sweatshirt 3% off(~~£64~~)

3 Sweatshirts **£88.50**
£29.50 per Sweatshirt 8% off(~~£96~~)

4 Sweatshirts **£114**
£28.50 per Sweatshirt 11% off(~~£128~~)

Figure 12.21 – Pricing structure for printed clothes

Your country of residence will determine the currency and delivery times. I'm based in the UK, so these are my delivery options. There is always a free standard delivery option, and then a charged, quick turnaround option. If you're happy to wait a few days, go for the free option – I've found items often arrive quicker than expected.

Add in your delivery address and click **Continue** – it will then ask you to confirm and place your order.

Congratulations! You've created a product with your very own design.

Summary

What a fantastic journey we've been on throughout this book! In this chapter alone, you have learned how to set up a blank template for printing and understood what crop marks, print bleed, and margins are and how to add them to your design. You've discovered how to merge PDFs, upload and turn an existing PDF into an editable document, create multi-page documents, and print through Canva, creating your own designs and printing them directly onto products.

You have gone from being a Canva novice, getting set up and learning what Canva is all about, to becoming a Canva expert, and should now be able to create a multitude of designs, videos, and presentations, and create your own products.

Congratulations!

Index

G

H

I

L

M

P

Q

R

S

T

V

Packt.com

Subscribe to our online digital library for full access to over 7,000 books and videos, as well as industry leading tools to help you plan your personal development and advance your career. For more information, please visit our website.

Why subscribe?

- Spend less time learning and more time coding with practical eBooks and Videos from over 4,000 industry professionals
- Improve your learning with Skill Plans built especially for you
- Get a free eBook or video every month
- Fully searchable for easy access to vital information
- Copy and paste, print, and bookmark content

Did you know that Packt offers eBook versions of every book published, with PDF and ePub files available? You can upgrade to the eBook version at packt.com and as a print book customer, you are entitled to a discount on the eBook copy. Get in touch with us at customercare@packtpub.com for more details.

At www.packt.com, you can also read a collection of free technical articles, sign up for a range of free newsletters, and receive exclusive discounts and offers on Packt books and eBooks.

Other Books You May Enjoy

If you enjoyed this book, you may be interested in these other books by Packt:

Designing and Prototyping Interfaces with Figma

Fabio Staiano

ISBN: 978-1-80056-418-3

- Explore FigJam and how to use it to collect data in the research phase
- Wireframe the future interface with shape tools and vectors
- Define grids, typography, colors, and effect styles that can be reused in your work
- Get to grips with Auto Layout and the constraints to create complex layouts
- Create flexible components using styles and variants
- Make your user interface interactive with prototyping and smart animate
- Share your work with others by exporting assets and preparing development resources
- Discover templates and plugins from the community

Adobe Illustrator for Creative Professionals

Clint Balsar

ISBN: 978-1-80056-925-6

- Master a wide variety of methods for developing objects
- Control files using layers and groups
- Enhance content using data-supported infographics
- Use multiple artboards for better efficiency and asset management
- Understand the use of layers and objects in Illustrator
- Build professional systems for final presentation to clients

Packt is searching for authors like you

If you're interested in becoming an author for Packt, please visit `authors.packtpub.com` and apply today. We have worked with thousands of developers and tech professionals, just like you, to help them share their insight with the global tech community. You can make a general application, apply for a specific hot topic that we are recruiting an author for, or submit your own idea.

Hi!

I Laura, author of *Design Better and Build Your Brand in Canva,* really hope you enjoyed reading this book and found it useful for increasing your productivity and efficiency in Canva.

It would really help us (and other potential readers!) if you could leave a review on Amazon sharing your thoughts on *Design Better and Build Your Brand in Canva.*

Go to the link below or scan the QR code to leave your review:

`https://packt.link/r/1800569335`

Your review will help us to understand what's worked well in this book, and what could be improved upon for future editions, so it really is appreciated.

Best wishes,

Laura Goodsell

Download a free PDF copy of this book

Thanks for purchasing this book!

Do you like to read on the go but are unable to carry your print books everywhere? Is your eBook purchase not compatible with the device of your choice?

Don't worry, now with every Packt book you get a DRM-free PDF version of that book at no cost.

Read anywhere, any place, on any device. Search, copy, and paste code from your favorite technical books directly into your application.

The perks don't stop there, you can get exclusive access to discounts, newsletters, and great free content in your inbox daily

Follow these simple steps to get the benefits:

1. Scan the QR code or visit the link below

`https://packt.link/free-ebook/9781800569331`

2. Submit your proof of purchase
3. That's it! We'll send your free PDF and other benefits to your email directly

Made in the USA
Coppell, TX
22 August 2023